ISLAMIC THEOLOGY IN THE TURKISH REPUBLIC

Edinburgh Studies on Modern Turkey

Series General Editors: **Alpaslan Özerdem**, Dean of the School for Conflict Analysis and Resolution and Professor of Peace and Conflict Studies at George Mason University, and **Ahmet Erdi Öztürk**, Lecturer in International Relations and Politics at London Metropolitan University and a Marie Sklodowska-Curie Fellow at Coventry University in the UK and GIGA in Germany.

Series Advisory Board: Ayşe Kadıoğlu (Harvard University), Hakan Yavuz (University of Utah), Samim Akgönül (University of Strasbourg), Rebecca Bryant (Utrecht University), Nukhet Ahu Sandal (Ohio University), Mehmet Gurses (Florida Atlantic University), Paul Kubicek (Oakland University), Sinem Akgül Açıkmeşe (Kadir Has University), Gareth Jenkins (Institute for Security and Development Policy), Stephen Karam (World Bank), Peter Mandaville (George Mason University).

Edinburgh Studies on Modern Turkey is an outlet for academic works that examine the domestic and international issues of the Turkish republic from its establishment in the 1920s until the present. This broadly defined frame allows the series to adopt both interdisciplinary and trans-disciplinary approaches, covering research on the country's history and culture as well as political, religious and socio-economic developments.

Published and forthcoming titles

Policing Slums in Turkey: Crime, Resistance and the Republic on the Margin
Çağlar Dölek

Islamic Theology in the Turkish Republic
Philip Dorroll

The Kurds in Erdoğan's Turkey: Balancing Identity, Resistance and Citizenship
William Gourlay

Peace Processes in Northern Ireland and Turkey: Rethinking Conflict Resolution
İ. Aytaç Kadioğlu

The Decline of the Ottoman Empire and the Rise of the Turkish Republic: Observations of an American Diplomat, 1919–1927
Hakan Özoğlu

Religion, Identity and Power: Turkey and the Balkans in the Twenty-first Century
Ahmet Erdi Öztürk

Electoral Integrity in Turkey
Emre Toros

Erdoğan: The Making of an Autocrat
M. Hakan Yavuz

edinburghuniversitypress.com/series/esmt

ISLAMIC THEOLOGY IN THE TURKISH REPUBLIC

Philip Dorroll

EDINBURGH
University Press

To Liv

Edinburgh University Press is one of the leading university presses in the UK. We publish academic books and journals in our selected subject areas across the humanities and social sciences, combining cutting-edge scholarship with high editorial and production values to produce academic works of lasting importance. For more information visit our website: edinburghuniversitypress.com

© Philip Dorroll, 2021, 2023

Edinburgh University Press Ltd
The Tun – Holyrood Road
12 (2f) Jackson's Entry
Edinburgh EH8 8PJ

First published in hardback by Edinburgh University Press 2021

Typeset in 11/15 Adobe Garamond by
IDSUK (DataConnection)

A CIP record for this book is available from the British Library

ISBN 978 1 4744 7492 4 (hardback)
ISBN 978 1 4744 7493 1 (paperback)
ISBN 978 1 4744 7495 5 (webready PDF)
ISBN 978 1 4744 7494 8 (epub)

The right of Philip Dorroll to be identified as author of this work has been asserted in accordance with the Copyright, Designs and Patents Act 1988 and the Copyright and Related Rights Regulations 2003 (SI No. 2498).

CONTENTS

Acknowledgements	vi
Introduction	1
1 Origins	17
2 Nation	53
3 God	87
4 Humanity	123
5 Futures	164
Conclusion	201
Bibliography	210
Index	233

ACKNOWLEDGEMENTS

The research for this book began over a decade ago while I was a master's student in the Department of Near Eastern Languages and Cultures at Indiana University. Since that time, I have been met with support and encouragement from family, friends and innumerable others, without whom this book would have been impossible.

I have benefitted immensely from the support of numerous academic mentors in the United States, including Jacqueline Mariña, Stacy Holden, Thomas Ryba, Kevin Jaques, Kevin Martin, Zaineb Istrabadi, Vincent and Rkia Cornell, Gordon Newby, Scott Kugle, Devin Stewart, Richard Martin, M. Hakan Yavuz and Kecia Ali. Dr Ali provided particularly crucial guidance about this project that enabled its publication in the current form. In addition, numerous colleagues and professors in Turkey have provided me over the years with general guidance, feedback on my work, or helpful suggestions, including Sönmez Kutlu, Hülya Alper, Hanifi Özcan, İlyas Çelebi, Hadi Adanalı, Mehmet Bulğen, Şaban Ali Düzgün and Emine Öğük. I am very grateful to these mentors and colleagues.

I am also very thankful for the staff and resources of the research institutions that provided access to crucial documents and texts. These include the libraries of Wofford College, Indiana University, the University of Arizona, and Boğaziçi University; the Berlin State Library (Staatsbibliothek zu Berlin), the Centre for Islamic Studies in Istanbul (İslam Araştırmaları Merkezi), the

Süleymaniye manuscript library in Istanbul and the Turkish National Library in Ankara (Milli Kütüphane). I would also like to thank Emory University and Wofford College for research funding that supported my access to these collections and other institutions.

I also would like to offer my sincere thanks and gratitude to the Little River Coffee Bar and Roasting Company of Spartanburg, South Carolina; and to the teachers and caregivers at the Advent Episcopal and Trinity United Methodist Children's Centers in Spartanburg, South Carolina. It would have impossible to complete this project without you.

I am also very grateful to Wofford College, where I teach. The experience of teaching 'Introduction to Islam' and other courses on Islamic Studies in a small liberal arts college setting provided me with the inspiration to write about topics that I think are important, and hopefully do so in ways that are accessible and helpful to many different audiences.

Most of all, I would like to thank Dr Courtney Dorroll, for truly insightful comments on all of my work, and for support that cannot be measured. Any work that I do of significance is utterly impossible without you. And I would like to thank Liv, for simply being who she is.

INTRODUCTION

This book concerns the tradition of Islamic religious thought written in the modern Turkish language in the modern nation of Turkey. This book argues that Islamic theology in the Turkish Republic constitutes a distinct tradition of reflection on the Islamic doctrine of the Oneness of God (*tawḥīd* in Arabic; *tevhid* in Turkish) as it relates to the intellectual, social and political context of modernity. Put simply, Islamic theology in the modern Turkish language, or what will simply be called 'modern Turkish theology' throughout this book, revolves around the question of what it means to believe in the One God in the context of modernity.

This book will thematically explore the ways in which Islamic theology in the Turkish Republic seeks to answer the question: what are the implications of believing in *tevhid* in the modern era? What does it mean to believe in *tevhid* in the context of modern social thought, modern political thought, modern scientific cosmology or modern conceptions of gender and sexuality? Through a thematic analysis of modern Turkish theologians' handling of these and other related topics, this book will trace how Islamic theology in the Turkish Republic can be viewed holistically as a tradition that developed in order to answer what it means to be a Muslim believer in the One God in the specific context of modernity and modernisation.

Islamic theology in the Turkish Republic constitutes a distinct tradition of Islamic thought because it emerges within the new language of modern

Turkish, and in the new social and political context of the modern Turkish Republic. The context of rapid social and political modernisation in the late nineteenth century in the Ottoman Empire, culminating in the founding of the Republic of Turkey in 1923, has framed the way in which Islamic theology in the Turkish Republic has developed. Modern Turkey was the outcome of processes of radical change, and it was into this experience of flux and instability that modern Turkish theology was born. Moreover, Islamic theology in the Turkish Republic is written in the genuinely new language of modern Turkish, a language that simply did not exist until the opening decades of the twentieth century. In a quite literal sense, Islamic theology in the Republic of Turkey has always spoken the language of modernity.

Modern Turkish theology is therefore the product of genuinely unprecedented linguistic and social structures. Yet its topic, God, is the very definition of unchanging reality. The question that has conditioned the development of modern Turkish theology is the same question that has animated all Islamic theological traditions: what is the relationship between the Creator and the created? Who is the One God, and what is the relationship between human beings and this God? As this book will demonstrate, the modern Turkish theological tradition seeks to answer these questions in ways that are shaped by the intellectual, social and political circumstances of the Turkish Republic. Due to its emergence in the processes of modern change, modern Turkish theology has sought to explore the traditional Islamic theological question of *tevhid* by relating this question to the problem of change and permanency in the modern world. Modern Turkish theology has developed as a way to answer the question posed to it by modernisation: what is the relationship between unchanging truth and the changing world? In other words, what is the relationship between the Creator and the created, when we view this relationship in the context of modernity?

What is Islamic Theology?

With respect to Islamic theology as a larger tradition, this book follows Sabine Schmidtke's definition. She argues that Islamic theology focuses on two main themes: 1) God's nature and existence; and 2) God's interactions with God's creation, most especially human beings.[1] As Schmidtke points out, the bases of Islamic theological discourse are the descriptions of God in the Qur'an, which Muslims believe to be God's final revelation to humankind. As Ingrid Mattson argues, the Qur'an is the ultimate source of divine guidance for Muslims on how to understand and enter into relationship with God.[2] In Martin Nguyen's apt phrase, 'theology unfolds in relation to God', meaning that Islamic theology is always a process of forming faith in, and relationship with, the One God.[3] This relationship is based on systematic reflection on God's revelation to humanity. The vehicle of this final revelation is the Prophet Muhammad, whose life and tradition thus become both sources and subjects of theological reflection.

Islamic theological thought can take numerous forms and can be found in numerous genres of religious writing. The genre of Islamic thought that is most specifically devoted to systematic reflection on the nature of God and the nature of God's creation is called *kalām*. The term *kalām* refers to rational systematic Islamic theology that concerns the cardinal doctrines of Islamic belief.[4] The *kalām* method of theology forms the intellectual basis of the most fundamental components of Islamic dogma, and for this reason it is often referred to in English simply as 'Islamic theology'. *Kalām* can therefore also be thought of as Islamic dogmatics or doctrinal theology. Because *kalām* played this role in the Ottoman Empire and the Turkish Republic, when the term 'Islamic theology' is used in this book it is used in reference to traditions stemming from this particular Islamic theological method.

Moreover, the word used in modern Turkish to refer to 'theology', or systematic religious thought, comes directly from the *kalām* vocabulary. This term is *ilahiyat*. This word in Turkish literally translates into English as 'divinity' or 'matters divine'.[5] In the *kalām* texts used in the Ottoman Empire that form the historical basis of modern Turkish theology, *ilahiyat* was the term used to denote topics of theological discussion that concerned the existence, nature and attributes of God. Thus, the technical term in modern Turkish for 'theology', *ilahiyat*, is directly derived from the Sunni tradition of rational dogmatic theology – *kalām*. This is another reason why the tradition of *kalām* and the modern Turkish developments of this tradition are prioritised in this book. *Kalām* is quite literally the source of the concept of 'theology' itself in modern Turkish.

The word '*kalām*' means 'speech' and refers to the theological method of dialectic and debate. This term points to the origins of systematic Islamic theology in the pluralistic religious environment of the late-ancient Near East within which Islamic thought developed. In such an environment, rational debate on key points of religious doctrine became a common intellectual practice among theologians within the same faith, and between theologians of different faiths.[6] As products of this cultural environment, Muslim theologians felt the need to elaborate and defend their faith through rational argument and dialectic. *Kalām* developed over time into an enormous and diverse tradition of rational systematic theology devoted to the discussion and defence of the bases of Islamic belief, such as belief in the One God and the prophecy of Muhammad. This is why *kalām* can be considered the most fundamental form of Islamic dogmatic theology: it is the type of Islamic theology that developed in order to explicate the most essential beliefs of the faith.

Though a wide variety of theological movements and schools developed among Sunni Muslims from the seventh century onwards, two *kalām* schools that trace their origins to two tenth-century theologians gradually emerged as the main representatives of Sunni theological orthodoxy. These two schools of theology are the Ash'ari and the Maturidi schools, named for Abu al-Hasan al-Ash'ari (d. 935–6)[7] and Abu Mansur al-Maturidi (d. 944).[8] Their theological methods were similar, as both al-Ash'ari and al-Maturidi used syllogistic and dialectical reason as their theological method of explicating and defending the basic points of Sunni Islamic doctrine. Their theological goal was similar as well – to secure the foundations of Islamic doctrine through the application of universal reason to the specifics of Quranic revelation and Prophetic tradition. Most importantly, they both argued for the existence, loving mercy and power of the One God and the finality of the message of the Prophet Muhammad.

The differences between al-Ash'ari and al-Maturidi were a result of which attributes of God they tended to emphasise the most in their respective theological systems. As a consequence of their dialectical methods, they present their theology in the format of a series of rational answers to difficult theological questions, such as the question of the relationship between human freedom and God's power. In order to answer these questions, each theologian tended to emphasise certain attributes of God as a way to rationally resolve theological paradoxes. Al-Ash'ari, on the one hand, tends to emphasise God's attribute of omnipotence and the centrality of the text of revelation.[9] Al-Maturidi, on the other, tends to emphasise God's attribute of wisdom and the ability of human reason to understand God's creation and the meaning of God's revelation.[10] Neither would have rejected the other's basic theological claims on these points. At the same time, the differences in their emphases did at times lead to serious controversy between their followers in the first few centuries after their death.[11] Over time, however, both systems came to be accepted within Sunnism as equally valid ways to approach the most crucial questions of Islamic belief.

Over the course of the next two to three centuries, the reflections and specific arguments put forward by these two towering figures of Sunni theology were organised by later thinkers into ever more systematic and rationalistic theological texts. This resulted in a highly sophisticated tradition of systematic theology that flourished across the Sunni world. The *kalām* tradition developed into a highly nuanced and disciplined method of reflecting on the fundamental questions of Islamic religious belief, most especially *tevhid*. From its beginnings, this tradition emphasised the cardinal importance of reason and proof in both the elaboration and defence of the most important elements of the Muslim worldview. Al-Maturidi's definition of *kalām*, for instance, emphasised that it is the discipline of Islamic religious thought that uses reasoned proof and reflection in order to establish the objective truth of religious belief.[12]

The later *kalām* theologians, whose work formed the core of the Ottoman theological tradition, further refined this definition in ways that would come to be central to how theology is understood in the modern Turkish tradition. According to 'Adud al-Din al-Iji (d. 1355), *kalām* theology is designed to refute doubts about the truth of Islamic belief by utilising systematic rational argumentation and reflection.[13] Al-Sayyid al-Sharif al-Jurjani (d. 1413), whose commentary on al-Iji's work became one of the most important works in Ottoman theological study, outlined a definition of theology that has particularly strong resonance across the late Ottoman and modern Turkish theological tradition. For al-Jurjani, theology concerns two sets of topics. These are the nature of the Creator, and the nature of the created. With respect to the Creator, theology concerns what the human mind can comprehend about God's essence and attributes. With respect to creation, theology investigates the forms and attributes of the physical world insofar as they relate to their ultimate origin and ultimate destiny.[14] In other words, according to al-Jurjani's highly influential conception, theology rationally investigates the world insofar as it relates to God.

All of these elements became the core of the modern Turkish term '*ilahiyat*', the conceptual basis for the kinds of systematic reflection on religious belief signified in the English term 'theology'. Moreover, all of these elements are different ways of phrasing the cardinal doctrine of *tevhid*. Modern Turkish theology, following in this tradition, places *tevhid* in all of its various aspects at the centre of its reflections. At the same time, modern Turkish theology's focus on *tevhid* has a distinctly modern character. Establishing the truth of *tevhid*, and exploring all of its complex implications, becomes key to modern Turkish theology because it asserts something about the created world that is often called into question by modernity. It asserts that the world has sacred value because it points to its Creator. The world is not merely a collection of material elements that mechanically coalesce or dissipate according to blind natural laws. The world is the creation of the One God.

Moreover, the world is ordered by God in ways that reflect God's infinite wisdom and loving mercy. The world in its endless beauty and complexity points towards the truly Infinite, Ultimate character of its Creator. Modern Turkish theology focuses so intently on *tevhid* not only because it is the core of the *kalām* tradition but because it asserts something fundamentally, unchangeably true about the cosmos that is frequently dismissed in the modern intellectual and social context. As we will see throughout this book, modern Turkish theology is keen to discuss a wide variety of modern social, political and intellectual phenomena precisely because, as al-Jurjani asserts, all things are ultimately related to God's bringing them into being, and God's will for them in this life and the next.

The methods and specific arguments of modern Turkish theologians are often distinct from the traditional methods and specific arguments of Sunni *kalām*. The modern period sometimes puts forward different theological questions that need to be answered. However, due to the roots of modern Turkish theology in the Ottoman systematic *kalām* tradition, the basic technical concepts explored by *kalām* are still the central concepts explored in modern Turkish theology. These include the existence and nature of God, the parameters of Prophetic tradition and the nature of religion itself. And as described above, the essential characterisation of theology itself in the *kalām* tradition remains the basis for Islamic theological reflection in Turkey up to the present day. This book therefore explores the Sunni Muslim thinkers writing in the modern Turkish language whose work is the direct descendant of the Ottoman *kalām* tradition, and whose theology concerns the most essential questions of Islamic religious belief. This is the tradition that this book refers to as 'modern Turkish theology', or Islamic theology in the Turkish Republic.

The Study of Modern Turkish Theology

Critical and historical Turkish-language studies of Islamic thought in the Turkish Republic have focused on the development of this tradition as it relates to the cultural politics of modern Turkey. These studies have been crucial for shedding light on the question of the Islamic authenticity of modern Turkish theology. Tahsin Görgün's important work, for example, argues that the basic cultural problematic of modern Turkey is the goal of Westernisation, enshrined in every part of its modern social and political structures. This poses a particular dilemma for Islamic religious thought. Traditional Islamic thought is not drawn from Western culture, though the political and social framework of modern Turkish society is drawn from the West. He thus phrases the problem of theology in modern Turkey this way: Are Islamic religious disciplines of thought possible within a Westernised social and political framework? Is it possible to change Turkish society without changing its religion?[15]

As Görgün explains, the traditional forms of religious thought in Islam do, in fact, presume continuing social change. In other words, theology in modern Turkey can indeed be considered to be authentically Islamic, even if some of its questions and conclusions are different from the pre-modern Islamic tradition. This is because Islamic religious thought is designed to connect human life with religious truth. The various branches of this vast tradition, from dogmatic theology to sacred ritual practice to mystical experience, are all devoted to enabling Muslims to unite their present context with the eternal truths of Islam. Far from denying or denigrating the changeable nature of human society, traditional Islamic thought sees this historical flux as part of the natural order of things. It is therefore the task of Islamic religious thought to acknowledge, influence and/or guide social experiences and development on the basis of the eternal truths of the Islamic faith.[16]

The fact that Islamic theology in the Turkish Republic is so deeply influenced by its specifically modern social and historical circumstances is thus not a mark of its inauthenticity. On the contrary, it is proof that modern Turkish theology is part of a dynamic and complex heritage of Islamic thought that has deep roots in the past. As this book will demonstrate, the vitality of modern Turkish theology comes precisely from its ability to put traditional Islamic theological concepts into dialogue with modernity, thus producing novel theological insights that are also grounded in Islamic tradition.

This book therefore proceeds from the premise that Islamic theology written in the modern Turkish language and in the modern political context of the Turkish Republic can indeed be considered an authentically Islamic theology that deserves to be understood on its own terms. Considering it in this way allows for a nuanced and detailed analysis of its most sophisticated conceptual components, which might otherwise be neglected in our understanding of the modern Islamic intellectual tradition. On this basis, this book endeavours to take the study of modern Turkish theology forward by analysing its specific theological arguments and insights as interlocking pieces of a complex and dynamic, but coherent and distinct, tradition of Islamic thought.

The study of modern Turkish theology in the English language is indebted to two works in particular, Felix Körner's *Revisionist Koran Hermeneutics in Contemporary Turkish University Theology: Rethinking Islam* (2005) and Taraneh R. Wilkinson's *Dialectical Encounters: Contemporary Turkish Muslim Thought in Dialogue* (2019). These pioneering studies were the first book-length treatments in English of the topics and works of contemporary Turkish academic theologians. Both books treat in detail the work of selected living Turkish theologians. Körner's book focuses on the Quranic hermeneutics of influential Turkish theologians working in the Ankara University Faculty of Theology. Wilkinson's book focuses on the work of two contemporary theologians in particular, Recep Alpyağıl and Şaban Ali Düzgün. It is important to make clear that the present work is not presented as a critique or modification of either Körner or Wilkinson's work, but instead seeks to accomplish a different goal by outlining the historical development and broad themes in Turkish theology from the late nineteenth century to the present day.

Körner's and Wilkinson's works have presented numerous foundational insights into the nature of modern Turkish theology that deserve analysis here. Indeed, it is hoped that the present work contributes historical depth and breadth to these insights. Körner was the first scholar writing in English to treat modern Turkish theology as a distinct tradition of thought worthy of extensive analysis. His work identifies the institutional locus of modern Turkish theology as the modern Turkish faculty of theology, the academic departments of Turkish universities that house theological and religious scholarship.[17] His work demonstrates that the study of modern Turkish theology is a necessary corrective to the excessive focus on Arabic-language Islamic theology.[18] As Körner points out, Arabo-centric conceptions of Islamic identity are endemic in modern scholarship in Islamic Studies, particularly in the study of Islamic thought and theology.

Körner's work also laid out the basic historiographical parameters of the study of modern Turkish theology. He notes that the modern Turkish faculty of theology is the ancestor of both pre-modern Ottoman and modern Turkish academic traditions, a key point that this book tries to develop into a clear historical narrative.[19] Körner also referred to the nationalist political context of the development of modern Turkish theology, pointing out that Turkish theology developed in the context of Turkish social modernisation. As he indicates, Islam in the modern Turkish Republic has functioned as the basis of 'national coherence and ethical motivation'.[20] This book tries to develop these key historiographical insights through a detailed intellectual history of the modern Turkish theological tradition.

Wilkinson's book offers necessary correctives to Körner's and the present author's previous work, and breaks new ground in the study of modern Turkish theology. Wilkinson demonstrates that this previous scholarship did not take full account of the internal complexity of modern Turkish theology, arguing that nationalist political categories such as 'traditional' and 'modern' are understood in very nuanced and complex ways by modern Turkish theologians. Wilkinson's work reveals that modern Turkish theology exhibits a 'dialectical' structure that puts three major traditions into dialogue with one another: Ottoman, classical Arabic and Persian, and Western European.[21]

Wilkinson shows that modern Turkish theology exhibits a 'plurality of conceptual provenance': it references and critically engages with these different traditions, and arises from the dialogue between them.[22] In other words, Wilkinson's key insight is that all three of these traditions of thought are considered authoritative for modern Turkish theologians, and are at the same time engaged with critically and constructively when modern Turkish theologians do their work. Wilkinson, therefore, very precisely identifies the elusive quality that makes Turkish theology distinctive: it is, in her words, the 'dialectical encounter' between these traditions of thought.

Wilkinson's insight is a significant criticism of, and advancement beyond, some of the present author's previous work on modern Turkish theology.[23] The historical perspective in the present book is inspired by her critique and by the need to offer an historical outline of modern Turkish theology. This book therefore builds on the insights offered by both Körner and Wilkinson by drawing a historical narrative that begins in the late Ottoman period and covers the state of Turkish theology up to the present day. This book provides an historical and conceptual map to the vast territory of modern Turkish theology, in the hope that it will be of use to anyone interested in understanding the key features of modern Islamic theology in the nation of Turkey.

Summary of Chapters

Chapter 1, 'Origins', argues that the modern Turkish tradition of theology is composed of three main influences: 1) the legacy of Sunni Ottoman systematic theology (*kalām*); 2) late nineteenth- and early twentieth-century Islamic modernism; and 3) late Ottoman and early Republican Turkish sociological theory. The chapter examines these influences by tracing the development of these streams of thought and the institutions that housed them, namely the Ottoman system of religious education, the *medrese* system; and the development of modern faculties of theology in the Republic of Turkey. The chapter therefore lays the groundwork for understanding modern Turkish theology as a distinct tradition of thought by revealing its institutional and conceptual bases in Ottoman and early Republican history. As will be seen throughout the rest of the book, these bases would form the main conceptual ingredients for how modern Turkish theologians would attempt to understand *tevhid* in relation to modernity, in all of the variety of their approaches to this question.

Chapter 2, 'Nation', discusses the most important social and political context of modern Turkish theology that continues into the present day – the context of Turkish nationalism and national identity. This context is key to understanding how modern Turkish theology tackles the question of how to relate *tevhid* to the modern world, because modernity in Turkey developed within the context of nationalism. Specifically, the chapter argues that secular Turkish nationalism actually nurtured the growth of modern Turkish theology by providing a new social and political context for theological reflection. Through an analysis of the work of a wide range of both late Ottoman and Republican-era theologians, the chapter reveals how the social and ideological framework of nationalism provided ways for modern Turkish theology to develop creative forms of reflection that would not have been possible outside of this framework.

This analysis reveals how concepts inherited from discussions of the new national community, such as the notion of national progress and the concept of the Turkish nation, provided modern Turkish theologians with new ways to assess their pre-modern theological tradition. One example that will be discussed in detail is the renaissance of the study of al-Maturidi's theology that has taken place in Turkey as a direct consequence of his inclusion in the modern definition of Turkish national heritage. The remaining chapters of the book will also demonstrate in their own discussions just how influential Maturidi theology has become in contemporary Turkey. At the same time, the concept of the nation also spurred debates about the relationship between religion and the secular state, giving rise to important conservative theological critiques of the Turkish national project that will also be analysed in this chapter.

Chapters 3 and 4 focus on how modern Turkish theologians directly address the fundamental distinction at the heart of the doctrine of *tevhid*, the distinction between the Creator and the created. Chapter 3, 'God', focuses on the cardinal doctrines of God and the nature of religion itself that have played the most essential role in the history of modern Turkish theology. This chapter argues that modern Turkish theology defines God in terms of God's Oneness and God's loving care for creation and humanity. These are the fundamental and unchangeable truths about the universe. The truths of God's Oneness and God's loving concern for the world are crucial to the modern Turkish theological tradition because they affirm that the world is sacred and possesses transcendent value, and is not merely a product of mechanistic material forces. The world possesses this value because it is composed of signs that point to these truths about its Creator. This argument becomes so important to modern Turkish theologians because it reveals the genuinely sacred meaning of the cosmos in an age when secular materialism has called the religious worldview into question. The main components of this theological argument are analysed in this chapter through the work of four of the most important theologians in the modern Turkish tradition, İsmail Hakkı İzmirli (or İzmirli İsmail Hakkı) (1869–1946), Bekir Topaloğlu (1932–2016), Hülya Alper and Emine Öğük.

Chapter 4, 'Humanity', focuses on the created world, the second half of the Creator/created distinction within the doctrine of *tevhid*. This chapter therefore looks at questions of the human and the changeable. The chapter argues that modern Turkish theology discusses the created world as a constantly changing sphere of ethical action within which humans are commanded by God to live out God's eternal will and to reflect God's loving mercy in the world. The chapter reveals how modern Turkish theologians emphasise the dynamism of historical change via their appropriation of late Ottoman sociology, and thus stress the need for theological reflection on the challenges of living out God's will the complex and ever-changing context of modernity. Specific issues that are analysed in this context include consideration of the relationship between Islam and representative democracy, and the conception of gendered social norms and gender relations. Alongside a discussion of numerous other theologians, this chapter features a detailed consideration of the importance of the work of Hüseyin Atay (b. 1930) on human freedom and ethical action, and a similarly detailed examination of the work of Hidayet Şefkatli Tuksal, the author of the first systematic feminist theological text in modern Turkish.

Chapter 5, 'Futures', considers the possible future directions of modern Turkish theology by analysing how the statist policies of the Turkish Republic have decisively influenced the development of theology in modern Turkey. The chapter argues that the way the Turkish state intervenes in theological discussions has been, and will continue to be, the most influential factor that conditions the possibilities for future development of Islamic theology in the Turkish Republic. The chapter explores this dynamic by examining the kinds of theological voices that have been promoted and marginalised by the Turkish state at various points throughout the twentieth and twenty-first centuries, paying particular attention to the history of theology under the administration of the current governing party, the AKP (in English, the Justice and Development Party). The chapter includes a close analysis of the extraordinary expansion of female religious authority under the AKP, and the first emergence of LGBTI+ affirming systematic theological discourse in modern Turkey as case studies to understand the capacity of the Turkish state in the AKP administration to both promote and marginalise certain kinds of theological discourse.

A Note on Audiences and Inspirations for this Book

This book is meant for any reader interested in theology in the modern world. While it is written from the perspective of someone within the academic field of Islamic Studies, it is designed to be of use beyond that field, particularly in a comparative context. The questions asked by modern Turkish theologians are very often the same ones asked by monotheistic believers in the modern period the world over, and so will potentially be of interest to practitioners, scholars and theologians in other traditions. When discussing the key theological arguments mentioned in the book, special emphasis has been placed on including the key Quranic verses that these theologians use to make their points, so that the reader can trace and consider the scriptural bases of these arguments. Key Islamic religious terms (such as *fiqh* or *Shari'ah*) that are crucial to understanding the book's arguments, but that may be unfamiliar to non-Muslim or non-specialist readers, are provided with explanatory endnotes and references for further reading upon their first appearance in the text. Moreover, in these cases care has been taken to direct the reader to English resources that are considered both authoritative and highly accessible.

One major goal of this book is to introduce readers both within and without Islamic Studies to the richness of modern theology in a country that is familiar to many, but whose language is foreign to most. As a result, care has been taken to focus on works and theologians that are widely known and influential in the modern Turkish theological tradition. This includes the work of highly influential women such as Hülya Alper whose work is essential reading in contemporary Turkish faculties of theology, but which is very unfortunately neglected in studies of contemporary global Muslim theology. Another goal of this book is to demonstrate the historical connections between the classical Arabic Sunni theological tradition and the concepts used by modern Turkish theologians. These connections are explored in detail in Chapters 3 and 4 in particular. Demonstrating these connections not only reinforces the arguments made in this book about the historical roots of modern Turkish theology but also helps to connect readers familiar with the classical *kalām* tradition with its modern elaborations.

Finally, this book also attempts to include in its historical narrative voices that are theologically significant but may also be controversial or even marginalised in the contemporary Turkish intellectual environment. While this book takes the form of a traditional history of theology (or perhaps even historical theology), it tries to be inclusive in its scope. Feminist theology and LGBTI+ affirming theology are discussed in detail because they are profound and universally important meditations on the key themes of modern Turkish theology in general, even though these voices may unfortunately be marginalised in some Turkish academic contexts (as they are in many academic contexts worldwide). On this point in particular, the present author is deeply indebted to the revolutionary, and yet deeply tradition-connected, work of Kecia Ali and Scott Siraj al-Haqq Kugle.[24] Their theological meditations taught the present author to think inclusively when attempting to understand and chart the development of theology in the modern world. These theologians have demonstrated the capacity of religious tradition to manifest the guidance and loving mercy of God in unexpected but utterly necessary ways.

A Note on Translation and Transliteration

The large majority of primary texts referenced in this book have not been translated into English. All translations from Arabic and Turkish are the author's own unless otherwise indicated. Arabic names and titles have not been transliterated in the main text, and CE dates have been used throughout. The transliterated forms of words can be found in the bibliography, following the transliteration system of the *International Journal of Middle*

East Studies. All English translations of Quranic verses have been taken from *The Study Quran*.

Notes

1. Schimdtke, 'Introduction', 2.
2. Mattson, 'How to Read the Quran', 1593.
3. Nguyen, *Modern Muslim Theology*, 23.
4. For a summary of the history and development of *kalām*, see Treiger, 'Origins of Kalām'.
5. This and similar terms were used by Ibn Sina and later Sunni theologians to refer to either metaphysics or rational theological discussions that concern the nature of God. It is in the latter sense that the term is used in Ottoman-era theological texts. See Eichner, 'Handbooks', 500; and Körner, *Revisionist Koran Hermeneutics*, 55–6.
6. See on this point Yafeh, Cohen, Somekh and Griffith, eds, *The Majlis: Interreligious Encounters in Medieval Islam*; and Treiger, 'Origins', 27–34.
7. For English translations of Ash'ari's theological works, see McCarthy, *The Theology of Ash'ari*. For recent studies of Ash'ari's life and theology in English, see Frank, 'Elements'; Schmidtke, 'Early Aš'arite Theology'; Siddiqui, *An Intellectual Portrait of al-Juwayni*; and Thiele, 'Between Cordoba and Nīsābūr'.
8. For recent studies of Māturīdī's life and theology in English, see Brodersen, 'Divine and Human Acts'; Correa, *Testifying Beyond Experience*; Dorroll, 'The Universe in Flux'; and Rudolph, *Sunnī Theology in Samarqand* and 'Ḥanafī Theological Tradition and Māturīdism'.
9. Frank, 'Elements', 183–7; McCarthy, *The Theology of Ash'ari*, 33, 53.
10. Brodersen, 'Divine and Human Acts', 359; Rudolph, 'God's Wisdom', 45–8.
11. Rudolph, 'Das Entstehen der Māturīdīya', 394–404.
12. Al-Maturidi, *Kitab al-Tawhid*, 65–6, 480.
13. Al-Iji, *Al-Mawaqif*, 1:1:1
14. Al-Jurjani's definition is quoted and analysed in Topaloğlu, *Kelam İlmine Giriş*, 50. This definition is widely quoted in modern Turkish textbooks and studies as a classic starting point for understanding Islamic theology.
15. Görgün, 'Batı Medeniyet İçerisinde İslami İlimler Mümkün müdür', 1–12.
16. Görgün, 'Batı Medeniyet İçerisinde İslami İlimler Mümkün müdür', 25–6.
17. These departments - *ilahiyat fakülteleri* - are sometimes called 'divinity faculties'. This book follows Wilkinson's consistent usage of the English 'theology faculty' or 'faculty of theology' when translating this term.

18. Körner, *Revisionist Koran Hermeneutics*, 48.
19. Körner, *Revisionist Koran Hermeneutics*, 48–50.
20. Körner, *Revisionist Koran Hermeneutics*, 54.
21. Wilkinson, *Dialectical Encounters*, 5.
22. Wilkinson, *Dialectical Encounters*, 65.
23. See Dorroll, 'The Turkish Understanding of Religion'.
24. See in particular Ali, *Sexual Ethics and Islam*, and Kugle, *Homosexuality in Islam*.

1

ORIGINS

The central claim of this book is that modern Turkish theology constitutes an extended and diverse tradition of meditation on the consequences of the Islamic doctrine of the Oneness of God (*tawḥīd/tevhid*) for modernity. In other words, modern Turkish theology seeks to answer the question: what does it mean to believe in the One God in the context of modernity? This chapter will outline the historical and institutional background that laid the groundwork for the modern Turkish theological tradition's reflection on this question. Specifically, this chapter argues that the modern Turkish tradition of theology is composed of three main influences: 1) the legacy of Sunni Ottoman systematic theology (*kalām*); 2) late nineteenth- and early twentieth-century Islamic modernism; and 3) late Ottoman and early Republican Turkish sociological theory.

This chapter will delineate the intellectual and institutional history of these three components, beginning in the institutional development of the Ottoman system of Sunni Islamic education, the *medrese* system, and ending in the rise of the modern system of theology faculties in Turkish universities. As the rest of the book will elaborate through further thematic analysis, these components came together to form the institutional and conceptual structures that modern Turkish theologians used to meditate on the truth of God's existence and nature, and the implications of this truth for the modern world.

This chapter will trace the historical and institutional developments that allowed these three components to interact with one another, leading to the emergence of a distinct tradition of Sunni Islamic theology in the modern Turkish language at the beginning of the twentieth century. Theology was an important part of Ottoman intellectual life due to its place in the Ottoman religious educational system, the *medrese* system. The highly bureaucratic organisation of this system allowed for a specific set of theological texts and traditions to become part of Ottoman Islamic intellectual culture until the end of the empire and the beginning of the republic. In this way, modern Turkish theology was able to build on classical Sunni theological discourses. The highly organised structure of religious education in the Ottoman Empire also laid the groundwork for the development of the modern Turkish faculty of theology, the current institutional home of Islamic theology in Turkey.

This strong institutional context that bridged the Ottoman and Republican periods allowed sophisticated intellectual discourses to interact productively with one another. Within late Ottoman and early Republican reformed educational institutions such as the *Darülfünun* and the Ankara University Faculty of Theology, traditional Sunni systematic theology, Islamic theological modernism and sociological theory became particularly popular topics of discussion and analysis among theologians and Muslim intellectuals. This chapter will thus describe in detail the history of the ways in which these influences merged in the late nineteenth and early twentieth centuries to form the basis of modern Turkish theology.

The Pre-modern Ottoman Empire and the *Medrese* System

Sunni Islamic theology under the Ottoman Empire was distinguished by its institutionalisation in the highly bureaucratised state religious education system, the *medrese* system. By providing a stable institutional structure, this imperial context gave Ottoman Sunni theology its unique contours and parameters. Between the fifteenth and nineteenth centuries, certain texts and theological traditions from medieval Sunnism became standard features of Ottoman theological education. It is important to outline these major texts and traditions here, because these were the immediate backdrop to the development of Sunni theology in the Turkish Republic. As we will see in the coming chapters, the principal texts and theological traditions that coalesced in the Ottoman period would form the basis for the development of a uniquely modern Turkish theological tradition.

The transition of the Ottoman state from a warring, tribal principality to a settled imperial government accompanied a shift in Islamic discourse in the territories of the empire.[1] At the beginning of the fourteenth century, the Islamic educational institutions that were under direct Ottoman control were largely limited to rural Sufi lodges associated with the multitudes of popular charismatic saints that spread Islam throughout the Anatolian countryside (variously termed *şey*, *derviş* or *baba*).[2] These institutions had a loose relationship with state authorities, but had much deeper roots in Anatolian folk Islamic traditions.[3] The needs of the Ottoman state, however, quickly favoured the creation of a settled class of Sunni Islamic authorities who would be a much more stable and reliable source of dynastic legitimacy.[4] This new class of Sunni Muslim scholars would come from a uniquely Ottoman institution, the *medrese* (from the Arabic term, *madrasa*). These Islamic educational institutions had much in common with their institutional predecessors in the medieval Islamic world and drew on their scholarly traditions.[5] Like the madrasas, the Ottoman *medrese*s focused their studies on Islamic religious disciplines,[6] leaving scientific traditions such as medicine and astronomy to be developed in separate schools created for that purpose.[7] The Ottoman *medrese*s also built on the legacy of Seljuq madrasas that predated the Ottoman control of Anatolia.[8]

At the same time, Ottoman *medrese*s differed in important ways from other educational institutions in the medieval Islamic world. Theological education in medieval cities such as Baghdad and Cairo was based on the individual relationship between a teacher and student.[9] Students acquired expertise based on the individual teachers under whom they studied. Thus, academic prestige resided in, and was transmitted through, the personal authority of well-known teachers who could teach in a variety of formal and informal contexts. Theological education flourished both under state patronage and outside of it; some institutions were closely connected with state authority and others were run exclusively by private endowment. Teachers could be attached to a specific centre of learning, the court of a ruler, or a variety of other institutional contexts. In other words, in medieval Sunni Islamic societies before the Ottoman Empire, there was no tradition of a wholly state-run and thoroughly centralised system of theological education.

The Ottoman system of *medrese*s introduced an entirely new model of Sunni religious education. The first *medrese* in Ottoman territory was founded in 1331 in Iznik. The *medrese* offered instruction in all the Islamic religious disciplines, which would have included theology.[10] Between 1331 and 1451 (the beginning of the second reign of Mehmet II, the conqueror of Constantinople, r. 1444–6 and 1451–58) at least eighty-four separate *medrese*s were founded; by then, a new system of education had fully supplanted the independent Sufi lodges and small independent Qur'an schools that had previously dominated the countryside.[11] This new system of *medrese*s was fully under state control and provided education for state functionaries. Beginning with educational reforms under Mehmed II and Süleyman the Magnificent (r. 1520–66), Ottoman *medrese*s were classified by the state according to a rigid system of promotion and prestige. Successive Ottoman administrations further refined, reorganised and consolidated the hierarchy of this system over the course of Ottoman history.[12]

Though the details of the system varied over time, *medrese*s were grouped according to criteria of prestige. A precise order of career advancement by appointment at increasingly more prestigious institutions was set out in Ottoman law. This career path began at the lowest levels of countryside *medrese*s and could culminate in appointment at higher academic levels, such as professoriates at highly ranked *medrese*s in Istanbul or various high-ranking *qāḍī* (imperial judge) positions throughout the empire. The relative ranks of individual *medrese*s and the other specificities of this system varied in accordance with periodic changes in Ottoman administrations and the policies of a given Sultan, but the graded and bureaucratised structure of the system remained in effect until the end of the empire.

The centralisation of religious authority under the state was a feature of Ottoman governance from its beginning. As far back as Orhan I, Muslim religious scholars had played a role in sanctioning the use of state power;[13] now, the Ottoman state had fully integrated the Islamic religious scholarly class, the *'ulamā'*, into the machinery of the Ottoman government. In the apt phrase of Ahmet Yaşar Ocak, the Ottoman Empire effected an 'assimilation of the state with Islam' that was unprecedented in Islamic history.[14]

This assimilation was made possible by a sacralisation of state authority that had never been achieved to such an extent under previous regimes in Islamic lands. The Ottoman state from the fifteenth century on, in opposition to the rising Shi'i Safavid Persian empire to its east, promoted Sunni orthodoxy within its borders, and the *medrese*s became the intellectual backbone of state religious orthodoxy. While the utilisation of notions of Sunni orthodoxy in the legitimation of the state were a feature of other dynasties such as the Seljuqs, the complete incorporation of the *'ulamā'* and Sunni religious institutions into the state bureaucracy seems to have been unique to the Ottomans.[15]

The Ottoman Empire also established a centralised state office of Sunni Islamic religious authority as part of its incorporation of Sunni Islamic religious institutions into the machinery of the Sultan's state. In 1425, Murad II (r. 1421–44 and 1446–51) established the office of the *Şeyhülislam*, the highest position at the top of the Sunni religious hierarchy in the empire.[16] This position was originally established to issue Islamic juristic opinions supporting government decisions, but it grew to have broad institutional authority. It always remained, however, subordinate to the Sultan himself.[17] The first person appointed to this position was Molla Fenari (d. 1431), a renowned scholar from a village near İnegöl, a city in northwestern Anatolia not far from the former Ottoman capital of Bursa. Molla Fenari's own theological background would have major consequences for the development of Ottoman theology. Molla Fenari was one of the first Ottoman-era scholars to produce large numbers of students and original works. His adherence to the tradition of philosophical Ash'arism helped to establish this school's dominance in the theological curricula of Ottoman *medrese*s, as will be discussed in more detail below.[18]

This Ottoman merger between religious and state power was not properly a theocracy, as Ocak usefully points out: religious institutions were explicitly subordinated to the state, not the other way around.[19] In Ottoman political theory, religion (*din*) and the authority of the ruler or the state (*devlet*) were distinct concepts. Religion provided sacred legitimacy to the Ottoman ruling dynasty, but did not have the authority to wield worldly power or to operate the government itself. The ruler and the state were vested with the duty of ensuring the flourishing of Islamic religious life, in exchange for the sacred blessing of the religious establishment.[20] In other words, in the Ottoman Empire, religion and state supported one another, but were distinctly different kinds of authority. Religion had to do with adhering to the will of God and thus attaining eternal reward, while the state had to do with preserving earthly order and justice. The emperor, the Sultan, was ultimately in control of both of these hierarchies.

This conceptual distinction between religion and state corresponded to a legal distinction in Ottoman law, the distinction between *kanun* and *Shari'ah* (Islamic ritual practice).[21] *Kanun* comprised public code that was promulgated by the Sultan and the ministers of state. *Shari'ah* governed the private sphere of Muslim subjects of the Ottoman realm, and was sanctioned and supported by the Ottoman state. This distinction in legal practice and norms was not only found in Ottoman society, but was also a common feature of pre-modern Muslim states more broadly.[22] Though these Ottoman conceptual and legal distinctions do not correspond precisely to the modern 'secular'–'religious' binary, they do illuminate the pre-Republican backdrop to the kinds of theological and social debates that will be explored more fully in the final two chapters of this book.

The Main Features of Sunni Theology in the Ottoman *Medrese*s

Crucially for the history of modern Turkish theology, one of the distinguishing features of the Ottoman *medrese*s was the important place accorded to Sunni systematic theology (*kalām*) in this system. Due to a lack of consistent documentary evidence, it can be difficult to determine which exact subjects and texts were taught in which institutions at a given time or place in Ottoman history. The extant curriculum lists vary with respect to which subjects were included for study and instruction. What is clear is that Sunni *kalām* did occupy a central place in *medrese* curricula and academic life throughout the history of the empire.[23] Due to its speculative and rational nature, *kalām* did at times provoke controversy outside the *medrese* system. Despite its capacity for controversy, however, *kalām* continued throughout Ottoman history to be a staple of *medrese* education, and therefore of elite Sunni academic discourse in general. Providing key examples of this will help illustrate how a Sunni theological tradition formed under the Ottoman Empire that could then be passed down to modern Turkish theologians.

As noted above, it is likely that systematic theology in some form was taught at the first Ottoman *medrese* founded in Iznik in 1331. The oldest extant imperial laws associated with the *medrese*s are those attributed to Mehmed II. Though this material is thought to contain significant anachronisms, it does give a sense of Ottoman legal tradition from the 15th and 16th centuries.[24] One curriculum list drawn from this legal corpus lists important works that were taught in *medrese*s during this period, including a commentary on the creed of 'Adud al-Din al-Iji (d. 1355) and the commentary of Al-Sayyid al-Sharif al-Jurjani (d. 1413) on the *Tajrid al-I'tiqad* of Nasr al-Din Tusi (d. 1274). The great Ottoman polymath Katip Çelebi (d. 1657) also provides information on works that Sultan Mehmet the Conqueror ordered to be taught: these include al-Jurjani's commentary on al-Iji's *Mawaqif fi 'Ilm al-Kalam*, and Sa'd al-Din al-Taftazani's (1322–90) *Sharh al-Maqasid*.[25] One extant curriculum list for higher-level *medrese*s under Süleyman, however, does not list *kalām* among its subjects.[26]

Further evidence for the place of *kalām* in Ottoman Islamic education can be found in the records left by individual scholars. A number of prominent scholars from the classical Ottoman period personally detailed the books they studied during their education and even the *medrese*s where these books were taught. According to the Ottoman scholar Taşköprülzade (d. 1561), al-Jurjani's commentary on al-Tusi's *Tajrid* was taught at the lower level *medrese*s, while al-Jurjani's commentary on al-Iji's *Mawaqif* was reserved for instruction at the higher level *medrese*s. Documentary evidence from 1741 attests that *kalām* was taught in mid-level *medrese*s.[27] Other evidence from the eighteenth century suggests that some students preferred to study philosophy rather than the standard works by al-Iji and al-Jurjani.[28] In other words, theology remained an important, if at times controversial, scholarly discipline throughout the history of the Ottoman Empire. The exact nature of its importance and popularity depended heavily on the policies of Sultans and the opinions of scholars, which of course varied widely over the course of the six centuries of Ottoman history.

Certain theologians and their works did, however, attain canonical status in Ottoman theological circles. The most important of these were a-Iji, al-Jurjani and al-Taftazani. Commentary on and discussion of these theologians' work in particular formed the core of most theological thought and scholarship in the Ottoman period.[29] Al-Jurjani's commentary on al-Iji's *Mawaqif* was the most common work taught at the advanced levels of instruction in theology.[30] Al-Jurjani's and al-Iji's theology represented the most outstanding examples of what is often referred to as the 'late' tradition of Sunni theology, a tradition that begins with Fakhr al-Dan al-Razi's (1149–1210) incorporation of the philosophical concepts of the great Ibn Sina (d. 1037) into orthodox Sunni theology.[31] This tradition of Sunni theology combined the Ash'ari school of Sunni dogmatic theology with the philosophical structure of Ibn Sina's metaphysics to produce a genre of theology that set out a systematic and rationalistic vision of Sunni Islamic belief. This is the particular style of theology that became dominant within the Ottoman *medrese* system.

Al-Taftazani's *Sharh al-Maqasid* was also a major text of instruction at the advanced levels of theology. Al-Taftazani's text is perhaps best described as a synthesis of both of the major schools of Sunni dogmatic theology, Ash'arism and Maturidism, and as such represents another important dimension of the development of Sunni theology in the Ottoman period: Sunni theological synthesis.[32] Though al-Razi's version of Ash'arism seems to have formed the basis of Ottoman formal education in Sunni theology, the inclusion of al-Taftazani in the Ottoman curriculum (who wrote a famous and widely read commentary on the Maturidi creed of Abu al-Barakat al-Nasafi, d. 1310) points to the fact that many Ottoman theologians saw no fundamental conflict between different schools of Sunni dogmatics, such as the Ash'ari and Maturidi schools.

This spirit of synthesis is most clearly on display in the extremely popular (and misleadingly named) *ikhtilāf* ('disagreement') genre of texts that detail the points of divergence between the Maturidi and the Ash'ari schools. In fact, the goal of these texts was to examine supposed differences one by one and demonstrate that they were not actually substantive differences after all, or at the very least were not differences that justified accusations of heresy from either side. Indeed, this attitude seems to have prevailed particularly in the fifteenth century, when scholars were found writing commentaries on Maturidi and Ash'ari creeds in almost equal numbers. For instance, one early Ottoman specialist in theology, Hayali Ahmed Efendi (d. 1470), wrote very popular and influential commentaries on both al-Iji and al-Taftazani.[33]

These comparative *ikhtilāf* treatises epitomise the Ottoman tendency towards synthesis as well as its acceptance of Sunni theological diversity. The earliest example in this genre seems to have been authored by the Mamluk-era scholar, Taj al-Din al-Subki (d. 1370), *Nuniyya al-Subki*.[34] Al-Subki's work comparatively examines the key theological positions of these two schools and concludes that most of the points in which they differ are merely semantic, and that those points that are substantive disagreements are not so serious as to necessitate accusations of heresy. This two-part argument became the standard form for all subsequent texts in this genre, which, like al-Subki's, conclude that the differences between these two Sunni traditions offer no basis for animosity among their adherents.[35] Some Ottoman authors, such as Kara Halil Pasha Çorlulu (d. 1775–6), even made the case that all disagreements between the two schools were merely semantic.[36]

In sum, theology in the Ottoman period developed a broad notion of Sunni theological consensus that was bureaucratised and co-opted by the Ottoman state. Theological education, and thus the development of theological thought more generally, became an important part of the specific policy decisions of each successive emperor's government. This unprecedented level of institutionalisation in Sunni theology meant that a certain body of theological works would be passed down as authoritative right up until the development of the modern Turkish state in the early twentieth century. This provided modern Turkish theology with a readily available basis in, and organic connection with, pre-modern Sunni theological traditions. It also meant that the development of theology in the Turkish Republic would be decisively influenced by the intervention of the Turkish state, because the modern Turkish Republican government would also assert authority over religious education in the country (as will be discussed in the last chapter of this book).

The Ottoman Islamic intellectual tradition was able to form the basis of modern Turkish theology because it endured in a coherent and institutionalised form well into the modern period. Because the Ottomans had so thoroughly integrated Islamic religious education into their state structure, and because a specific tradition of systematic Sunni theology played a key role in this system of religious education, Sunni systematic theology from the Ottoman tradition formed the foundation for the emergence of modern Turkish theology. Systematic Sunni theological reflection became such a marked feature of modern Turkish Islamic intellectual history because a strongly systematic and strongly pan-Sunni tradition of thought had already been shaped by the Ottomans, and this tradition was the basis of the education of the late Ottoman theologians who, as we will see, would go on to begin the process of developing modern Turkish theology.

The Life of Mulla Hafiz

In order to help bring all of the above historical information into better focus, it is helpful to summarise the biography of one scholar in particular, Hafiz al-Din Muhammad ibn Ahmad Basha ibn 'Adil Pasha (better known as Mulla Hafiz). His life, described in Taşköprülzade's *Shaqa'iq al-Nu'maniyya*, provides an illustrative example and case-in-point of the unique features of the Ottoman *medrese* system analysed above.[37] Born in Persia sometime in the late fifteenth century, Mulla Hafiz moved to Ottoman territory and began his studies under the scholar 'Abd al-Rahman ibn al-Mu'ayyad, and subsequently presented his work to Sultan Bayezid II (r. 1481–1512). Impressed with his scholarship, Bayezid awarded him headship of a *medrese* in Ankara. After teaching *fiqh* there, he then became a professor at a *medrese* in the town of Merzifon in northwestern Anatolia. After composing a supra commentary on al-Jurjani's commentary on al-Sakkaki's (1160–1229) widely read work on rhetoric (*Miftah al-'Ulum*), he presented this work to his former teacher, Ibn al-Mu'ayyad, who approved of his work.

Mulla Hafiz then travelled to Istanbul where he became a professor at the *medrese* of the minister Ali Pasha, during which time he composed a supra commentary on al-Jurjani's commentary on al-Iji's famous systematic theological work mentioned above, *al-Mawaqif fi 'Ilm al-Kalam*. He was then appointed professor of a *medrese* in Iznik, where he wrote an apparently widely known treatise on prime matter. He then became a professor at one of the famous 'Eight Medreses', a complex at Fatih Mosque in Istanbul widely regarded as one of the most prestigious centres of learning in the empire at the time. During this period of his life, he authored a commentary on al-Tusi's *Tajrid*. Finally, he became a professor at Ayasofya *medrese*, at the top of the Ottoman higher educational system. During his tenure at Ayasofya, Mulla

Hafiz authored a text called 'The City of Knowledge' (*Madinat al-'Ilm*) where he synthesised sections of major works on Quranic hermeneutics, *kalām* and *fiqh*. After leaving this position, he was offered a retirement stipend of seventy dirhams a day, and died around 1550.

Mulla Hafiz's career summarises the professionalisation and synthesis of Islamic education that took place in the Ottoman period. His career arc takes him from the edges of the empire to the heart of imperial power, in a gradual ascent from less prestigious institutions to the Ayasofya *medrese*, one of the greatest academic institutions in the empire. Moreover, this series of promotions was based on his own individual work as a scholar, which spanned numerous disciplines. Finally, his academic work exemplifies how theology played a crucial role at various stages of higher education in the *medrese*s. Throughout his life, Mulla Hafiz participated in a highly structured and regularised system of education that was under the direct control of the Ottoman state and which rewarded him at the end of his illustrious career with a rather generous retirement income.

The Late Ottoman Empire I: Islamic Modernism

The transition to modern Islamic theology in Turkey from the pre-modern Ottoman Islamic theological tradition was part of a much larger social and political shift experienced in the territories of the late Ottoman Empire. At the end of the eighteenth century and throughout the nineteenth century, Ottoman elites first put into action their centuries-old debates over the causes of the apparent decline in the political and economic pre-eminence of their empire. This was the era of constant reform, a series of dramatic political and social engineering carried out by the Ottoman state with the intention of modernising Ottoman society to such an extent that it was able to economically and militarily compete with developing West European powers.[38] These reforms began with attempts to reverse the decline of Ottoman military power by remodelling Ottoman armies along European lines. Gradually, and most especially during the Tanzimat period in the middle of the nineteenth century, these top-down reform programmes attempted to dramatically alter the social fabric of Ottoman life by establishing equal legal treatment for religious minorities and economically integrate the Ottoman Empire with the growing international market.

These reform programmes set in motion a period of social transformation that culminated in the disintegration of imperial loyalties into a rapid succession of national independence movements, each claiming a mandate to establish a modern republic to defend the interests of a new national community. Modern Turkey emerged as a result of this process, as Turkish nationalists defended the contemporary borders of the Turkish Republic as the historical centre of a Turkish national community, winning control of this territory in a struggle against the attempts of the Allied powers to divide it among themselves at the end of the First World War. In the transition from empire to nation state, nearly all aspects of social life were reconfigured and reimagined in the light of the understanding that the Turkish-speaking inhabitants of Anatolia constituted an historical community distinct from centuries of Ottoman imperial civilisation. In other words, the concept of nation and its attendant political system, republican democracy, led late Ottoman intellectuals to re-examine conceptions of religion, gender, social hierarchy and economic theory, and under the influence of West European philosophical currents even the nature of the world and humanity itself.[39] The history of modern Islamic theology in Turkey begins with these reimaginings, most particularly the redefinition of religion, religiosity and national community.

The legacy of Ottoman reformism reached its radical conclusion after the collapse of the Ottoman Empire following the First World War. In the early years of the new Turkish Republic, founded in 1923, the first president of Turkey and nationalist leader Mustafa Kemal Atatürk and his government undertook a series of drastic social reforms that aimed, in his words, to 'form Turkish society into a modern society in every aspect'.[40] The Ottoman Sultanate was abolished (1924), the Caliphate was abolished (1924), fezes and turbans were declared illegal (1925), all Sufi shrines and lodges were outlawed (1925), and legal reforms designed to solidify the equality of women and men under Turkish law were continued throughout the decade, including granting women full suffrage and rights in political participation (in 1935, eighteen female representatives were elected to the Turkish parliament). In 1924, all religious institutions were brought under the control of a single government ministry for religious affairs, now called the *Diyanet İşleri Başkanlığı*, or simply 'the Diyanet'.

All education was brought under the control of the state also in 1924, and *medrese*s were abolished entirely. In 1928, the Latin alphabet was introduced as the basis for the new Turkish alphabet, replacing the Ottoman use of Arabic script, as part of a massive programme of linguistic reform. In addition, in 1926 a civil legal code based on West European models was implemented (replacing any legal function that *Shari'ah* had fulfilled to that point), and in 1937 the principle of laicism was included in the Turkish constitution. These social transformations reached every aspect of Turkish society, and were meant to replace loyalty to the Ottoman dynasty, the Sunni Caliphate or the worldwide Muslim community (the *Umma*) with loyalty to the Turkish Republic, the Turkish nation and the principles of strict secularism along the lines of the French model of laicism.[41]

This climate of reform and innovation led to the development of a distinctly Ottoman and modern Turkish version of Islamic modernism. Islamic modernism is one of the most influential intellectual movements in the modern Muslim world, having its roots in a synthesis of classical Islamic intellectual traditions with political and social questions that emerged in the eighteenth and nineteenth centuries. Islamic modernism is based on the argument that there exists a fundamental distinction between religious beliefs and practices that reflect eternal truths, and religious beliefs and practices that are the products of human contingency and thus subject to reform or abrogation.

As Abdolkarim Soroush points out, the distinction between the 'unchangeable' and the 'changeable' in Islamic belief and practice has been the key theological motif in Islamic modernist thought since its early development.[42] The effort to define the true essence of the Islamic faith is at the heart of the modernist project: returning to the essence of Islam means the necessary reform of the faith in the light of modern social and technological change.[43] This reform was also seen as necessary to strengthen the Muslim community to resist the onslaught of Western imperialism and colonialism.[44] Determining what constitutes 'true' Islam is the precondition for both social progress and the defence of the most necessary elements of Islamic tradition. The Islamic modernist distinction between the changeable and the unchangeable in religion would go on to be highly influential in modern Turkish theology, as successive chapters and analyses in this book will demonstrate.

This distinction played a key role in debates over gender and social reform in Muslim societies in the late nineteenth and early twentieth centuries. These debates emerged as a consequence of the encounter with Western imperialism, and they took place in the context of nationalist modernisation and legal reform.[45] As Ziba Mir-Hosseini points out, the theological distinction between the changeable and the unchangeable in Islam was a particularly important part of Islamic modernist discussions on gender in the Arab world and elsewhere. She refers, for example, to the work of the Tunisian Tahir al-Haddad, whose 1930 work on women in Muslim legal practice was based squarely on this distinction between the eternal and the contingent, the essential and the contextual, in Islamic religious belief and practice.[46]

As Aysha Hidayatullah points out, the Islamic modernist project is also based on a strong vision of theological rationalism. Islamic modernists explicitly described Islam as a religion compatible with Enlightenment conceptions of natural reason, modern progress and empirical scientific discovery.[47] For Islamic modernists, the best of what modern progress had to offer had already been anticipated in the achievements of classical Muslim theology and religious culture. In their view, change brought on by rational investigation represented the dynamism of the faculty of reason gifted by God to the human being. The great Egyptian modernist theologian Muhammad 'Abduh (d. 1905), for example, described theology in the same rationalistic way as the Ottoman reformists. He famously argued that classical *kalām* was based on a rejection of traditional intellectual authority and a purely rational method that reflected the progressive and modern essence of the true spirit of Islam.[48] 'Abduh was deeply admired by many of the Ottoman reformists, and key themes in his work re-emerged throughout late Ottoman intellectual culture.[49]

At the same time, Islamic modernism is not merely reducible to Enlightenment rationalism. Much like the Ottoman reformers who were influenced by his work, 'Abduh was conscious of the potential dissonance between Enlightenment rationalism and traditional Islamic thought. Like other Islamic modernists, he recognised a dynamism in Islamic theology that mirrored the dynamism he perceived in modern thought, but he did not ignore the uniqueness of Islamic religious identity. As Samira Haj has argued,

Islamic modernism sought to navigate a middle course between the conservative reactionism of the existing Muslim scholarly establishment of the time, and a simplistic acceptance of all things Western.[50] In other words, Muslim modernists in the Ottoman Empire and elsewhere saw European modernity as a stimulus and inspiration for a critical and rational re-evaluation of their own traditions.

Modern Turkish theology grew from the interaction of classical Ottoman theology with the newly developing Ottoman Islamic modernism in the late nineteenth and early twentieth centuries.[51] This Ottoman-Turkish strain of Islamic modernism came to be referred to in modern Turkish by the term *yenilenme*, or 'renewal', meaning the renewal of traditional Islamic theological thought in the context of modern social and technological change.[52] The Islamic modernist distinction between the changeable and unchangeable thus became key to the development of the modern Turkish theological tradition. The task set before Muslim modernism, to rediscover the true essence of Islam, became central to the mission of modern Turkish theology. As this book argues, modern Turkish theology takes up this task by meditating on the essential theological belief of Islam – the existence of the One God and the consequences this belief has in the ever-changeable social context of modernity.

The development of Ottoman Islamic modernism began in the mid-nineteenth century. In 1865, a cadre of Ottoman intellectuals established a secret society called *Ittıfak-ı Hamiyet*, or 'Patriotic Alliance'. These intellectuals, later known as the Young Ottomans, advocated the establishment of a constitutional state and of a liberal political regime. Their comprehensive intellectual programme included a theory of religion that foreshadowed debates and conceptual distinctions that developed in modern Turkish politics, social thought and theology. In their famous *Letter from Paris* (their place of exile), they argued that religion pertains to the domain of the spiritual and the afterlife, and is to be distinguished from the worldly laws of the state.[53] This argument was not meant to denigrate the value of religion, but rather to protect its true value. Distinguishing between eternal truth and the contingent circumstances of social life is necessary in order to protect the essential truth of religion and the value of this truth as a properly transcendent guide to the higher purpose of social life.

These words express a momentous shift in Ottoman Islamic thought: in the late nineteenth century, the essence of religion came to be thought of as something conceptually distinct from politics and social policy, as something that primarily referred to the 'eternal'.[54] Political concepts that in the Ottoman period found their legitimacy in religious discourse, such as sovereignty or rights, were now being welded to West European philosophical notions of popular sovereignty and natural rights. The influential intellectual Namık Kemal (1840–88), for instance, argued that what was moral was determined based on conformity to the notion of the Good, which itself was created by God.[55] Sovereignty, however, rested in the people, though their natural rights came from God. In this way a modernist Islamic discourse emerged that attempted to synthesise classical Islamic theological ideas with the liberal constitutionalist political discourses of the late nineteenth century. Namık Kemal's understanding of *Shari'ah* also reflected his acknowledgement that religious truth could be decoupled from social reform; thus, he held that the concrete rulings of the *Shari'ah* (the *aḥkām*) could be changed over time.[56]

Modernist Islamic discourse emerged in the unique intellectual climate of the late Ottoman Empire that flowered in the period following the great wave of comprehensive Ottoman reform known as the Tanzimat and ended with the establishment of the Turkish Republic (roughly 1839–1923). During this period, three dominant strains of thought emerged in answer to the question of how to pull the Ottoman Empire back from the brink of financial and political ruin and restore it to its former position of pre-eminence in global affairs. These were Westernism, Islamism and Turkism.[57] These three ideologies were not exactly well-defined, but instead were broad intellectual tendencies that could be present to a greater or lesser degree in a single thinker or set of discourses. Westernists argued for wholesale adoption of Western philosophical commitments (such as philosophical materialism, positivism and secularism) and concepts of governance, such as the establishment of a secular republic and the complete removal of Islam from political power. Islamists, on the other hand, argued that Islam must remain the ideological basis of the state, but that autocracy should be replaced with some form of constitutionalism.

A third current of thought emerged that utilised the concept of Turkish nationality to mediate between the competing demands of Islamism and

Westernism. Turkism saw the concept of a shared Turkish identity to be the most suitable means for both preserving a sense of cultural distinctiveness and enabling the adoption of West European social models and technologies conducive to modernisation. Turkism argued that Islam was part of the Turkish national story, and thus could not simply be discarded as a relic of an Oriental past. At the same time, certain West European forms of governance and social policy (most notably democracy and gender equality) represented the true ideals of the Turkish national culture, long lost under the influence of Ottoman imperialism. The negotiation of these disparate theoretical elements achieved lasting cohesion in the formulations of Ziya Gökalp (1878–1924),[58] perhaps the most influential intellectual voice of modern Turkish thought. His sociological reflections on Turkish identity and Islam's role in Turkish history would become highly influential in the development of a modern Turkish Islamic theological tradition.

The Late Ottoman Empire II: Ziya Gökalp and Sociology

Ziya Gökalp was born Mehmed Ziya in Diyarbekir province in 1878; he later adopted the surname 'Gökalp', or 'sky hero', as an homage to old Turkish folklore. As a leading intellectual of his day, he actively participated in the Young Turk movement that resulted in the overthrow of the absolute Ottoman monarchy in 1908. Gökalp's thought had wide impact beyond this period, however. His analysis of Turkish nationhood synthesised the intellectual tendencies of Westernism, Turkism and Islam into a coherent intellectual Turkish nationalism that became foundational for modern Turkish intellectual and cultural history.

Besides politics and military reform, the Ottoman reform movements of the nineteenth century also extended their efforts to the translation and dissemination of European philosophy and social thought. The influence of French thought in particular extended deeply throughout nearly all areas of Ottoman elite society. A British traveller to Istanbul in 1847–8, Charles MacFarlane, was once told to his surprise by a student at the Galatasaray Medical School that he and the rest of the students at the school were followers of Voltaire.[59] This French influence carried over to the nationalist period just before and after the Young Turk Revolution of 1908, that is, the period of Ziya Gökalp's most influential intellectual activities. Like other intellectuals of his time, Gökalp was particularly influenced by French sociology in general and by the works of Emile Durkheim in particular.[60] Sociology became for Gökalp the key to a correct understanding of history, religion and politics: sociology was for him the most effective intellectual tool in approaching the question of Turkish identity. In 1912, Gökalp became the first professor of sociology at the *Darülfünun* (discussed below), putting him in a particularly strong position to influence the direction of Turkish theological thought.[61]

Gökalp famously rejected any racial definition of nationhood, arguing that race simply cannot be correlated with any particular social formation.[62] Likewise, he regarded the notion of ethnic purity as a complete myth: the historical reality of intermarriage and the intermingling of peoples made it impossible in his view.[63] Instead, Gökalp argued for a national identity based on a shared culture inculcated by societal norms and social education. The 'nation' is the society into which a person is born and through which a person is shaped according to its ideals. The bond of unity between people of the same nation is their shared experience of a single social context.[64] Gökalp saw the individual's experience of society as absolute: everything that makes an individual person who they are is provided to them in a social setting, through the social inculcation of values.

In describing the essence of national culture, Gökalp made a crucial conceptual distinction that would become instrumental in the definition of 'Turkishness' in later periods of modern Turkish history. Gökalp distinguished between 'culture' and 'civilisation', arguing that culture refers to the values and sentiments inculcated by a given society into an individual.[65] These values are innate to the individual: they are organic and authentic, and cannot be changed by individual initiative. They are what people refer to when talking about the 'national'. These are the cultural characteristics imparted to any individual who is raised in the Turkish national society, whether their race is of Turkic descent or not. Again, what it means to be Turkish is not imparted by racial or ethnic characteristics, but the experience of being raised in Turkish society. The term 'civilisation', however, refers to those aspects of human culture that are created by human initiative, and thus can be harmoniously shared by peoples of different nations. These include science, aesthetics, technology or any other form of culture that is a product of human creativity and not the result of being born into a certain social environment.

For all the apparent artifice of this distinction, this conceptual move authorised a highly important feature of modern Turkish intellectual life: the assumption that the adoption of West European social and cultural institutions does not conflict with Turkish national distinctiveness. This conceptual distinction allowed Gökalp to declare that the Turkish nation should discard Ottoman civilisation for 'Western' civilisation, and become Western in civilisation while remaining Turkish in culture. Becoming Turkish in culture was to be accomplished by Ottoman elites spending time among Turkish peasants to learn the folkways of Turkish national culture. At the same time, these same elites were to impart Western civilisation to the Turkish masses.[66] In fact, Gökalp saw no contradiction between authentic Turkish national values and Western civilisation. Gökalp's theory may help explain why mainstream Turkish intellectual culture has usually had little objection to certain social institutions and conceptions that were originally imported from Western Europe, such as representative democracy and the secular state.

Gökalp viewed religion (and all other aspects of a human being's internal life) in Durkheimian terms. Durkheim famously describes religion as the reflection of the social group: religion is produced by society and is a concrete manifestation of a given society's norms, institutions and values.[67] This conception of society produced Gökalp's attempt to reform *Shari'ah* jurisprudence (*fiqh*), by the creation of what he called 'social *fiqh* theory' (*ijtimā'ī uṣūl-i fiqh*).[68] This theory sought to incorporate the insights of modern social science into the study of the sources of Islamic legal rulings, thus allowing for the flexibility and adaptation of classical Islamic jurisprudence to modern social needs. Gökalp argued that religious principles based on divine revelation are not subject to change; however, religious rulings rooted in social conditions are liable to change along with those social conditions.[69] As will be discussed in Chapter 4, these arguments foreshadowed similar claims that would be made by Turkish theologians throughout the history of the Turkish Republic.

Gökalp also inherited the Young Ottomans' view of religion as an essentially internal experience. This meant a separation between religion and worldly affairs such as politics and the state. In his words, '[t]he state and the *medrese* are two separate worlds'.[70] Like many Muslim intellectuals of the period, Gökalp separated the legislative power of the state from religion, arguing that religion only referred to matters of private belief and worship (*itikat* and *ibadet*).[71] Like the Young Ottomans, he argued that this separation was necessary to protect the inner transcendent essence of religion from worldly corruption. Gökalp also argued that this distinction was a basic principle of Islam itself, referring to Qur'an 4:59, which he interpreted as a command to believers to obey the rulers of the societies in which they live. In his view, this verse implicitly recognises a distinction between religious authority and secular authority by separating the authority of God and the Prophet from the power of temporal rulers.

Gökalp adopted the term *diyanet* to refer to personal religious practice, arguing that this is the true definition of what constitutes religion, rather than adherence to any particular model of politics or government.[72] These matters, as the Qur'an demonstrates, are left to the discretion of individuals and societies. In this way Gökalp argued that the establishment of such modern notions as equality between the sexes and democratic government is in no way in conflict with Islamic values, but instead serves as the expression of their essential truths in a modern social context. As Markus Dressler points out, Gökalp's body of work argued that the moral values and spirit of Islamic culture and the development of novel modern social institutions could be seen as fundamentally compatible with one another.[73]

Gökalp's elaboration of religion as a sociological and cultural phenomenon exemplifies the broad intellectual climate in which modern Turkish Islamic theology came into being. As outlined above, the intellectual ferment of the late Ottoman Empire encouraged discussions of Islamic theology that grew from the *medrese* tradition, but quickly acquired their own distinctive character. These new parameters took into account the notion of a Turkish national community, the establishment of liberal participatory forms of governance, the privatisation of religion and the acceptance and even encouragement of radical social change such as changes in gender norms.

These socially and politically reformist currents of thought were not alone, of course, in this intellectual environment. However, due to their official patronage by the Ottoman state and their continuing support by Turkish national governments, these currents of thought acquired a unique level of importance and pre-eminence during the period of Young Turk rule from 1908–18 and the subsequent establishment of the Turkish Republic after the

First World War in 1923. This meant that these ideas would become foundational to modern Islamic theology in the Republic of Turkey, and certain key academic institutional formations allowed them to consolidate and perpetuate their authority in Turkish Islamic intellectual life. Chief among these institutions was the large network of theology faculties (*ilahiyat fakülteleri*) that today form part of the Turkish state and private university system. These faculties are the outcome of a process of the reorganisation of Islamic intellectual life in the late Ottoman Empire and the Turkish Republic, a process that laid the foundations for the institutional context of contemporary Turkish Islamic theology.

The History of the Faculty of Theology in the Turkish Republic

The national vision of the Turkish Republic provided the framework for an entirely new institutional context for Sunni theology in Turkey. That new institution, the modern Turkish theology faculty, is the subject of the final section of this chapter. Just as the Ottoman state asserted control over all Islamic religious education in the empire, the new nationalist administration would assert the same level of control over religious education in the new Turkish Republic. State control over theological education in the Republic was part of the larger effort to completely reorganise and modernise Turkish society along the lines described above. The transformation of late Ottoman theological academia into the modern Turkish system of the theology faculties under the early Turkish nationalist regime is therefore one of the key historical processes that enabled the emergence and development of modern Turkish theology. It was in the theology faculties of the Turkish Republic that the three intellectual roots of modern Turkish theology (classical Sunni Ottoman systematic theology, late Ottoman Islamic modernism and late Ottoman sociological theory) were woven together in the modern Turkish language for the first time.

The first modern university in the Ottoman Empire, the *Darülfünun*, opened its doors in 1864 as part of a *medrese* reform movement occurring during the Tanzimat period. This institution also produced the first Faculty of Theology in the Ottoman Empire. Situated next to the imperial mosque of Ayasofya, in the heart of the Ottoman capital of Istanbul, the *Darülfünun* was meant to lead the empire in a series of modernising educational reforms in imitation of the modern university system taking shape in Western Europe. It operated until 1933, when it was reorganised as Istanbul University, still one of the most prestigious universities in Turkey today.

Throughout its history the *Darülfünun* experienced a series of reorganisations and reforms, and only included a faculty of theology during certain periods of its existence.[74] In 1912, the first section of the *Darülfünun* devoted to the traditional Islamic religious disciplines was established, but was closed soon thereafter in 1919.[75] This section was called variously *Ulum-u Aliye-i Diniyye* (The Higher Religious Sciences) or *Ulum-i Şer'iyye* (The *Shari'ah* Sciences). The curriculum of this *Shari'ah* sciences section featured courses on Quranic interpretation, the study of Prophetic traditions, the jurisprudence of Islamic ritual practice (*fiqh*), *fiqh* theory and methodology (*uṣūl al-fiqh*), systematic theology (*kalām*), ethics, Sufism, Prophetic biography, Arabic literature and philosophy, the history of philosophy, the history of Islam and the history of religions.[76] In other words, there was a heavy focus on the study of traditional Islamic religious disciplines organised according to the institutional demands of a modern university and combined with a significant offering of modern Western disciplines such as the history of philosophy and the history of religions. The programme reflected the Islamic modernist outlook of the members of its faculty, who advocated the enrichment of the traditional Islamic intellectual worldview with the insights of the modern West European social and humanities disciplines.

The theology section of the *Darülfünun* was reopened in 1924 and then closed again permanently in 1933 with the rest of the institution. This second incarnation of the faculty featured at least one key difference from its predecessor: it no longer offered courses in *fiqh*, except in the context of historical study. It also focused heavily on modern social science research methodologies.[77] The faculty was officially titled the 'Faculty of Theology' (*İlahiyat Fakültesi*), the first time this term had ever been used to denote an educational institution.[78] The faculty journal (*Darülfünun İlahiyat Fakültesi Mecmuası*) also published articles on research and reform in Islamic disciplines, and published in particular numerous articles by Durkheim, translated into Turkish.[79]

During this brief period the *Darülfünun* theology faculty was home to the most important figures in Islamic theological reform in the late Ottoman and early nationalist period; such important theological reformists as İsmail Hakkı İzmirli (or İzmirli İsmail Hakkı) (1868–1946), Mehmed Şerefettin Yaltkaya (1879–1947) and Yusuf Ziya Yörükan (1887–1954) taught there.[80] This generation of theologians was particularly important for the development of Islamic thought in the Turkish Republic, and so deserves some detailed discussion here. These theologians shared a desire for the Islamic modernist style of renewal (*yenilenme*) of Islamic thought in the Ottoman Empire. This distinguished them from more conservative Islamic intellectuals and *'ulamā'* of the time.[81]

İzmirli articulated his project of renewal in terms of a 'new Islamic theology' (*Yeni İlm-i Kelam* – this theological project will be featured in particular detail in the third chapter of this book). This project was motivated by his study of traditional *kalām* and its shortcomings in the modern philosophical context. He describes his theological methodology as a combination of the core theological insights of the classical Sunni tradition and the methodological and scientific insights of Cartesianism and the modern Western philosophical tradition more broadly. Moreover, İzmirli described this project as a service to Islam itself, as it would enable modern Muslims to secure the essentials of their faith in the modern context.[82] He therefore conceived of Islamic theology as a discipline always in dialogue with its social and intellectual context, and argued that it was time to change its philosophical interlocutors. In the past, *kalām* scholars were versed in the philosophical thought of figures such as Plato, Aristotle and the Greek Pre-Socratics because these constituted the intellectual vernacular of the period.[83] However, İzmirli argued that modern Islamic theology had to be reconstructed along the lines of a reconstructed *kalām*: it must be reconceived to take into account the Western philosophical currents of the modern age.[84]

Instead of integrating the defence of Muslim dogma with the philosophical insights and precepts of the ancients, İzmirli argued that the new Islamic theology must both thoroughly integrate, yet also be prepared to critique, the bases of modern Western philosophy, including Bacon, Descartes, Spinoza, Leibniz, Malebranche, Hume, Kant, Hegel, Comte, Mill and Bergson.[85] Not only did these philosophers for him represent significant advances in human thought but, perhaps most importantly, İzmirli observed that they were becoming the standard reference for the new generation of

Turkish Muslims and that the new Islamic theology had to both appreciatively and critically engage with them in order to secure the foundations of Islamic belief for succeeding generations of young Muslims in Turkey and around the Muslim world.[86]

İzmirli stressed that his new Islamic theology would never conflict with the conclusions of empirical scientific investigation. On the contrary, it would seek to use the conceptual tools of modern scientific knowledge, combined with Quranic theology, to demonstrate the truth of Islamic belief.[87] He also emphasised the importance of reason in Islam, arguing that though revelation may include precepts that are inaccessible to reason, it does not include precepts that are fundamentally irrational.[88] On the contrary, Islam by nature encourages the free use of reason and the rejection of the unthinking imitation of authority.[89]

Without embarking on such a comprehensive theological undertaking, Yaltkaya made very similar arguments. He was also a vocal champion of religious progressivism and believed in the fundamentally 'reasonable' and 'scientific' nature of Islam. In his view, Islam evinces 'complete harmony' between empirical science and the principles of Quranic theology.[90] Yaltkaya also stressed the importance of human free will and imitative in the true understanding of religion.[91] Like İzmirli, Yaltkaya was also concerned to remain within the bounds of Islamic theological orthodoxy and emphasised that the existential root of Islam is revelation. God, whose existence can be demonstrated by reason alone, is recognised through a very personal relationship with the believer who locates their belief in God in their innermost heart and approaches the divine from a stance of awe and reverence.[92]

Unlike İzmirli, however, Yaltkaya did not locate the roots of a new and modern Islamic theology in philosophy. Instead, he turned to Gökalp's sociology as the foundation for reform in Islamic thought.[93] Yaltkaya was a strong supporter of Gökalp's proposal for reform in Islamic law based on social contingency and even argued that 'the social is the birthplace of the spirit of the sacred'.[94] In fact, Yaltkaya was even known to have been a close associate of Gökalp.[95] Like Gökalp, Yaltkaya was clearly a follower of Durkheimian sociology and viewed religion in general and Islam in particular in these terms.[96] This is in fact the point at which he and İzmirli part ways: though they served on the same reformist theological faculty, they participated in different reformist theological circles. İzmirli belonged to the group of Ottoman Islamic reformers that published in the well-known modernist journal *Sırat-ı Müstakim* (The Straight Path; 1908–25) that also included translated articles by Muhammad 'Abduh and Jamal al-Din al-Afghani.[97] He was famously opposed to Gökalp's sociological framework for reform in *fiqh*, and published extensive refutations of his position and in favour of reform based on classical *fiqh* methodologies, albeit understood in a modernist context.[98]

İzmirli's works notably betray little trace of nationalism, and he famously declared that he owed no allegiance to any particular classical Islamic theological school, Ash'ari or other.[99] This reflected the syncretistic nature of Sunni Ottoman theology discussed above, which focused on the similarities between Sunni schools of thought instead of declaring allegiance to one in particular. İzmirli's older contemporary, Manastırlı İsmail Hakkı (d. 1912), reflected this outlook. He argued that the Ash'ari and Maturidi schools were of equal value in defending the Islamic creed, and that neither could accuse the other of being heterodox.[100] İzmirli and many of his contemporaries in late Ottoman Sunni theological circles therefore had no interest in defining a specifically Turkish heritage of Islam or of focusing on one Sunni theological school over another. Yaltkaya, by contrast, published in the modernist Islamic journal *İslam Mecmuası* (Journal of Islam; 1914–18) which had clear Turkish nationalist tendencies and strongly supported the works of Gökalp in this regard.[101]

Yaltkaya was eventually appointed to the headship of the Turkish government's central ministry for religious affairs, the Diyanet, in 1942, and served in that capacity until his death in 1947. His colleague at the *Darülfünun*, Yusuf Ziya Yörükan, however, continued to serve in an academic capacity even after the closing of the theology faculty in 1933. After this, the only academic venue to teach higher Islamic Studies was provided at Istanbul University by the Institute of Islamic Sciences, attached to the Faculty of Letters.[102] Yaltkaya and Yörükan taught at this institute as well, but Yörükan would be the only professor of Islamic theology to go on to teach in the first theology faculty founded during the Turkish Republic, the Ankara University Faculty of Theology.[103]

Yörükan's career played an important role in the development of modern Islamic theology in Turkey because it spanned the transition from late

Ottoman to early Republican theological academia. He was a product of the late Ottoman *medrese* system, taught in the first reformed institutes of religious education at the end of the Ottoman Empire (during which time he also participated in outlining the widely influential Islamic reformist agenda discussed above), and then went on to become one of the first professors at the first faculty of theology founded in the Republic of Turkey. He also wrote the first article in the first issue of the Ankara University Faculty of Theology's faculty journal, a short catechism of Islam comprised of Quranic verses translated into Turkish. Yörükan conducted his work as a specialist in Islamic theology at the Faculty of Theology at Ankara University by solidifying the modernist and reformist trend of thought that he had promoted in the late Ottoman period. The combination of Islamic modernism and Turkish laicism that characterises Yörükan's work will be discussed more extensively in the last chapter of this book, as it concerns both the past and future political dynamics of the history of theology in modern Turkey.

The Ankara University Faculty of Theology

To sum up the main arguments of this chapter: The roots of modern Turkish theology consist of three intellectual strands: (1) the legacy of Sunni Ottoman systematic theology (*kalām*); (2) late nineteenth- and early twentieth-century Islamic modernism; and (3) late Ottoman and early Republican Turkish sociological theory. These three strands were woven together by the institutional context of the Ottoman Empire, and then the early Turkish Republic. In the Ottoman period, the highly centralised and state-controlled *medrese* system ensured that a coherent and stable body of Sunni Islamic systematic theology was available to late Ottoman theologians as they confronted the challenges of social and political modernity in the late nineteenth and early twentieth centuries.

In the course of their efforts to confront these challenges, late Ottoman theologians and religious intellectuals developed their own version of Islamic modernism. They also thoroughly incorporated the insights of European sociology into their deliberations on the nature and future directions of Islamic and Turkish society. When the Ottoman Empire collapsed and gave way to the Turkish Republic, a new institutional context emerged that would bring these three intellectual strands together: the modern Turkish faculty of theology. Just as the Ottoman *medrese* system provided a stable institutional context for the growth of pre-modern Sunni systematic theology, the modern Turkish theology faculties provide the stable institutional context for the development of systematic Sunni theology in modern Turkish.

In order to more clearly conceptualise all of these complex historical developments, this chapter will close with a brief discussion of the first faculty of theology founded in the Turkish Republic: The Ankara University Faculty of Theology. This faculty remains one of the most prestigious in the country, and its history served as the model for the development of every successive theology faculty in modern Turkey. Founded in 1949, the Ankara University Faculty of Theology was intended to further the modernisation of Islamic belief and practice in the new Turkish Republic.

The records of the parliamentary debate leading to the establishment of the faculty indicate that the mission of religious modernisation was the main reason its establishment was supported by the Turkish state. The prominent intellectual İsmail Hakkı Baltacıoğlu (1886–1978) contrasted the new theology faculty with the traditional *medrese*, arguing that faculties of theology embody scientific, 'objective' (*objektif*) studies, replacing the *medrese*'s irrational and 'subjective' (*sübjektif*) methodologies.[104] Baltacıoğlu also emphasised the key role the new faculty would play in fostering the social sciences. The Minister of Education at the time declared that the new faculty 'would be worthy of the Atatürk Revolution' and would even serve as a bulwark against conservative reactionary opposition to the new Republic and its social policies.[105] The first year of instruction at the faculty (1949–50) included the following courses: Arabic, Persian, English, German, French, Sociology, logic and philosophy of the sciences, history of Islam, history of Islamic schools of thought (taught by Yörükan), history of Islamic art and comparative history of religions.[106]

The curriculum of the faculty in its first year of operation is particularly informative about the character of this innovative institution. Unlike the curriculum of the first *Darülfünun* theological faculty (1912–19, the faculty of *Shari'ah* sciences) discussed above, the Ankara faculty's first year of course offerings did not include a single subject related to *Shari'ah*. In 1953 and 1954, courses were added in classic Turkish religious texts, psychology and sociology of religion, Qur'an, Prophetic traditions, fine arts, pedagogy, history of Sufism, foundations of Islamic belief, Islamic philosophy, history of the Turkish Revolution and 'Islamic law' (İslam hukuku).[107]

The courses offered at the Ankara faculty followed in the footsteps of the second *Darülfünun* faculty (1924–33) by focusing on *Shari'ah* as an object of primarily historical study. This is unsurprising, considering that implementation of the *Shari'ah* at the state level was by that point illegal in Republican Turkey. Though a course in Islamic law was added in 1953 and 1954, the subject remained subordinated to the historical study of Islamic thought and Islamic history. Overall, the early Ankara theology faculty courses exhibited a strong focus on intellectual history and the study of the historical legacy of Islamic thought and culture. This focus helped foster the kind of intensive study of the classics of Islamic intellectual history that is at the foundation of most systematic Islamic theological projects in Turkey today. The Ankara faculty also incorporated elements of Turkish nationalism, with its inclusion of courses in Turkish religious classics and Turkish Republican history.

From the earliest years of the faculty both male and female students were enrolled.[108] The faculty also came into being during a period of great intellectual openness to international influences. For instance, the famous German scholar of Islam and Sufism, Annemarie Schimmel, taught in the faculty from 1954 to 1959. In addition, throughout the 1940s the Turkish government commissioned the translation and popularisation of classics of world (largely West European) literature and philosophy. In 1952, a similar project was launched for the translation of classics from the Islamic world originally written in Arabic, Ottoman Turkish and other historical languages of the Muslim world.[109]

The Faculty of Theology at Ankara University would prove to be the most influential Islamic academic institution in the first decades of the Republic. In 1990, only nine faculties of theology existed in Turkey, and six were headed by graduates of the Faculty of Theology at Ankara University (as will be discussed in the final chapter of this book, the number of theology faculties has skyrocketed in the 2000s).[110] The faculty also served as a model for later institutions, and inaugurated the critical and sociological study of Islam in Turkish intellectual life. It remains best known (and sometimes critiqued) for its modernist leanings.[111]

The Turkish state throughout the twentieth century asserted a high degree of control over the activities of the theology faculties, mirroring how the old Ottoman government had dealt with the *medrese* system for centuries before. In an effort to depoliticise the activities of religious scholars, a law was passed in the Turkish parliament on the very same day that the Ankara faculty was opened which declared that anyone who attempted to use religion as the basis for 'judicial, social, economic, or political order' or to in any way undermine Turkish laicism would be liable to imprisonment.[112] This provision of the Turkish penal code (Article 163) was abolished in 1992; however, higher education remains under close state supervision.[113] The political context of theology in Turkey that results from this state supervision will be discussed in detail in the final chapter of this book.

Through a thematic analysis, the rest of this book will elucidate how the three main streams of influence, 1) the legacy of Sunni Ottoman systematic theology (*kalām*); 2) late nineteenth- and early twentieth-century Islamic modernism; and 3) late Ottoman and early Republican Turkish sociological theory, interacted with one another to produce a modern tradition of theology in the Turkish linguistic and republican national context. The historical developments outlined above created an institutional context within which these streams of thought could interact with one another. At the same time, the new linguistic context of the modern Turkish language provided a new space for the creation of a distinct theological tradition. In this way, modern Turkish theology was born when elements of classical and Ottoman Islamic tradition were melted down and reformed in the crucible of the modern Turkish language and the modern Turkish nation.

Notes

1. Kafadar, *Between Two Worlds*, 41.
2. İhsanoğlu, 'Emergence', 289–90.
3. On Anatolian charismatic Sufism represented by such figures as Ahmet Yesevi and Yunus Emre, see Fuad Köprülü, *Early Mystics in Turkish Literature*. These figures are described as wonder-working champions of popular piety, and as such represented an inherent challenge to settled Islamic authorities such as the traditional religious scholars of the sacred law and theology, the *'ulāma'*.
4. İhsanoğlu, 'Emergence', 291; Zilfi, *The Politics of Piety*, 34.

5. İhsanoğlu, 'Emergence', 289–90.
6. These are called in Arabic the *'ulūm al-dīn*, literally 'sciences of religion'. This group of disciplines comprises the larger, interdependent whole of Islamic religious thought, and includes fields such as Quranic interpretation, the study of the saying and deeds attributed to Muhammad (the hadith), the study and elaboration of Islamic sacred law and ritual practice (*fiqh*), Islamic mysticism (Sufism) and systematic theology.
7. İhsanoğlu, 'Emergence', 289. On scientific *medrese*s see also Shefer-Mossensohn, *Ottoman Medicine* and Zorlu, 'Medical *Medrese*'.
8. İhsanoğlu, 'Institutionalisation of Science', 272.
9. İhsanoğlu, 'Institutionalisation of Science', 265; Makdisi, *The Rise of Colleges*, 9; 'Muslim Institutions of Learning', 10–17; Berkey, *The Transmission of Knowledge in Medieval Cairo*, 17–18.
10. Demirci, 'Osmanlı'da Kelam Eğitimi', 24; İhsanoğlu, 'Institutionalisation of Science', 273.
11. İhsanoğlu, 'Emergence', 297.
12. Ahmed and Filipovic, 'The Sultan's Syllabus', 183–5; Atay, *Osmanlılarda Yüksek Din*, 82–3; Berger, 'Interpretations of Ash'arism and Māturīdism', 694; Inalcik, *The Ottoman Empire*; Repp, 'Ottoman Learned Hierarchy', 17–32; Repp, *The Müfti of Istanbul*, 27–72; Zilfi, *The Politics of Piety*, 24.
13. İhsanoğlu, 'Emergence', 293.
14. Ocak, 'Islam in the Ottoman Empire', 188.
15. On the use of Sunni Islam in the legitimation of the Seljuq state, particularly under the vizierate of Nizam al-Mulk (1018–92), see Safi, *The Politics of Knowledge*, 90–100. Safi describes how Nizam al-Mulk sought through his patronage of the madrasa system to ease tensions within Sunni factions in order to present a unified front of Sunni orthodoxy against competing Isma'ili powers such as the Fatimids. These policies foreshadow the Ottoman pan-Sunnism that would be deployed against its Shi'i imperial rival, the Safavids.
16. İhsanoğlu, 'Emergence', 297.
17. See Erdem, 'Religious Services in Turkey'.
18. Aydın, *Türk Kelam Bilginleri*, 51; and Aydın, 'Kelam between Tradition and Change', 105.
19. Ocak, 'Islam in the Ottoman Empire', 189.
20. Sariyannis, 'Ottoman political thought', 87–92.
21. *Shari'ah* is usually translated in English as 'Islamic law', but this common translation is misleading for a number of reasons. The literal meaning of the term itself

is 'path'. *Shari'ah* refers to the ideal way of life that God commands Muslims to follow. The term *fiqh* refers to the body of jurisprudential texts that attempt to outline in detail the specifics of this lifestyle. The most important aspect of *Shari'ah* is ritual practice, such as daily prayer, giving charity, fasting during the holy month of Ramadan, and the pilgrimage to Mecca. However, *fiqh* texts are not exactly 'legal' texts in the way this term is usually used in English, because the majority of their content does not have to do with legal ordinances enforceable by the state. Thus, the phrase '*Shari'ah* law' is misleading. As Mohammad Hashim Kamali puts it, *Shari'ah* 'is a path to religion, [and] is primarily concerned with a set of values that are essential to Islam and the best manner of their protection'. See *Shari'ah Law: An Introduction*, 2. As Jerusha Tanner Lamptey points out, 'Shariah is *not* a codified, static or agreed upon collection of laws' but rather a collection of principles the interpretation of which constitutes the framework of Muslim sacred tradition. See 'Boko Haram: Not My Shariah'.

22. Imber, 'Ottoman Law', 90.
23. See on this point Demirci, 'Osmanlı'da Kelam Eğitimi', 38. There is some disagreement among specialists on just how much prestige and importance *kalām* possessed in the Ottoman system. Berger, for instance, argues that it 'retained an honourable place' but that it was considered inferior to other disciplines such as the study of Prophetic traditions (hadith) (694). Demirci's and Atay's extensive documentary work on this topic, however, suggests that it was often considered among the most elite genres of religious learning. It seems most likely that the exact level of prestige theology possessed as a religious discipline varied depending on the perspective of the scholar or Sultan in question. What is clear from the documentary evidence is that theology was a generally respected and widely studied field of religious learning throughout the entire history of the Ottoman Empire.
24. Repp, *The Müfti of Istanbul*, 32–41.
25. Atay, *Din*, 77–100.
26. Ahmad and Filipovic, 'The Sultan's Syllabus', 207.
27. Atay, *Din*, 191.
28. Khaled El-Rouayheb, 'The Myth of "The Triumph of Fanaticism"', 205.
29. Dhahani, 'Commentaries', 375; Özervarlı, 'Theology in the Ottoman Lands', 572.
30. Atay, *Din*, 80, 85, 87, 88.
31. Dhahani, 'Commentaries', 375; Eichner, 'Handbooks', 497–8; Oliver Leaman and Sajjad Rizvi, 'The Developed *Kalām* Tradition', 85–6.

32. See Ansari, 'Taftazani's Views'.
33. Aydın, *Türk Kelam Bilginleri*, 56. Aydın's extremely useful list of Ottoman-era theologians and theological works cites twenty-five separate commentaries or supra commentaries on al-Iji's *Mawaqif*, five on al-Taftazani's *Maqasid*, six on Hızır Bey's *Qasida*, seventeen on al-Nasafi's creed, and twelve on al-Tusi's *Tajrid*. This amounts to thirty-seven commentaries by separate authors on Ash'ari texts and twenty-eight on Maturidi ones. This indicates, again, a slight favouritism towards Ash'arism, which was most likely due to its institutionalisation early on. This data also, however, demonstrates that Maturidism had a significant presence in theological debates and writings, despite its under-representation in the curriculum.
34. Edward Badeen (ed.), in *Sunnitische Theologie in Osmanischer Zeit*, 2–18.
35. The most widely known example of this genre is Hasan ibn Abi 'Udhba's *Rawdat al-Bahiyya fima bayna al-Asha'ira wa-l-Maturidiyya* (Badeen, ed., 2008 and 'Ali Farid Dahruj, 1996). Other examples include: *Risalat al-Ikhtilaf bayna al-Asha'ira wa al-Maturidiyya fi ithnatay 'ashara masa'la* by Ibn Kamal Pasha (d. 1534), one of the most prolific theologians of the Ottoman period (Badeen, ed., 2008); *Risala fi al-farq bayna madhhab al-Asha'ira wa-l-Maturidiyya by Yahya Efendi ibn 'Ali al-Nawa'i* (1533–98) (Badeen, ed., 2008); *al-Masalik fi bayan al-madhahib li-l-Ḥumama' wa al-Mutakallimun wa al-Ash'ariyya wa al-Maturidiyya* by 'Abdullah ibn Osman ibn Musa Mestcizade (d. 1737) (Süleymaniye Kütüphanesi İstanbul, Hekimoğlu Ali Paşa 402); *Sharh al-Khilafiyyat bayna al-Ash'ari wa-l-Maturiiī* by Muhammad ibn Veli ibn Resul al-Kırşehri (d. 1752) (Süleymaniye Kütüphanesi İstanbul, Şehit Ali Paşa 1650); and *Risala Tata'allaqa bayna Kalam al-Maturidi wa-l-Ash'ari* by *Abu al-'Abbas Ahmad ibn Hasan al-Jawhari* (d. 1768–69) (Topkapı Sarayı Müzesi, İstanbul, 2004).
36. Kara Halil Pasha Çorlulu, appendix to *al-Masa'il al-Mukhtalifa bayna-l-Ash'ariyya wa al-Maturidiyya*, Süleymaniye Kütüphanesi İstanbul, Hafid Efendi 150/20.
37. Taşköprülzade, *Al-Shaqa'iq al-Nu'maniyya*, 267–8.
38. For summaries of the reformist period, see Ahmad, *The Making of Modern Turkey*, 15–30; Quataert, *The Ottoman Empire: 1700–1922*, 54–74; and Zurcher, *Turkey: A Modern History*, 9–92.
39. On social change in the early Republican period, see Zafer Toprak, 'Family, Feminism, and the State'; Weiss 'Turkish Republican Woman'; and Hale, *Modern Turkey*.
40. Quoted in Karal, 'The Principles of Kemalism', 15.

41. Karal, 'The Principles of Kemalism', 28. See also Ahmad, *The Making of Modern Turkey*, 77–9; Ahmad, 'The Political Economy of Kemalism', 152; Ozbudun, 'Kemalist Political Regime', 79–192.
42. Soroush, 'The Changeable and the Unchangeable', 9.
43. For the most influential early nineteenth-century Muslim perspective on these changes, see Rifa'a Rafi' al-Tahtawi, *An Imam in Paris*. As his translator Daniel Newman points out, the encounter with European technological power spurred reflection on the future of Islamic societies among travellers and government officials such as al-Tahtawi. One of the main issues that al-Tahtawi explores in his account is the need to adopt European scientific and technological learning in order to enable Muslim societies to regain their former positions of geopolitical power and influence. As Newman explains, al-Tahtawi recognised that these scientific and technological developments were in many ways founded on the achievements of medieval Muslim scientists whose learning was transmitted to Western Europeans. Al-Tahtawi thus argued that returning to the forgotten essentials of the Muslim faith would lead to progress in the modern age because Muslim history itself showed that Islamic culture was a crucial component in the historical development of modern science and technology.
44. Wood, *Christian Criticisms, Islamic Proofs*, 17–23.
45. Mir-Hosseini, 'Muslim Legal Tradition', 19–20.
46. Mir-Hosseini, 'Muslim Legal Tradition', 20.
47. Hidayatullah, *Feminist Edges*, 28.
48. 'Abduh, *The Theology of Unity*, 29.
49. Bein, *Ottoman Ulema, Turkish Republic*, 31.
50. Haj, *Reconfiguring Islamic Tradition*, 87.
51. On *kalām* reformists in late Ottoman/early Republican Turkey, see also Aydın, 'Kelam between Tradition and Change'; Özervarlı, 'Attempts to Revitalize Kalām', 90–105; and Özervarlı, *Kelamda Yenilik Arayışları*.
52. Çelebi, 'Modern Dönem Kelam Çalışmalarının Temel Sorunları Üzerine', 81.
53. Berkes, *Secularism in Turkey*, 208–9.
54. On the 'privatisation' of the notion of religion in Tanzimat-era Ottoman elites, see also Mardin, *The Genesis of Young Ottoman Thought*, 118.
55. Mardin, *The Genesis of Young Ottoman Thought*, 211.
56. Mardin, *The Genesis of Young Ottoman Thought*, 211.
57. For comparative discussions of these three currents of thought, see Berkes, *Secularism in Turkey*, 337–408; and Ö. M. Alper, 'Islamic Philosophy in Turkey'.

58. On Gökalp's social and religious thought, see Erşahin, 'Ziya Gökalp's Diyanet Ishları Nazaratı', 182–98; Karpat, *The Politicization of Islam*, 374–88; Özervarli, 'Transferring Traditional Islamic Disciplines'; Şentürk, 'Intellectual Dependency'.
59. Özervarli, 'Transferring Traditional Islamic Disciplines', 317.
60. Özervarli, 'Transferring Traditional Islamic Disciplines', 326; Şentürk, 'Intellectual Dependency', 303–4.
61. Dressler, 'Rereading Ziya Gökalp', 512.
62. Gökalp, *The Principles of Turkism*, 12; Karpat, *The Politicization of Islam*, 376–7.
63. Gökalp, *Principles*, 13.
64. Gökalp, *Principles*, 15.
65. Gökalp, *Principles*, 22–4.
66. Gökalp, *Principles*, 37.
67. Durkheim, *The Elementary Forms of Religious Life*, 318.
68. Özervarli, 'Transferring Traditional Islamic Disciplines', 321–4; Şentürk, 'Intellectual Dependency', 304–10.
69. Özervarli, 'Transferring Traditional Islamic Disciplines', 323; Senturk, 'Intellectual Dependence', 308; Dressler, 'Rereading Ziya Gökalp', 515–16. As Dressler notes, Gökalp's argument here is very similar to 'Abduh's, and therefore other Muslim modernists who as described above base their argument for progressive reform on the distinction between the changeable and the unchangeable in religion.
70. Quoted in Erşahin, 'Ziya Gökalp's Diyanet Ishları Nazaratı', 188.
71. Erşahin, 'Ziya Gökalp's Diyanet Ishları Nazaratı', 188. On the privatising of Islam to matters of belief and worship see also: Ocak, 'Günümüz Türkiye Müslümanlığına Genel Bir Bakış', and Cetinsaya, 'Rethinking Nationalism and Islam', 354.
72. See Berkes, *Development of Secularism in Turkey*, 416; Erşahin, 'Ziya Gökalp's Diyanet Ishları Nazaratı'.
73. Dressler, 'Rereading Ziya Gökalp', 526.
74. On the history of the theology faculties in the *Darülfünun* see Aydar, 'Darülfünun'un İlahiyat Fakültesi'; Koştaş, 'Ankara Üniversitesi İlahiyat Fakültesi'; and Pacaci and Aktay, 'Higher Religious Education'.
75. Koştaş, 'Ankara Üniversitesi İlahiyat Fakültesi', 2; Pacaci and Aktay, 'Higher Religious Education', 123.
76. Koştaş, 'Ankara Üniversitesi İlahiyat Fakültesi', 2–3.
77. Koştaş, 'Ankara Üniversitesi İlahiyat Fakültesi', 6.
78. Aydar, 'Darülfünun'un İlahiyat Fakültesi', 26.
79. Aydar, 'Darülfünun'un İlahiyat Fakültesi', 30.

80. Koştaş, 'Ankara Üniversitesi İlahiyat Fakültesi', 7. On *kalām* reformists in late Ottoman/early Republican Turkey such as İzmirli and others, see Aydın, 'Kelam between Tradition and Change'; Özervarlı, 'Attempts to Revitalize Kalām' and Özervarlı, *Kelamda Yenilik Arayışları*.
81. Özervarlı, 'Alternative Approaches to Modernization', 82–3.
82. Hizmetli, 'İzmirli İsmail Hakkı'nın İlmi Şahsiyeti', 20–1.
83. Aydın, 'Kelam between Tradition and Change', 114–15; Hizmetli, 'İzmirli İsmail Hakkı'nın İlmi Şahsiyeti', 19; Özervarlı, 'Alternative Approaches to Modernization', 87.
84. Hizmetli, 'İzmirli İsmail Hakkı'nın İlmi Şahsiyeti', 19; Özervarlı, *Kelamda Yenilik Arayışları*, 60–2.
85. Aydın, 'Kelam between Tradition and Change', 115.
86. Özervarlı, 'İzmirli İsmail Hakkı'nın Kelam Problemleriyle İlgili Görüşleri', 109.
87. Hizmetli, 'İzmirli İsmail Hakkı'nın İlmi Şahsiyeti', 21.
88. Özervarlı, 'İzmirli İsmail Hakkı'nın Kelam Problemleriyle İlgili Görüşleri', 123.
89. Özervarlı, 'İzmirli İsmail Hakkı'nın Kelam Problemleriyle İlgili Görüşleri', 123.
90. Yaltkaya, *Dini Makalelerim*, 56.
91. Yaltkaya, *Dini Makalelerim*, 57.
92. Yaltkaya, *Dini Makalelerim*, 57, 11–13; Özervarlı, *Kelamda Yenilik Arayışları*, 67.
93. Özervarlı, 'Transferring Traditional Islamic Disciplines', 324.
94. Özervarlı, 'Transferring Traditional Islamic Disciplines', 325. I have slightly modified Özervarlı's translation of this phrase.
95. Duman, 'Şerafeddin Yaltkaya', 54.
96. Özervarlı, *Kelamda Yenilik Arayışları*, 65.
97. Özervarlı, 'Alternative Approaches to Modernization', 82.
98. Özervarlı, 'Alternative Approaches to Modernization', 92. See for instance his pieces 'Sosyal Bir İslam Fıkıh Usulüne İhtiyaç Var mı?' and 'İcma, Kıyas ve İstihsanın Esasları'.
99. Özervarlı, 'Alternative Approaches to Modernization', 84.
100. Manastırlı, *Telhis'ül Kelam fi Berahini Akaid'il İslam*, 23–4.
101. Özervarlı, 'Alternative Approaches to Modernization', 84. *İslam Mecmuası* was actually funded by the nationalist ruling party of the time, the Committee of Union and Progress. See on this point Azak, 'Nationalist Search for Vernacular Islam', 161–79.
102. Koştaş, 'Ankara Üniversitesi İlahiyat Fakültesi', 7.

103. At least one other professor from the *Darülfünun* accompanied him there, Hilmi Ömer Budda, who taught courses in comparative religion and religious history. See Koştaş, 'Ankara Üniversitesi İlahiyat Fakültesi', 7–11.
104. Koştaş, 'Ankara Üniversitesi İlahiyat Fakültesi', 8.
105. Quoted in Köylü, 'Religious Education in Modern Turkey', 54.
106. Koştaş, 'Ankara Üniversitesi İlahiyat Fakültesi', 11.
107. Reed, 'Revival of Islam', 274.
108. Of the 80 students who completed the first semester of the faculty, 22 were women (28 per cent). Of the 40 students who graduated in the first class of 1953, 9 were women (22 per cent). See Pacaci and Aktay, 'Higher Religious Education'.
109. Reed, 'Revival of Islam', 270.
110. Koştaş, 'Ankara Üniversitesi İlahiyat Fakültesi', 8.
111. Subaşı, 'İlahiyat(çı)lar Üzerine'.
112. Quoted in Köylü, 'Modern Turkey', 54.
113. Müftüler-Baç, *Turkey's Relationship with a Changing Europe*, 88.

2

NATION

The late Ottoman and early Republican period produced the basic institutional and intellectual structures that laid the foundation for modern Turkish theology. The same period also saw the creation of the political and social community of the Turkish Republic: the Turkish nation. This chapter argues that secular Turkish nationalism aided in the growth of modern Turkish theology by providing a new social and political context for theological reflection. The conceptual shifts engendered by the nationalist context did not arrest the development of Sunni theology in Turkey, but instead helped to produce creative theological responses to the novel challenges posed by this new political environment. Modern secular Turkish nationalism did not destroy vital and profound religious thought in the new Republic, as might be assumed. On the contrary, it helped infuse modern Turkish theology with its own distinct character and creativity.

This chapter will therefore discuss how the novel conceptual framework of Turkish nationalism provided key concepts that have come to constitute core features of modern Turkish theological thought, such as notions of progress, national history and the relationship between religion and the secular state. In other words, the redefinition of community provided by the framework of secular nationalism allowed for a new tradition of Sunni theology to be born that responded specifically to the Turkish national context. This redefinition allowed for new forms of theological thought to be explored and developed, as the task of moving the Turkish nation forward while at the same time delineating its ancient heritage took on urgent importance. This nationalist agenda both gave new life to theological reflection in modern Turkish and at the same time gave rise to a century's worth of controversy over the relationship between secularism, nationalism and Islam that continues to this day in modern Turkey. This chapter will chart this complex relationship between modern Turkish theology and modern Turkish nationalism, including the theological critiques that Turkish nationalism has received from multiple points on the Turkish ideological and political spectrum.

Theology and National Progress

During the late Ottoman period, notions of social progress and evolution became key modes of Islamic theological argumentation, especially among Ottoman Muslim modernists. Many of the most influential Ottoman Sunni theologians of the time agreed that Islam and Islamic thought supported, strengthened or even epitomised social progress and evolution. In an article titled 'Islam and Progress' published in 1904, the Ottoman *Şeyhülislam* Musa Kazım (1858/59–1920)[1] argued that the most basic elements of Islamic thought and practice supported human social progress and that it is Islam itself that is the basis of a nation's progress and process of civilisation. His particularly striking words on this point deserve quoting here: 'the religion of Islam is not an obstacle to progress. On the contrary, it is that which commands and encourages progress; it is the very reason for progress itself'.[2] In the same piece, Kazım argues that the basis of this progress and national civilising process is liberty, also a core value of Islam.[3] Kazım defines progress as the development of fundamental humanity and human values in a national community, based on the ethical underpinning of Islamic religious faith and practice.

Along very similar lines, Elmalılı Muhammed Hamdi Yazır (1878–1942)[4] argued in his 1923 article 'The Islamic Religion is not the Obstacle to Progress, it is the Basis of Progress' that true progress is defined as progress in moral virtue and human goodness, and that it is only Islam that can form the basis of this moral development in the modern context.[5] According to Yazır, the basis of virtue is self-sacrifice on behalf of one's community, from which the individual draws their own strength and vitality. Religion, which commands and inculcates virtue in the individual, constitutes the affective basis and urge to perform necessary acts of self-sacrifice on behalf of others Thus, religion is the basis both for society itself and for the virtuous individual impulses that sustain social progress.[6] Yazır appeals to the Qur'an as the foundation of this view. He cites 19:73–6 to argue that Islam provides the necessary moral guidance that is the basis for doing good deeds in the world. Therefore, Islam provides the moral foundation for the implementation of new ideas and practices insofar as these constitute genuine moral and social improvement for humanity.

For nineteenth- and early twentieth-century Ottoman thinkers, progress was to be ensured by the rational and modern reorganising of society and government into a new system of social and political order (*nizam*). The concept of 'reform' (*ıslah*) became the impulse at the heart of social progress and order. As Rıdvan Özdinç points out, these terms were first used in an administrative sense within Ottoman government circles. They became central concepts for a larger project of social and individual reform, a project that was integrated into Ottoman theological language during the post-Tanzimat period.[7] In his theological magnum opus published in 1923–4 (*Yeni İlm-i Kelam*), İsmail Hakkı İzmirli wrote that the entirety of the Islamic religion, including all of its religious rulings, is directed towards the reform of human reason, human action and the human heart in accordance with truth and justice.[8]

Modernist Ottoman theologians of this period also began to coalesce around a general consensus that one feature of proper modern social order is a conceptual distinction between religion and the form of the state. Their wide array of suggestions for political and governmental reform were based on the theological proposition that the Qur'an and Hadith did not prescribe any particular form of human governance or politics, but asked only that state and politics accord with the basic religious principles of Islam.[9] In their view these Islamic principles included human virtue, respect for humanity and the rights of individuals, and (as described above) the fundamental importance of social progress and change.

A key feature of these late Ottoman theologians' ethical philosophies is their use of the traditional Islamic concept of *adalet* (justice) to frame their theological arguments for universal human rights and social progress outlined above. According to İzmirli, one of the key goals of the revision of Islamic thought in the modern period is its contribution to the establishment of justice in this world by helping to lay the foundations for harmonious and ordered social relations. Justice is the purpose of the practical elements of *Shariʿah*, that is, the elements of Islamic legal practice that are subject to continual reform on the basis of their ability to foster and maintain justice in a given social context. These practical elements of *Shariʿah* practice include governmental policies, law and administration – all elements of *Shariʿah* that must be evaluated or re-evaluated on the basis of their ability to contribute to a just social order.[10]

Kazım made a similar point by arguing that the essence of true civilisation is the establishment of justice at all levels of society, which ensures the prosperity and general welfare of the entirety of the people.[11] Yazır went so far as to describe justice as the most important concept in Islam used to describe proper relations between people. Furthermore, according to Yazır, justice means the establishment and the defence of human rights (*hukuk-ı beşer*).[12] In order to support his view, Yazır cites the well-known saying attributed to the Prophet that one year of justice is better than seventy years of worship.[13]

On these bases, Ottoman theology in this period elaborated a new framework for the discussion of ethical values. Concepts that lay at the heart of human rights discourses such as liberty and equality came to be seen as divinely mandated forms of the basic Islamic ethical value of justice. The process of inculcating these notions of human rights into the populace and governmental structure in an Islamic theological idiom came to be understood as vital with regard to the process of creating a truly moral and modern civilisation. Inherited from the philosophy of the French Revolution, the concepts of liberty and equality in particular became watchwords of the Ottoman intelligentsia in this period. Özdinç points out that the notion of liberty (*hürriyet*) came to be a positive point of reference in nearly all forms of late Ottoman thought, a kind of universal term for all forms of positive social change and development.[14]

In his 1908–9 article titled 'Liberty-Equality', Kazım envisioned liberty as a kind of liberation from any kind of pressure to deviate from the free exercise of religious observation and national customs.[15] He stressed the moral dimension of liberty, arguing that it must incorporate both responsibility and order.[16] Like Yazır, he saw the willingness of the individual to sacrifice for the good of society as a fundamental part of social order, and therefore a necessary correlate to any understanding of unrestricted human action.[17] According to Kazım, liberty lay at the heart of Islam's social vision, which requires that members of the government take great pains to respect individual rights and vigorously oppose any unjust violation of them.[18] In his view, the concept of equality did not mean absolute sameness among individuals, but rather total equality in all individual rights and social relations, and in the eyes of the law.[19]

Kazım also argued that men and women possessed equal rights, though he interpreted this argument in characteristically nineteenth-century terms of gender complementarity and difference.[20] According to Kazım, the distinct natures of men required that they play distinct and separate roles in society.[21] Kazım framed this argument as a requirement of human order and civilisation. He also took pains to point out that his recommendations for gender relations should not be construed as a legal question enforceable by the coercion of the state, but rather as a recommendation for proper religious practice and moral rectitude.[22] Yazır also uses notions of equality and liberty to argue for the social equality of Muslims and non-Muslims. He argues that the Qur'an makes it clear that it is a grave sin to infringe on the rights of minorities, as in 29:46, where God commands Muslims to express their differences with Jews and Christians in a civil and non-coercive manner.[23]

Ottoman progressivism found its most radical expression in the political agenda of the nationalist Turkish state under the leadership of Mustafa Kemal Atatürk. According to Atatürk, social progress was the ultimate goal of the entire Turkish nationalist project. Progress here meant assimilation to West European modernity, and any Ottoman social institution that resisted this assimilation was simply abolished and replaced with a copy from a West European model. Conformity to Western modernity meant Enlightenment, while resistance to it meant superstition.[24] This conception of progress turns on a very strict positivist dichotomy between the modern and the traditional and invests the state with the role of rescuing the people from ignorance and moulding them into model citizens of the modern world.[25]

Yet one of the main arguments of this chapter is that the emergence of this Turkish nationalist notion of progress actually aided the development of modern Turkish theology. This almost millenarian conception of secular progress resulted in the severe repression of conservative religious piety, as will be discussed further in this chapter. At the same time, however, the shifting of the frames of reference for Muslim identity in the territory that would become the modern Turkish Republic spurred modern Turkish theologians to rethink the framework of Islamic theology itself. These efforts resulted in new paradigms of theological analysis, including concepts of religious change and renewal that, as the rest of this book will demonstrate, would become vital to the development of Islamic theology in modern Turkey.

In other words, though radically secularist notions of progress often proved unworkable or even hostile to Islamic religiosity, the concept of social change as an authentically Islamic value did become central to modern Turkish theology. Theologians whose work bridged the transitional period between the collapse of the Ottoman Empire and emergence of the Turkish Republic translated Ottoman-era Islamic modernist notions of progress into the Republican context. This allowed modern Turkish theology to develop a concept of progress that was acceptable to the new secular nationalist political context, and organically connected to Islamic tradition.

The work of Ahmet Hamdi Akseki (1887–1951)[26] exemplifies this transition and translation. In 1944 Akseki wrote that the 'evolution of humanity' constitutes the central goal of Islam itself.[27] Akseki also defined progress in moral terms, as that which protects social harmony and cohesion.[28] Akseki argues that the goals of Islam's religious rulings (*ahkam*) are 'individual and social evolution' and happiness and success in this life and the next.[29] Islam is based on universal principles that can be used as a guide for meeting the particular social needs of every age.[30] He also goes to great lengths to argue that human reason is one of the most important of these bases, at that according to Islam the exercise of human reason is the foundation of authentic religious belief.[31] He also argued in 1948 that *Shari'ah* rulings are subject to reinterpretation and renewal over time, in accordance with the need to continually adjust the application of Islam's universal principles to changing social environments.[32]

Unlike the radicalism of secularist Turkish nationalists, however, Akseki saw progress as an incremental process that when properly executed and managed actualised the true essence of human nature and the ultimate goals of religion itself. Social progress and individual human virtue were two sides of the same religious coin in his view. As with Kazım, Yazır and many other Ottoman theologians, according to Akseki Islam constituted the moral centre of modern human social and individual development. For both late Ottoman and early Republican theologians, it was only by a return to the essence of Islam itself that true progress and social evolution (on the way to a truly moral and modern civilisation) was possible.[33]

Akseki's writings also stress the importance of liberty and the protection of human rights as Islamic ethical values. He argues that Islam's ethical vision allows no individual to exercise command over a person's spirit, reason or conscience.[34] Akseki argues that Islam is dedicated to the protection of natural rights (*tabii haklar*), such as life, liberty, private property and equality. According to Akseki, these individual rights are restricted only insofar as their exercise attempts to disrupt social order.[35] He further clarifies that if individual liberty has a limit, it is located at the border of someone else's individual liberty.[36] Individual liberty includes protections of the freedom of the press, freedom of conscience and political freedom. The responsible use of this individual freedom is, in fact, the basis of virtue (*fazilet*).[37] Akseki also argues that individual liberty encompasses freedom of belief and worship, and that Muslims are religiously obligated to protect the rights of belief and worship of others.[38]

The Theological Limits of Progress

Given the potential audacity of the Turkish nationalist discourse on progress, it is important to determine what the limits of progress were from the perspective of modern Turkish theology. Though conceptions of progress and change would become central to modern Islamic thought in Turkey, already in the late 1920s the limits of radical change in Islamic practice had begun to emerge. The limits of this change corresponded to a distinction that we will see emerge time and again in modern Turkish theology: the distinction between the essentials of Islamic theological belief and worship practice, and social norms and institutions. In other words, as will be discussed in later chapters in particular detail, modern Turkish theologians converged on the argument that the basic beliefs of Islamic theology (most especially *tevhid*) and the traditional rituals of worship could not be changed. But religious rulings that did not have to do with these areas, such as rulings regarding marriage, family life, political life, and so on, could be changed.

İzmirli had already opened up this discussion at the very beginning of his magnum opus *Yeni İlm-i Kelam* (published in 1923–4). He argues that within Islam one can detect certain immutable beliefs and practices that comprise the essence of Islam; these have been elaborated on the basis of revelation using the various methods of human reason. At the same time, he argues that there are certain elements of Islamic practice that are subject to change and reform in order to ensure that these elements of practice are able to accomplish their essential goals within changing human societies. In this sense, İzmirli distinguishes between theological judgements and practical judgements: the former are established as rationally certain and cannot change, while the latter have elements that may change as social needs develop over time.[39] Theological judgements such as *tevhid* cannot be changed, and practical judgements concerning the specifications of worship and ritual practice cannot be changed. Practical judgements related to human interaction, however, can change over time.

We can discern the hardening of this distinction already in the late 1920s by analysing the reception of one widely discussed proposal for religious reform. In 1928 The *Darülfünun* theology faculty produced a report on the question of reform and modernisation in religion, a document that would have wide influence among government circles in the early years of the Turkish Republic. This report on reform was prepared by a committee headed by the esteemed scholar of Turkish religious history, M. Fuad Köprülü (1890–1966), and included İzmirli, Mehmed Şerefettin Yaltkaya and Yusuf Ziya Yörükan. However, Yörükan claimed in 1947 that this report had been published without the knowledge of most of the members of the faculty.[40] It is likely that Yörükan and others opposed some of its more radical suggestions such as the wearing of shoes during worship. However, Yörükan, İzmirli and other members of this reformist circle did publicly support and help implement the basic precepts of the document (such as the translations of religious texts into Turkish, the call for national religious reform and the establishment of the modern Turkish theology faculty).[41]

The report is remarkable for its succinct inclusion of the most basic precepts of Turkish Islamic theological modernism. These include the sociological analysis of religion, the identification of (and the need to foster) a national Turkish religious tradition, the religious commitment to democracy and the claim that religious practices are subject to constant change in accordance with changing social conditions. Numerous elements of the suggestions in the report were actually carried out by the Turkish government after it was released, and the report was also published on the front pages of the daily Istanbul newspaper *Vakit* in 1928.

The report begins by stating its explicit intent to reform the religion of Islam in the larger cause of the 'Turkish Revolution', referring to the radical social and political reforms being carried out by the Turkish state at the time.[42] In the view of the document's authors, the essence of the religion of Islam is separate from particular social manifestations of religious truth, and thus formal religion must be open to change as society changes throughout history. Religion was a necessary part of the nationalist project in their view; however, arcane and irrelevant forms of religious life had to be discarded to enable the true essence of Islam to be actualised in modern social circumstances.

The report clearly outlines the sociological bases of this conception of religion. It states outright that '[r]eligion is a social institution'. It emphasises that constant change and 'evolution' is the hallmark of social life, and therefore religion is subject by nature to change and evolution. Moreover, this change and process of renewal in religious practice is driven by the needs of 'Turkish democracy'.[43] Reminiscent of Gökalp and Durkheim, the document clearly understands religion in sociological terms, and analyses it as a product of social forces. Thus, religion is suitable for periodic change, as the original social conditions that continually act as its foundations change as well.

At the same time, the document stresses that the part of religion that must 'evolve' through the process of modernisation is not the part that makes religion what it essentially is; the inner truth of religion is rigidly distinguished from social and political contingencies. Thus, the document makes another key point that, as will be demonstrated in Chapter 4, will be developed throughout the history of Turkish theology in the twentieth and twenty-first centuries: the distinction between the 'divine' and 'human' elements of religion. The document draws a fundamental distinction between the human (*beşeri*) and the absolute (*mutlak*), the latter term referring to the Quranic revelation and the essential theological and moral principles of the Islamic faith.[44] This means that religion possesses both changeable and unchangeable aspects, the former being related to varying social conditions and the latter relating to divine truth.

The report also goes on to call for a number of specific religious reforms that it argued would enable the true nature of Islam to best be revealed in the context of the nascent Turkish Republic. These suggestions included an emphasis on orderly worship, the proper training of preachers, praying in the mosque while wearing shoes and the use of musical instruments in communal prayer. The document also called for the use of Turkish as the language of worship. This provision was famously carried out by Atatürk's government, which meant that until Atatürk's party (the Republican People's Party, *Cumhuriyet Halk Partisi*) was voted out of power in 1950 all calls to prayer were made in Turkish instead of Arabic. This recommendation had first been made by Ziya Gökalp in his book *The Principles of Turkism*, published in 1923.[45] The document ends by calling for the development of a modern Turkish theology faculty to serve as the locus for these reform efforts.[46]

It was precisely the proposals for changes to the specifics of ritual worship that were rejected. As mentioned above, the use of modern Turkish as a ritual language in place of the traditional Arabic was entirely abandoned, and it is of course still the case that it would be unthinkable to wear shoes inside the worship space of a mosque. One the other hand, the document's sociological understanding of religion, its emphasis on Turkish democracy and national solidarity, and its call for better education of Islamic religious authorities all became widely accepted principles of modern Turkish religious life. In other words, changes to religious rulings on social interaction, so long as they were enacted in accordance with broader Islamic moral principles, came to be accepted and encouraged by modern Turkish theologians. Changes to the specifics of ritual worship, on the other hand, were decisively rejected. This conceptual distinction between the changeable and the unchangeable in Islamic religious practice, already here emerging in the first years of the Republic, would emerge again and again as a key theme of modern Turkish theology, in a wide variety of specific theological contexts and debates.

Theology and National History

This chapter asserts that the ideological context of Turkish nationalism enabled new and creative forms of Sunni theology to flourish that would have been impossible outside of this context. One particularly striking piece of evidence for this assertion is the modern Turkish rediscovery of the work of the great Sunni dogmatic theologian Abu Mansur al-Maturidi (d. 944).[47] According to research based on reliable manuscript evidence and published in Turkish over the past few decades,[48] al-Maturidi was a well-known and widely respected theologian and scholar during his lifetime. His theology systematises the fragments of theological arguments found in works attributed to Abu Hanifa (d. 767), the eponymous founder of the Hanafi school of Sunni ritual practice and theology.[49] Al-Maturidi's theology defended the bases of traditional Sunni belief, but sought to do so in a way that was not dependent on irrational submission to religious tradition. His theological methodology was characterised by a moderate rationalism and epistemological realism, and he was stridently critical of both speculative rationalism and excessive traditionalism. His work can therefore be described as moderate Sunni theological rationalism, which makes his thought very characteristic of the *kalām* genre of theology in general (as discussed in the Introduction and Chapter 1).

Al-Maturidi was born and spent the entirety of his life in Central Asia, the region of the world that Turkish nationalists at the beginning of the Republic asserted was 'the homeland of the Turks'.[50] His name refers to Maturid, either a village near, or a neighbourhood within, the city of Samarqand in present-day Uzbekistan. Though al-Maturidi's theological views and academic circles in his native Samarqand are well-documented, nothing is known with certainty about his 'ethnic' lineage or even his native language. He seems to have spent little, if any, significant time away from Samarqand throughout his life, and was probably not a native speaker of Arabic, based on the highly idiosyncratic syntax of his extant theological works. As will be described in detail below, however, Turkish nationalists reasoned that al-Maturidi was ethnically Turkish on the basis of his Central Asian origins.

The adoption of al-Maturidi into the Turkish nationalists' definition of Turkish national heritage was, in fact, a positive development in the history of modern Turkish theology. The redefinition of the Muslim community in the Turkish Republic as a national community meant the reclamation of parts of Islamic theology neglected or underdeveloped in the Ottoman period. Because al-Maturidi came to be understood as a part of Turkish national heritage, this enabled the retrieval and revival of his theology in the Turkish Republican context. This opened up new possibilities for modern theology in Turkish that have not been explored in any other modern Sunni tradition, where interest in al-Maturidi remains marginal. In addition, though it is impossible to establish al-Maturidi's 'ethnic' identity, it is indisputable that his theology has been a key component of the pre-modern Islamic traditions from Central Asia, Anatolia and the Ottoman territories that form the historical lineages of modern Turkish Islamic thought and practice.[51]

This particular theological development, like the others examined so far, had roots in the late Ottoman period but came to full fruition only in the Republican context. As explained in Chapter 1, the Ottoman *medrese* curriculum strongly favoured Ash'arism and coexisted with a strong tradition of theological synthesis. However, alongside these developments, some Ottoman theologians maintained a preferential attitude towards Maturidism. A near-contemporary of Molla Fenari, Hızır ibn Jalal al-Din al-Rumi (known as Hızır Bey; d. 1458), authored the first explicitly al-Maturidi theological work in the Ottoman period, *al-Qasida al-Nuniyya*, a work which found many interested readers and commentators in the following centuries.[52] Other authors throughout the Ottoman period evinced an open preference for Maturidism, though in this era of synthesis they were far more reluctant to accuse Ash'arism of heresy than their intellectual ancestors had been.

The Bosnian scholar Kafi Hasan Efendi al-Aqhisari (1544–1616), for example, authored a treatise, *Rawdat al-Jannat fi Usul al-I'tiqadat*, that he said was inspired by his happenstance discovery of a manuscript of al-Maturidi's *Kitab al-Tawhid* in Mecca.[53] Aqhisari's treatise is essentially a summary of the Sunni articles of faith with a distinct Hanafi-Maturidi bent to issues such as the definition of belief. Ahmad ibn Hasan Bayadi Zadeh (d. 1687), the son of a Bosnian immigrant to Istanbul who had the good fortune to count the *Şeyhülislam* of Süleyman the Magnificent, Abu Sa'id Efendi (d. 1662) as one of his teachers and who also enjoyed an illustrious career that culminated in his accession to a professorship at the Ayasofya *medrese*, authored two famous compilations of (and commentaries on) the theological sayings of Abu Hanifa.⁵⁴ It is interesting to compare Bayadi Zadeh's professional success with the biography of Mulla Hafiz mentioned in the previous chapter. Both of these scholars during roughly the same time period were promoted to one of the highest academic posts in the empire, a professorship at Aya Sofya, yet each of them possessed contrasting theological inclinations.

The most dramatic assertion of a distinctly Maturidi theological identity in the Ottoman period came in the form of a heated theological controversy that emerged in the eighteenth century over the understanding of the classic Maturidi term for human free will, *ikhtiyār* (choice). A genre of treatises that emerged in the eighteenth century to defend this position identify themselves as Maturidi alone in theological affiliation, and offer a trenchant critique of the Ash'ari understanding of human freedom. All of these treatises involve an implicit critique of Ash'arism and sometimes even outright accuse the Ash'aris of the heresy of determinism, a charge that must have seemed rather odd in the syncretistic Ottoman intellectual environment.⁵⁵ One copyist of Davud al-Karsi's (d. 1756) treatise, for example, makes the rather striking declaration that he thanks God for making him and his colleagues members of the Maturidi theological school.⁵⁶

The emergence of Turkish nationalism provided a unique opportunity to reshape and revitalise this pre-existing Ottoman interest in al-Maturidi, this time as a way to develop a distinctly Turkish national heritage of Sunni theology. As government programmes and prominent intellectuals elaborated the Turkish national heritage in music, art, architecture, language and a whole range of other cultural institutions, Turkish theologians began to argue for the existence of a distinctly Turkish-Islamic theological heritage that they argued was distinct in content, style and methodology from other Islamic nations, such as Arabic or Persian Islamic thought.⁵⁷

Ziya Gökalp made statements to this effect in *The Principles of Turkism*, arguing that Maturidism belonged to Turkish national culture.⁵⁸ During the late Ottoman period, as Rıdvan Özdinç's important work makes clear, some reformist theologians began to argue that al-Maturidi constituted a uniquely important resource for modern theology because of his thoroughgoing focus on the importance of human reason and human freedom.⁵⁹ During the same period, some theologians began to describe al-Maturidi as ethnically 'Turkish', meaning that his work should have special interest for the development of modern theology in the emerging Turkish national community. According to Özdinç, the earliest mention of al-Maturidi as 'Turkish' came in 1869 in a work by Ali Suavi (1839–78).[60]

The first theologian writing in modern Turkish to claim that al-Maturidi was an actual member of the Turkish nation was Mehmed Şerefettin Yaltkaya, who published an article in the *Darülfünun* theology faculty review in 1932 bearing the title, 'Turkish Theologians'.[61] Yaltkaya's article is a list of medieval scholars of *kalām* presumed to have been 'Turkish', though the article does not spell out just what this means. It seems likely, however, that Yaltkaya understood this term in much the same way that Gökalp did, that is, as cultural and not racial in content. However the term may have been meant, this article represents the first text in modern Turkish (written as it was only a few years after the completion of the Turkish language reform) that speaks of al-Maturidi as being a Turk.

Yaltkaya's article does not actually include much information about al-Maturidi, and only refers to his success at debating with opposing Muslim theological schools and the importance of his work to Sunni theology.[62] The article is highly significant, however, in that its argument and basic assumptions seem to have quickly become normative in Turkish religious historiography. Contemporary histories of Turkish Islamic thought in Turkish still reproduce Yaltkaya's main schema and list of personalities. In general, Yaltkaya includes figures who are mentioned in earlier biographical texts as having a connection to Turkish peoples or who were born or active in Transoxania and the Maturidi school, as well as major theologians of the Ottoman period.

This is a rather mixed group of individuals, which includes Ibn al-Ikhshid (d. 937–8), a Sunni theologian whose father was Turkish according to the medieval scholar Ibn Hazm; al-Maturidi, a resident of Samarqand whose ethnic lineage is nowhere discussed in existing sources; and a host of Ottoman-era theologians born in various parts of that vast empire. Nevertheless, Yaltkaya's specific list of 'Turkish' theologians served as a model for later writers. Its format has been reproduced in a wide array of introductory and reference texts in modern Turkish. Ömer Aydın's work *Türk Kelam Bilginleri* (Turkish Theologians; 2004) is essentially an expanded version of Yaltkaya's list using similar criteria, though Aydın makes it clear at the outset of his work that for him the term 'Turk' does not refer to the race of these figures, but to their having been raised in and contributed to 'Turkish-Islamic culture'.⁶³

The most recent version of this genre of theological history, based consciously on Yaltkaya, is Metin Yurdagür's *Ünlü Türk Kelamcıları: Maveraünnehir'den Osmanlı Coğrafyasına* (Prominent Turkish Theologians: From Transoxiana to the Ottoman Territories, 2017). Like Aydın, Yurdagür emphasises that his work is not meant to refer to ethnicity alone, but rather trace the history of a certain 'scholastic and cultural mindset'.⁶⁴ Yaltkaya's article, therefore, represented a significant first step in the elaboration of the notion of a specifically Turkish Islamic theology that includes al-Maturidi. This notion evolved from a concept of Turkish heritage that was connected with ethnicity in the early nationalist period, to a concept of Turkish Islamic theological history that places less emphasis on asserting al-Maturidi's specific 'ethnic' background. Contemporary Turkish discussions of al-Maturidi's importance are less concerned with his family origins and more with his significance for Turkish theological history.

As we will see in significant detail in subsequent chapters, theological motifs from al-Maturidi's work have been revived across contemporary Turkish theology to address a wide variety of theological issues, from the relationship between reason and revelation to the relationship between religion and the state.⁶⁵ Following the new importance given to al-Maturidi's work by his inclusion in Turkish national and cultural identity, renewed academic attention to his work in modern Turkey has made this creative reappropriation possible. In 2002, Bekir Topaloğlu published his translation of al-Maturidi's *Kitab al-Tawhid*, which has been reprinted several times since and has made al-Maturidi's original work accessible to Turkish readers for the first time. In 2003, Topaloğlu and Muhammad Aruçi published the newest and still most widely used critical edition of this Arabic text. Under Topaloğlu's direction, a new critical edition of the Arabic original of al-Maturidi's massive Qur'an commentary, *Ta'wilat al-Qur'an*, was published in sixteen volumes between 2005 and 2011. An eighteen-volume Turkish translation of this text followed shortly thereafter.

According to the Turkish Council of Higher Education, since 1987 some eighty-nine master's and doctoral theses have been written concerning Maturidi theology.⁶⁶ Over that period, dozens of academic and popular works about al-Maturidi's life and theology have been published in Turkey. Numerous national and international conferences devoted to his theology have also taken place in recent years (including in Istanbul in 2009 and 2018, Eskişehir in 2014, Ankara in 2018 and Konya in 2018, to name a few). Consideration of al-Maturidi's theology has become a standard feature of theological discourse across Turkish academia. This is a truly remarkable development in the history of Islamic theology given that, as described in the previous chapter, al-Maturidi's original work had been inaccessible for centuries and was only accessed through later theologians and commentators of the Maturidi school. A true modern renaissance of Maturidism and Maturidi studies has developed as a consequence of the redefinition of the Muslim community enabled by the conception of the Turkish nation.

It is interesting to note here that the nationalist utilisation of al-Maturidi's life and theology has strong parallels with other developments in modern Turkish religious thought and practice. Mark Soileau's important analysis of modern Turkish scholarship on Sufi saints during the same period shows that Turkish nationalist historiography also incorporated the memory of towering figures of classical Islamic mysticism, such as Jalal al-Din Rumi (1207–73), into the new conception of Turkish national heritage. Soileau reveals that this incorporation was accomplished by a new Turkish historiography of Sufism that stressed its compatibility with modern notions of humanism and tolerance.[67] As Soileau argues, before the advent of nationalism, mystics were seen as paradigmatic examples of closeness with God; in the new context of Turkish nationalism, mystical spirituality served to connect Turkish national identity with the social values of modern humanism.[68] In a striking parallel with contemporary treatments of al-Maturidi, Turkish scholars at the beginning of the twentieth century argued that Rumi was in fact ethnically Turkish.[69]

As with the new Turkish re-evaluations of al-Maturidi's theology, these interpretations of Sufism during the 1910–50s focused on elements that were indeed crucial to the thought of these traditional figures, stressing how important their revival could be to confronting the social challenges of modernity. Al-Maturidi's theological analyses of human reason could speak to modern discussions of reason and progress, and the Sufis' mystical meditations on love could speak to modern discussions of tolerance and moral humanism. In both cases, Turkish nationalist historiography enabled the creative reappropriation of these traditional figures in a modern social and intellectual context, allowing their theological and spiritual messages to be successfully 'translated' into the new idiom of modernity.

The modern Turkish revival of al-Maturidi's theology also parallels the development of translations of the Qur'an into modern Turkish. As M. Brett Wilson's work has shown, the now widely accepted use of Turkish translations of the Qur'an for study and devotional purposes was not a development merely invented or forced by Turkish nationalists. The drive to translate the Qur'an into Turkish developed from the same late Ottoman Islamic modernist currents of thought that revived the study of al-Maturidi. Turkish nationalism accelerated, and provided a stable context for, the organic development of this scholarly effort, including funding for the project granted by the Turkish parliament in 1925.[70] As with Quranic translation, the modern revival of al-Maturidi's theology was the natural outcome of intellectual developments that had their roots in the Ottoman Empire, and which then grew into their natural maturity in the ideological and institutional context of the Turkish Republic.

The incorporation of al-Maturidi into the history of the Turkish nation contributed to the authenticating of modern Turkish Islamic theology by anchoring it in both traditional Islamic lineages of theological authenticity and in a new dimension of authenticity in this period: Turkish nationalism. It also demonstrates how Turkish nationalism as a political ideology enabled the development of new forms of Sunni theology. Despite its novelty, nationalism could in fact aid in the development of pre-national Islamic intellectual legacies, demonstrating its potentially salutary effect on the development of Islamic tradition in the modern period. Nationalism's relationship with Islamic identity is far from uncomplicated, however, and subsequent generations of Turkish theologians would call attention to the potential conflicts between secular nationalism and Islamic theological and communal identity.

Conservative Theological Critiques of Secular Turkish Nationalism

The emergence of Turkish nationalism in the late Ottoman period had already proved to be one of the main issues that caused severe tension among the earliest generation of modern Turkish theologians. As we have seen, these theologians shared a desire for the renewal of Islamic thought in the Ottoman

Empire.[71] They did, however, often disagree sharply over the issue of nationalism. This cleavage was one of the most significant tensions within late Ottoman theology that was then inherited by their intellectual descendants in the Turkish Republic. This tension can be clearly seen in a comparison between İzmirli and Yaltkaya, for instance.[72] As we have seen in the previous chapter, their works exercised immense influence at the beginning of the Republican period, but they disagreed sharply on the exact nature of theological reform and its relationship with Turkish nationalism.[73]

The nationalist and modernist theological visions described above met with particularly severe critique in the decades following the founding of the Republic and the eventual relaxation of its strict secularist policies. A concept of the national community did indeed become central to modern Turkish theological thought, but at the same time the question of how exactly to define the nation became one of the most important topics of debate in this tradition. Turkish nationalism placed the nation at the centre of modern Turkish culture, and modern Turkish theology has been debating its relationship with Islam ever since. Like progressive nationalist theologies, the first systematic theological critiques of nationalism in the Republic built on late Ottoman precedents and evolved into a distinct stream of discourse in modern Turkish theology.

These conservative critiques of secular Turkish nationalism are important to consider because they have constituted one of the most influential sources of conservative Turkish political activism, and also identified key ideological weaknesses in the secular Turkish national project. These critiques converge on the point that the progressive positivist morality of secular Turkish nationalism does not constitute a fulfilling moral vision. These critics argue that secular and ethnic nationalism marginalises the common human need for connection with the transcendent, and that such marginalisation of the sacred endangers moral order and individual happiness and fulfilment.

These criticisms were ruthlessly suppressed in the early years of the Republic, but experienced a revival after the end of the one-party period. In 1950, the first multi-party democratic elections in Turkish history were held. Erich Zurcher describes this event as the 'climax of the whole period of transition' that had occurred between the fall of the Ottoman Empire and the emergence of a democratic republic.[74] The repressive policies of the one-party state that had existed for over two decades were rejected by the voting public: with 80 per cent participation, 53.4 per cent of the votes went to the opposition Democrat Party (*Demokrat Partisi*) while 39.8 per cent of votes went to the Republican People's Party (*Cumhuriyet Halk Partisi*), resulting in a large Democrat Party majority in the Turkish parliament.[75]

One of the political platforms that helped carry the Democrat Party to victory was a promise to relax the repression of popular religion in the 1930s and 1940s and to encourage the expression of Islamic culture in the Republic. In fact, the activities of the Ankara University Faculty of Theology in the early 1950s were enabled partly by this shift. This period also saw a great increase in the influence and public profile of Islamic devotional movements such as the movement founded by Said Nursi (1877–1960), a charismatic intellectual who argued forcefully against the materialistic and naturalist philosophical currents of the late Ottoman Empire. Nursi's theology attempted to reinforce the strength of Islamic belief in an increasingly secular era without challenging the political bases of secular democracy.[76] His theology also represented the re-assertion of socially conservative Islamic activism in the Turkish Republic.

Nursi was not a member of the Istanbul Islamic intellectual elite, and spent most of his life spreading his message through informal study circles or advocating for educational reform in the provincial areas of the dwindling Ottoman Empire. His theological approach does, however, have some important similarities with that of reformists such as İzmirli who devoted their intellectual efforts to battling materialist interpretations of modern philosophy and science. Like İzmirli, Nursi did not reject all elements of modern society, and was famous for his support for science education in Islamic curricula. In his view, when properly understood, the modern sciences could be seen as the most powerful proofs for the truths of religion because they point towards the Creator of the world that is the focus of scientific inquiry. Nursi continually stressed in his work that the various disciplines of the empirical sciences provided their own specific forms of proof for the existence of God.[77] Rather than critique science itself, Nursi critiqued those who idolised it as a substitute for religion, calling them 'nature worshippers' (*tabiatperest*) or 'worshippers of natural causality' (*esbabperest*).[78]

Nursi also shared İzmirli's suspicion of the ethnocentrism of nationalist political thought and culture. He argued that nationalism is a fundamentally racist concept that orders society around the principles of coercion, conflict and the selfish and insatiable desires of an inward-looking community.[79] For Nursi, removing religion as the moral basis for society and replacing it with the ethnic nation meant removing the virtues of selflessness and service, and replacing them with the vices of bigotry and selfishness. This critique, combined with the socially conservative elements of his movement, earned him the ire of the secular Turkish nationalist establishment in the 1920s and drove his movement underground until the early 1950s. For instance, the segregation of genders often practised in his movement has been one its more distinctive features since its inception.[80] Nursi suffered greatly for his social conservatism and pious activism. He was arrested, prosecuted and imprisoned numerous times from the 1930s to the early 1950s. His followers were also imprisoned and abused by the government. Nursi's final trial and acquittal took place in 1953; he was then in his mid-seventies, only a few years before his death in 1960.[81]

Nursi clearly saw a stronger division between modernity and Islam than the Istanbul-based modernists (such as İzmirli, Yaltkaya and Yörükan). Nursi's theology, therefore, combined elements of İzmirli's Islamic modernist critique of materialism with a more explicitly conservative sensibility that made his project popular among conservative devotional movements that would later be known as the *cemaat*s, or 'associations'.[82] This combination accounts for Nursi's continuing popularity among Muslims in Turkey today. This theology emphasises support for modern scientific developments while validating the experiences of suppression that millions of devout, socially conservative Muslim believers encountered in the first few decades of the Turkish Republic.[83]

Despite his critique of secular nationalism, Nursi was not opposed to the new Turkish democracy. Rather than seek the overthrow of the democratic order (which he openly endorsed), Nursi instead focused his efforts on the revival of Islamic education and religious life in the secular Turkish Republic. In the 1950s, relaxation of the restrictions on religious expression from the previous decades allowed his movement to flourish and develop into countrywide networks that studied and disseminated his writings.[84] Not unlike other Turkish Muslim thinkers who were active in the late Ottoman Empire, Nursi located the essence of Islam in Islamic belief and spiritual practice, rather than identifying it with a specific political formation. Nursi's great historical importance lies less in his contributions to systematic theological thought and more in his tireless revival and dignifying of popular piety and spirituality in the newly secularised context of the Turkish Republic.

Other members of the mid-century Islamic activist current also tended to distance themselves from secular Turkish nationalism, instead speaking in the name of a broader pan-Sunnism. This critique of secular Turkish nationalism continued to be highly threatening to the secular elite, who punished these critics severely. One of the most influential critics was the poet and activist Necip Fazıl Kısakürek (1904–83), who, like Nursi, was imprisoned for his critique of the secular nationalist Turkish state. His work in particular epitomises the wider conservative Islamic critique of secular Turkish nationalism. From the 1940s until his death, he was among the most influential Islamist ideological voices in modern Turkey.

Kısakürek's literary output deals with a wide variety of subjects, and does not comprise a systematic theological project. Many of his specific arguments, however, became highly characteristic of conservative theological commentary on secular Turkish nationalism, and his life and activism inspired decades of political and theological critique.[85] During his studies in Paris in the 1920s, he became disillusioned with the materialism of the modern West and after he moved back to Turkey he turned towards the mystical piety of the traditional Sufi orders.[86] His theological critique of the secularisation of his homeland became so powerful precisely because it identified the spiritual vacuum created by the authoritarian modernisation programme of Atatürk's government.

Kısakürek defines religion as that which connects humanity with the only true Absolute, the One God who created the universe.[87] Kısakürek's critique of secular Turkish nationalism turns on his argument that this ideological programme fails because it replaces the one true Absolute with earthly idols, such as the ethnic nation. The only laws to which believers properly owe their allegiance are the laws of the One God. Islam, the truest expression of the religious impulse natural to all of humanity, is not merely a collection of beliefs and practices of worship. Instead, Kısakürek defines Islam as a totalising system that encompasses all realms of human life and experience. It speaks to the inner depths of the human individual, as much as it imbues very aspect of human society with moral order. Islam is a total social system, and the exact name of this system is *Shari'ah*. In exactly the same way that God is the absolute creator of the cosmos, Islam and *Shari'ah* are to be interpreted as absolute and founded by God.[88] Kısakürek argues that Islam, in contrast to secularism, provides true morality and freedom by recognising the inherently spiritual nature of humanity, and then organising all of life around this spiritual nature. Kısakürek's work, shaped by the totalising secularisation project of the early Republic, proposes as a critique a totalising vision of Islam as a social and political programme.

Kısakürek's critique of secular Turkish nationalism follows logically from his conception of Islam. If it is the case that Islam can only be conceived of as a totalising social project, then other social orders that compete for the loyalty and sacrifice of individual Muslims are potentially idolatrous replacements for our loyalty to God. Like other pan-Sunni Islamists, Kısakürek argues that the ethnic national distinctions that Muslims draw among themselves in the modern period (such as Turk, Arab, etc.) are earthly divisions that obscure Muslims' higher unity. Rather than think of themselves as loyal members of a given nation, Muslims should instead think of themselves as members of the global Muslim community, the *umma*. This traditional term for the Muslim community becomes in Kısakürek's usage a call to global pan-Sunni political struggle against secularism and nationalism. Kısakürek expresses his hope that all Muslims would be able to one day unite to create a truly Islamic order, in contrast to the morally decadent and vacuous culture of secular Western modernity.[89]

Following the struggles of critical thinkers and activists such as Nursi and Kısakürek, Turkey in the 1950s saw the formation of devotional associations that sought the revival of conservative religious practices, including the practice of Sufism. The prominent Nakşibendi sheikh, Mehmet Zahid Kotku, led this widely influential (though often underground) Sufi movement in Turkey throughout the 1950s and until his death in 1980.[90] Kotku also exercised a great amount of influence in Turkish politics in the 1970s and 1980s, especially through his contact with Necmettin Erbakan, the most influential Turkish Islamist politician of the 1970s to the mid-1990s and prime minister from 1996 to 1997.[91] Kotku's spiritual circle exemplifies the mid-century phenomenon of the rise of *cemaat*s, or Islamic devotional associations founded to promote socially conservative forms of Islamic spiritual practice, often through the utilisation of traditional forms of Sufi mystical piety. These conservative groups were instrumental in the growth of Islamic activism in the twentieth century in Turkey, having helped launch the career of Erbakan and thus the beginning of conservative Islamic politics that led eventually to the emergence of the AKP.[92]

Gökhan Bacık's work has also shown that these *cemaat*s are often suspicious of scientific reasoning if such reasoning is interpreted as weakening the conception of God's total sovereignty over the universe. These conservative mystical movements, in other words, often reject modern philosophical epistemologies as appropriate paradigms for understanding the world.[93] This tendency forms a notable contrast with theologians such as İzmirli who, as we have seen, stressed the need for direct and appreciative Islamic theological engagement with modern philosophy and science. Where the late nineteenth- and early twentieth-century Ottoman modernists often saw opportunities for dialogue with, and commonality between, pre-modern Islamic thought and modern Western philosophy and science, the mid-twentieth-century *cemaat*s often saw irreducible difference and opposition.

Similarly, Islamic theological engagement with nationalism would prove to be particularly unappealing to proponents of more radical theological critiques that emerged in the latter half of the twentieth century. Rather than following Nursi's acceptance of democratic governance, throughout the 1960s and lasting through the 1980s, many Islamist activists followed the path of Kısakürek and openly challenged the basic tenets of secular democracy. They argued instead for the re-establishment of the state in accordance with an Islamist ideology. This group of intellectuals (represented most prominently by Ali Bulaç) opposed the very notion of modernism, arguing that modernism represented the Western imperialist imposition of an inauthentic cultural identity on Muslim peoples.[94] According to Bulaç, religion and modernity are opposed in their very essences and fundamentally irreconcilable. They represent diametrically opposed views of the universe, and thus represent mutually contradictory ways of ordering social and individual life. Religion, considered here as a totalising concept along the lines envisioned by Kısakürek, is the only way of life that can be considered truly moral. Conceptions of the state and society that cannot be explicitly drawn from Islamic practice and precedent are to be considered alien to religion itself, and thus fundamentally dangerous and immoral.[95]

The 1980s and 1990s witnessed the re-emergence of discussions of the place of Islam in the history of the Turkish nation, and the possibilities for its renewed reconciliation with the secular republic. Partly as an attempt to co-opt the power of Islamic activist discourses, the leaders of the 1980 military coup adopted the right-wing nationalist ideology of 'Turkish-Islamic synthesis' (*Türk-İslam Sentezi*), which emphasised the importance of Islam and Turkic-Islamic dynasties in Turkish national history, as their official vision of the ideology of the Turkish state.[96] This inclusion of Islam in the Turkish national story was a continuation of the ideas of the earlier modernists mentioned above, and foreshadowed more sophisticated discussions of the relationship between religion and state that would take place in the 1990s and 2000s, as we will see throughout the rest of this book. Advocacy for the establishment of an explicitly Islamic state has weakened considerably since the late 1980s and the 'postmodern coup' of 1997, which unseated the government of the Islamist Prime Minister Necmettin Erbakan.[97] Yet as Chapter 5 will discuss in more detail, the 2000s saw the rise of the AKP and its transformation from a promoter of liberal democratic reform to an authoritarian regime. Though calls for the elimination of secularism or the establishment of an Islamist state are rare in mainstream Turkish discourse, conservative religious authoritarianism has emerged as a subject of major critique in Turkey in the 2010s.

Though Islamist activist strains have remained largely distinct from the academic theology of the theology faculties, there have been significant instances of overlap where theology faculty theologians have become involved in conservative politics. The widely influential scholar of Islamic law Hayreddin Karaman is representative of this potential overlap. Since the 1970s, Karaman has advocated for change and reinterpretation in *Shariʿah* practice. At the same time, his work is well known for its explicit questioning of the validity of a secular state, an institution whose utility he seems to accept but whose philosophical bases he frequently criticises. His work is a particularly widespread contemporary example of conservative Islamic theological critique of secular Turkish nationalist conceptions of the state.

Karaman depicts secularism as a system that Muslims have consented to live under, and a system to which they must learn to adapt as devout believers, but rejects the notion that the concept of a secular state can be supported by Islamic tradition.[98] Karaman argues that individual liberties must be protected by the establishment of a democratic state, but he critiques the concept of 'liberty' as fundamentally Western in origin and for its implication that God's sovereignty over human beings is not absolute.[99] He also argues that the concepts of human rights and even democracy itself are Western and imperialist in origin, and maintains that a fully functional democracy can be erected on the basis of an Islamic state.[100]

In recent years, Karaman has also distinguished himself from the usually apolitical intellectual projects of the Turkish theology faculties by openly aligning himself with the conservative political project of the current AKP government. Karaman has defended socially conservative positions associated with Recep Tayyip Erdoğan's government, such as disapproval of mixed-gender student residences. He has also argued that because Turkey is a majority-Muslim society, conservative Muslims have the right to assert the dominance of their value system in the public sphere, even if that means the suppression of alternative lifestyles (as will be discussed in detail in the last chapter of this book).[101] Though the current AKP government is the subject of growing criticism for its rising use of authoritarianism following the Gezi Park protests of 2013, and increasing with every political crisis since then (most notably the harrowing coup attempt of the summer of 2016), Karaman has very publicly supported AKP policies and has strongly backed the enforcement of socially conservative values in Turkish politics and government.[102] Karaman's avowedly activist stance has been an influential voice in contemporary Turkish Islamic activism, but it remains an unusual example of an academic theologian who has so forcefully entered the Turkish political sphere.

Liberal Theological Critiques of Secular Turkish Nationalism

Alongside conservative and broadly anti-secular voices, liberal theological critiques of secular Turkish nationalism have emerged in the 2000s. These approaches combine a commitment to secular liberal democracy with an Islamic theological perspective to produce a critique of the authoritarianism of secular Turkish nationalist ideology and state policy. In a noteworthy contrast with the conservative theological critiques of secular Turkish nationalism, these liberal theological critiques defend a basic conception of secularity as a natural part of Muslim governance and society. These theologians argue that secularism, if it is understood to protect individual freedom of religion rather than suppress it, can be seen as compatible with Islamic religious ideals. On this basis, therefore, these criticisms address the authoritarianism of twentieth-century secular Turkish nationalism, rather than engaging in a broad critique of the West or of all forms of secularity. Instead of seeing Islam as a totalising social system as the conservative theologians do, these theologians see a natural distinction between political power and Islam, and argue that these two social forces can work together harmoniously within the framework of the nationalist Turkish state.

These theological arguments clearly hark back to the modernism of the early Republican period, but they combine this progressivism with a nuanced contemporary engagement with secular national political ideology. These critiques form part of the post-1980 flowering of intellectual conversations surrounding Islamic history and culture in Turkey, conversations that featured a liberal democratic critique of the Turkish state's intervention into religious affairs.[103] In a sense, the strong belief in democracy and freedom of thought originally advanced by Atatürk's revolution has laid the foundations for its own critique, and has led to the accusation in Turkey that Turkish state authoritarianism has betrayed its own commitment to democracy.[104]

One highly influential theologian whose work focuses on these concerns is Sönmez Kutlu. Kutlu's wide body of work, beginning in the early 2000s in particular, has argued that secularity is actually a feature of Islam, rather than an alien import from the West. Kutlu argues that the distinction between religion and state is built into the Sunni Muslim religious ethos because Sunni Islam never developed a hierarchical priesthood.[105] Instead, Sunni ritual worship is based on individual practices, rather than on a corporate sacrament administered by a clerical figure. In other words, because Sunni Islam never developed an institution that was meant to compete with secular authority, it implicitly recognises the legitimacy of secular power and makes no claim to wield it. Sunnism does not require forcible secularisation because it already presumes and supports secularity. Christianity, on the other hand, did require secularisation in order to secure individual liberty precisely because it developed a hierarchical priesthood that acquired political power over time, thus blurring the natural distinction between worldly and sacred authority.

Kutlu argues that this is the reason why attempts to forcibly secularise Sunni society, such as the authoritarian nationalist secularism of the early Turkish Republic, result in tyranny rather than liberty. Because these social programmes are based on the Western experience of religion, they assume the existence of a clerical class that needs to be dismantled by the state. When such a programme is applied in a Sunni Muslim context, it results instead in the restriction of individual religious liberties, because there is no clerical class to target. Instead, the individual pious Muslim is targeted by the state.[106] This dynamic sets the stage for a conflict between the secular state and Muslim practitioners, a conflict that Kutlu argues has disastrous consequences for individual liberties. Not only will the state interfere with religious freedom, but this kind of governmental intervention into religious life will actually create an artificial Sunni clerical class that the state will seek to control. These conflicts and hardships are entirely avoidable if it is understood that the fact that some concept of secularity is needed to secure individual religious liberty is a truth that is already acknowledged and implied by the basic principles Islamic theology and practice.[107]

Rather than import conceptions of secularity from the West, what is needed is a theological exploration of the concept of the secular inherent within Sunni Islam itself in order to construct a just and free social order. More specifically, Kutlu argues that the Sunni Muslim concept of the secular can be derived from Maturidi theological tradition.[108] His work frequently refers to the *diyanet-siyaset ayrımı*, or the 'religion-politics distinction' that he sees as implicit in Sunni dogmatic theology. His theology constitutes an extended and nuanced reflection on how this distinction is implied by the most basic conceptual distinctions made by traditional Sunni dogmatics, such as the distinction between faith and works.[109] According to Maturidi theology, the most fundamental features of religion are beliefs about the One God, and these beliefs are apprehended primarily in the inner realm of the human being through the act of faith in the heart. Faith is an act of internal assent because this realm cannot be interfered with by others: it is a space of genuine free will.[110]

Acts are intimately related to faith which is their basis, but the confusion of the two risks imputing the contingency and changeability of the created world to the eternal and unchangeable content of faith itself. According to Kutlu's argument, confusing the religious and the political realms is exactly the same kind of error as confusing faith and works. The latter must of necessity proceed from the former, but this distinction must be maintained or the changeability of human politics might be mistaken for the unchanging content of divine revelation. Combining the political with the religious, as in the Islamist conception of Kısakürek and Bulaç, for instance, is according to Kutlu a theological mistake that risks the cardinal error of confusing the eternal with the contingent, the Creator with the created.

Arif Yıldırım made similar arguments when he wrote in 2006 about the points at which the goals of the secular state and the goals of religion intersect with each other. Like Kutlu, Yıldırım argues that religion and state constitute distinct spheres of life and activity, but they can and must work together because they share the same goal of establishing a just, free and moral society. Yıldırım asserts that the state naturally needs some metaphysical basis greater than itself to establish its legitimacy, and that if religion does not fill this role in supporting the goals of the democratic state, it will be supplanted by the outright sacralisation of the state itself. At the same time, religion cannot exist without the social framework provided by the state. Thus, though religion and state must be distinct and prevented from mutual interference, it must be recognised that they share the same basic social goals and should be arranged to support one another.[111]

Yıldırım's critique of the sacralisation of the state, and his concern to prevent conflict between state governance and free religious practice, are both comments on authoritarian secular Turkish nationalism. Rather than an authoritarian secularist system where the state dominates religious practice, or a theocratic system where religion attempts to play the role of the state, Yıldırım argues for a social system where the goals of religion and the secular state are recognised as mutually compatible and are allowed to work in harmony with each other.[112] Like Kutlu, Yıldırım therefore argues that secularism must be applied in a way that takes into account local religious conditions and attempts to work in harmony with the religious customs of the people.[113] And also like Kutlu, Yıldırım argues that Sunni theological tradition supports the general liberal humanist ethos that strives to protect individual freedom of religion for members of all faiths, while also recognising the right of the secular state to administer the public sphere and the general social order.[114]

In other words, liberal critics of secular Turkish nationalism focus their critiques not on secularity or nationalism per se, but rather on the authoritarian manner in which the Turkish Republic has implemented nationalism and secularism throughout the twentieth century. Unlike the conservative critics who identify authoritarian repression with secular nationalism, these theologians argue that secularism and nationalism are entirely compatible with the religion of Islam, but authoritarianism is not. Thus, they critique the secular Turkish nationalist repression of individual religious freedom not by rejecting secular nationalism, but rather by calling for a liberal secularism that is rooted in Islamic theological tradition. This reimagining of Turkish secularism, in their view, promises to end the religion–secular divide in Turkish politics and restore a harmonious relationship between devout religious practice and the secular state, which are both understood to be necessary for a well-functioning social order.

The relationship between Turkish theology and Turkish nationalism is therefore both generative and tense. While the conceptual resources of Turkish national belonging renewed the creativity and expanded the limits of Islamic theology in modern Turkish, they also produced a series of tensions between Islamic and national identity. Conservative theologians noticed this tension from the beginning of the Turkish national movement, and have elaborated theological critiques of ethnic nationalism since the beginning of the Republic. At the same time, the progressive conceptual framework provided by nationalism also sowed the seeds for its own critique, as Turkish theologians favouring more modernist approaches critiqued traditional Turkish nationalism as insufficient to live up to its own humanist and progressive ideals. This productive dialectic between modernity and the demands of systematic theology was generated by the innovative conceptual framework of Turkish nationalism, because this framework allowed Turkish theologians to reimagine the history and possibilities within Sunni theological tradition. As the rest of this book will demonstrate, this generative dialectic would emerge again and again as Turkish theologians tackled a wide array of philosophical, theological and social problems throughout the twentieth and into the twenty-first centuries.

Notes

1. Kazım was a widely influential archetypical example of the late Ottoman modernist theologian. He was also a strong supporter of the nationalist reform movement led by the Committee of Union and Progress. See Bein, *Ottoman Ulema*, 31.
2. Kazım, 'İslam ve Terakki', 123.
3. Kazım, 'İslam ve Terakki', 124.
4. Yazır was a widely regarded theologian who authored pioneering texts in Quranic commentary in Turkish. See Bein, *Ottoman Ulema*, 21, 119.
5. Yazır, 'Müslümanlık Mani-i Terakki Değil', 484.
6. Yazır, 'Müslümanlık Mani-i Terakki Değil', 485.
7. Özdinç, *Akıl, İrade, Hürriyet*, 15.
8. İzmirli, *Yeni İlm-i Kelam*, 1:21–4 (23–5). See note 6 in Chapter 3 for details on this text and how it is cited in this book.
9. Özdinç, *Akıl, İrade, Hürriyet*, 49.
10. İzmirli, *Yeni İlm-i Kelam*, 1:23–4 (23).
11. Kazım, 'Medeniyet-Din İlişkisi', 117.
12. Yazır, 'Müslümanlık Mani-i Terakki Değil', 496.
13. Yazır, 'Müslümanlık Mani-i Terakki Değil', 496.
14. Özdinç, *Akıl, İrade, Hürriyet*, 17, 46–7.
15. Kazım, 'Hürriyet–Müsavat', 109.
16. On the importance of virtue and morality to Kazım's understanding of progress and civilisation, see Kevin Reinhart, 'Musa Kâzım', 295–6.
17. Kazım, 'Hürriyet–Müsavat', 110.
18. Kazım, 'İslam ve Terakki', 124.
19. Kazım, 'İslam ve Terakki', 126.
20. Kazım, 'Hürriyet–Müsavat', 114.
21. Kazım, 'Hürriyet–Müsavat', 113–15.
22. Kazım, 'Hürriyet–Müsavat', 116.
23. Yazır, 'Müslümanlık Mani-i Terakki Değil', 498.
24. Atatürk, 'An Exhortation to Progress', 232.
25. Comte, *A General View of Positivism*, 2. For a thorough accounting of the ideological history of Kemalism, see Hanioğlu, 'The Historical Roots of Kemalism', 32–60.

26. Akseki's significance as a reformist scholar whose influence bridged the late Ottoman and Republican period is explored in detail in Bein, *Ottoman Ulema*, 114–16. As Bein points out, Akseki exemplified the typical 'middle-of-the-road' approach of reformist theologians of the period who were neither ardent Kemalists nor ardent opponents of the new regime. Akseki also served as the head of the Ministry of Religious Affairs from 1947 until his death.
27. Akseki, 'İslam Fitri, Tabii ve Umumı Bir Dindir', 868.
28. Akseki, 'İslam Fitri, Tabii ve Umumı Bir Dindir', 869.
29. Akseki, 'İslam Fitri, Tabii ve Umumı Bir Dindir', 870.
30. Akseki, 'İslam Fitri, Tabii ve Umumı Bir Dindir', 853.
31. Akseki, 'İslam Fitri, Tabii ve Umumı Bir Dindir', 846.
32. Quoted in Dorroll, 'The Turkish Understanding of Religion', 1042.
33. Özdinç, *Akıl, İrade, Hürriyet*, 19.
34. Akseki, 'İslam Fitri, Tabii ve Umumı Bir Dindir', 845.
35. Akseki, 'İslam Fitri, Tabii ve Umumı Bir Dindir', 864.
36. Akseki, 'İslam Fitri, Tabii ve Umumı Bir Dindir', 865.
37. Akseki, 'İslam Fitri, Tabii ve Umumı Bir Dindir', 865.
38. Akseki, 'İslam Fitri, Tabii ve Umumı Bir Dindir', 867.
39. İzmirli, *Yeni İlm-i Kelam*, 1:22–4 (23–6).
40. Yörükan, *Dini İnkilap ve İslahat Hakkında*, 10.
41. Azak, 'Nationalist Search for Vernacular Islam'; Berkes, *Development of Secularism in Turkey*, 487.
42. Adyar includes the full text of the report in his article, 37–9.
43. Aydar, 'Darülfünun'un İlahiyat Fakültesi', 37–8.
44. Aydar, 'Darülfünun'un İlahiyat Fakültesi', 37–8.
45. Gökalp, *Principles of Turkism*, 119.
46. Aydar, 'Darülfünun'un İlahiyat Fakültesi', 39.
47. For recent detailed analyses of Al-Maturidi's life and thought see Ak, *Büyük Türk Alimi Maturidi ve Maturidilik*; H. Alper, *İmam Matüridi'de Akıl-Vahiy İlişkisi*; Correa, *Testifying Beyond Experience*; Dorroll, 'The Universe in Flux'; and Rudolph, *Sunnī Theology in Samarqand*.
48. The basic insights of this highly important research, unfortunately still unavailable in English, are summarised in Dorroll (2016), 120–5.
49. The Hanafi school of Sunni law and theology is one of the four major Sunni schools of theology and sacred law (*fiqh*). For details on Abu Hanifa's life and theological views, see van Ess, *Theology and Society* Vol. I, 210–43. Abu Hanifa's most influential theological positions included his distinction between faith and works, and his use of rational and context-based scriptural hermeneutics.

50. Soileau, *Humanist Mystics*, 68–9.
51. See Bruckmayr, 'The Spread and Persistence of Al-Maturidi Kalām', and Madelung, 'The Spread of Māturīdism'.
52. Aydın, *Türk Kelam Bilginleri*, 53.
53. Badeen (ed.), 2008, 31–61.
54. See Çelebi, *İmam-ı Azam Ebu Hanife'nin İtikadi Görüşleri*.
55. Gümülcinevī, 2b; Karsī, 10b–10a; Isbiri, 62 (Isbirī's title also makes it clear that his treatise constitutes an implicit critique of the Ash'aris).
56. For an extended treatment of this theological controversy in English, see Haidar, *The Debates between Ash'arism and Māturīdism in Ottoman Religious Scholarship*.
57. On other efforts to 'nationalise' culture in the early Turkish Republic, see Bozdoğan, 'Architecture, Modernism and Nation-Building'; Öztürkmen, 'The Role of the People's Houses'; and Stokes, *The Arabesk Debate*.
58. Gökalp, *Principles of Turkism*, 126.
59. Özdinç, *Akıl, İrade, Hürriyet*, 108, 215–16.
60. Özdinç, *Akıl, İrade, Hürriyet*, 110.
61. Yaltkaya, 'Türk Kelamcıları', 1–19.
62. Yaltkaya, 'Türk Kelamcıları', 3.
63. Aydın, *Türk Kelam Bilginleri*, 11.
64. Yurdagür, *Ünlü Türk Kelamcıları*, 11.
65. The use of important Maturidi theological concepts in modern Turkish theology will be discussed in the following chapters via the work of Hülya Alper, Emine Öğük, Sönmez Kutlu and Hanifi Özcan, most notably.
66. See the search term 'Maturidi' in the Council's online database: <https://tez.yok.gov.tr/UlusalTezMerkezi/giris.jsp> (accessed 29 April 2020).
67. Soileau, *Humanist Mystics*, 84–91.
68. Soileau, *Humanist Mystics*, 90.
69. Soileau, *Humanist Mystics*, 119–25.
70. Wilson, *Translating the Qur'an in an Age of Nationalism*, 10–11, 133, 175.
71. Özervarlı, 'Alternative Approaches to Modernization', 82–3.
72. Bein discusses this split in greater detail on pp. 46–7 of *Ottoman Ulema*.
73. Özervarlı discusses this cleavage in some detail in *Kelamda Yenilik Arayışları*, 55–61.
74. Zurcher, *Turkey: A Modern History*, 217.
75. Zurcher, *Turkey: A Modern History*, 217.
76. On Nursi's life and thought see Mardin, *Religion and Social Change in Modern Turkey*; and Turner and Horkuc, *Said Nursi*.

77. Nursi, *The Words*, 170. See on this point also Mardin, *Religion and Social Change*, 203.
78. Nursi, *Sözler*, 628.
79. Nursi, *The Words*, 426.
80. Mardin, *Religion and Social Change*, 202.
81. Mardin, *Religion and Social Change*, 98.
82. Yildiz, 'Transformation of Turkish-Islamic Thought', 43; and Ocak, 'Günümüz Türkiye Müslümanlığına Genel Bir Bakış', 136. Important studies of these devotional groups include: Catharina Raudvere, *The Book and the Roses*, and Brian Silverstein, *Islam and Modernity*.
83. In this sense, Nursi was similar to other Islamic revivalists of the same period such as Mawlana Mawdudi, though Nursi shied away from wielding any kind of political power or discussing any notion of the Islamic state. Importantly, he demonstrated loyalty to the republican democratic order so long as it did not violate the rights of believers or prevent the expression of religious sentiments in politics, a stance that would become typical of many Islamic conservative thinkers in Turkey throughout the twentieth century.
84. Mardin, *Religion and Social Change*, 160.
85. See Guida, 'Stories of "Conversion"', 116–17.
86. Guida, 'Stories of "Conversion"', 102–4.
87. Kısakürek, *İman ve İslam Atlası*, 15.
88. Kısakürek, *İman ve İslam Atlası*, 35.
89. Kısakürek, *İman ve İslam Atlası*, 52–3.
90. Mardin, 'The Nakşibendi Order', 133–4.
91. Mardin, 'The Nakşibendi Order', 134.
92. Guida, 'Stories of "Conversion"', 117.
93. Bacik, *Islam and Muslim Resistance to Modernity in Turkey*, 223–32.
94. Karasipahi, *Muslims in Modern Turkey*, 7–12; Meeker, 'Muslim Intellectuals', 189–91; Ocak, 'Günümüz Türkiye Müslümanlığına Genel Bir Bakış', 129–30; 'İslami Düşüncenin Bir Tahlil Denemesi', 101–2.
95. Bulaç, *Din ve Modernizm*, 304.
96. Cetinsaya, 'Rethinking Nationalism and Islam', 374; Copeaux, *Türk Tarih Tezinden Türk-İslam Sentezine*, 79–89; Kurt, 'The Doctrine of "Turkish-Islamic Synthesis"', 113.
97. On the decline of the popularity of arguments for an explictly Islamic state in Turkish political debate, see Ocak, 'Günümüz Turkiye Müslümanlığına Genel Bir Bakış', 103; Yildiz, 'Transformation of Turkish-Islamic Thought', 41.

98. Karaman, 'Laikliğin Kur'an'la savunulması'. The online archives for this newspaper appear to be missing issues from 2004. Karaman wrote this piece as part of a series that refuted a series of pro-secularist pieces published by the Turkish MP Gündüz Aktan in the newspaper *Radikal*. A summary of their exchange is included in Uygur Aktan, 'İdeoloji, teoloji, ve devlet', *Radikal*, 12 November 2004. Available at <http://www.radikal.com.tr/yorum/ideoloji-teoloji-ve-devlet-728458> (last accessed 8 October 2020).
99. Guida, 'The New Islamists' Understanding of Democracy', 363.
100. Guida, 'The New Islamists' Understanding of Democracy', 364–5.
101. Kuru, 'Shari'a, Islamic Ethics, and Democracy', 170–2.
102. Kuru, 'Shari'a, Islamic Ethics, and Democracy', 170–2.
103. On the liberal critique of secularist Kemalism, see Karaveli, 'An Unfulfilled Promise of Enlightenment'.
104. Zurcher, *Turkey: A Modern History*, 289. On the questioning of secularist Kemalism since the 1980s, see also Kasaba, 'Kemalist Certainties and Modern Ambiguities', 18; and Somer, 'Democratization, Clashing Narratives, and "Twin Tolerations"', 36.
105. Kutlu, 'Diyanet-Siyaset Ayrımı', 69.
106. Kutlu, 'Diyanet-Siyaset Ayrımı', 69.
107. Kutlu, 'Diyanet-Siyaset Ayrımı', 69.
108. Kutlu, 'Diyanet-Siyaset Ayrımı', 61. See also Kutlu, 'Bilinmeyen Yönleriyle Türk Din Bilgini', 17.
109. Kutlu, 'Diyanet-Siyaset Ayrımı', 62.
110. Kutlu, 'Diyanet-Siyaset Ayrımı', 63.
111. Yıldırım, 'Ebu Mansur Matüridi'nin Din-Devlet İlişkisine Bakışı', 160.
112. Yıldırım, 'Ebu Mansur Matüridi'nin Din-Devlet İlişkisine Bakışı', 168.
113. Yıldırım, 'Ebu Mansur Matüridi'nin Din-Devlet İlişkisine Bakışı', 160.
114. Yıldırım, 'Ebu Mansur Matüridi'nin Din-Devlet İlişkisine Bakışı', 168.

3

GOD

This book argues that modern Turkish theology's fundamental concern has been to think through the consequences of the Islamic doctrine of the Oneness of God in the context of modernity. This tradition of thought is thus based on the cardinal Islamic theological distinction between the Creator and the created. This chapter will consider the first part of this distinction, the Creator. It will show how modern Turkish theology defines God in terms of God's Oneness and God's loving care for creation and humanity. For modern Turkish theologians, *contra* the claims of late Ottoman scientific materialism that this tradition of thought arose to oppose, the world is sacred and possesses transcendent value because it points to these truths about its Creator.

Meditation on the nature of God, the Creator of all, thus means determining what constitutes eternal and unchanging truth in order to defend and elaborate this truth during the rapid social changes of modernity. Religion, or *din*, constitutes this truth; but how exactly this truth is practised in the human world can be subject to change over time. Modern Turkish theology therefore seeks to identify which elements of Islamic religious tradition are eternally valid and thus cannot be changed; and which elements are liable to change in accordance with the rapid transformations of modern social life. This theological problematic, the definitions of and relationships between the changing and the unchanging within religion, is a direct result of the dramatic social change wrought by the founding of the Turkish Republic. This is what makes modern Turkish theology distinctive: it explores this theological problematic precisely because the very language that it is expressed in, modern Turkish, was born in an era of dramatic and revolutionary change. Because of this genesis, one of modern Turkish theology's primary goals has been to identify stability and permanence within a context of intense change.

This chapter focuses on some of the most important ways in which modern Turkish theology defines what is stable and unchanging about the world, and how human beings come to know this truth. In the Islamic context, this means the absolute truth of the existence of the One God, the ways in which God communicates with humanity, and how we interpret this communication and its significance for our lives. Specifically, modern Turkish theology approached these questions by critiquing materialist visions of the world prevalent during the late Ottoman Empire and among the secular Turkish political elite of the twentieth century.[1] The foundational works of modern Turkish theology in the early to mid-twentieth century are structured as critiques of materialist visions of reality that impute no inherent transcendent value to the created world.

In contrast with secular materialism, modern Turkish theologians describe the world as inherently sacred because it is a sign of the ultimately transcendent, its Creator. Moreover, human nature itself is sacred because it contains within itself consciousness of its Creator. The created universe and human existence are signs pointing towards the existence of the One God and God's loving care and concern for all of creation. Denying the transcendent significance of the universe and of human nature, as materialism does, means denying not only God's existence, but also the loving care of God for all of existence and thus the very meaning of existence itself. This is the foundational argument made in the earliest and most influential works in modern Turkish theology, and the specifics of this argument have been worked out in successive detail over the course of the twentieth and twenty-first centuries.

In order to sketch the contours of how the modern Turkish theological tradition engages with the question of absolute truth and how it is known by human beings, this chapter will focus on the works of four central figures in modern and contemporary Turkish theology: İsmail Hakkı İzmirli (or İzmirli İsmail Hakkı)[2] (1869–1946), Bekir Topaloğlu (1932–2016)[3], Hülya Alper[4] and Emine Öğük.⁵ İzmirli is widely considered the pre-eminent systematic theologian of the late Ottoman and early Republican period. Topaloğlu is widely considered one of the most influential theologians and scholars of theology in Turkey in the mid-twentieth century, and his work was deeply influenced by late Ottoman and early Republican theologians such as İzmirli. Alper and Öğük are two of the most distinguished living systematic theologians in Turkey, and their work develops in dialogue with both Topaloğlu and İzmirli.

The foundational systematic works of modern Turkish theology are designed to defend and restore the place of transcendence, sacredness and divinity in the modern Turkish understanding of humanity and the cosmos. İzmirli's *Yeni İlm-i Kelam* (*The New Theology*; published in 1923–4)⁶ constitutes the most influential late Ottoman theological work, and is explicitly oriented towards this goal. Later mid-century Turkish theologians, such as Bekir Topaloğlu, continued this tradition into the modern Republican period. His first major systematic theological text, *The Existence of God according to the Theologians and Philosophers of Islam (Establishing the Necessary Existent)* (1970)⁷ became one of the most influential treatises in modern Turkish theology for exactly this reason. Topaloğlu asserts that the challenge of philosophical materialism and positivism to religious belief that shook Europe in the nineteenth century has largely been defeated there in the present day, but that this threat remained potent in the Turkey of his day.⁸ Topaloğlu thus begins his work with a direct critique of the secular nationalist cultural and philosophical climate of Turkey in the middle of the twentieth century. Because God's existence is the basis of religion itself, Topaloğlu sets out to shore up belief in the One God in the highly secularised milieu of mid-twentieth century Turkish society.⁹

Contemporary Turkish theologians in the 2000s have elaborated their projects by focusing on and critically evaluating specific elements found within these much more expansive, but also more impressionistic, earlier works. Important examples of this include Hülya Alper's highly influential work on the relationship between human reason and divine revelation in contemporary Turkish theology,¹⁰ and the work of Emine Öğük on the nature of tradition and theological hermeneutics. The works of these four thinkers will therefore constitute the source of this chapter's discussion of the answer to the first part of the question asked in modern Turkish theology: what is unchanging truth, and how can this truth be known?

The Unchanging Truth: Defending Transcendence, *contra* Materialism

According to the theologians discussed above, religion is the only system of values and practices that acknowledges the sacredness, and thus the true dignity and worth, of the cosmos and the individual human being. Religion in general, and Islam in particular, concerns the truth of the existence and nature of the One God, and the need for human beings to establish justice and loving mercy towards one another in this world in accordance with the commands of the One God. The duty of all human beings to worship God and to have loving care and mercy for one another in the way that God does towards us is the basis of humanity's ultimate significance. The eternal truth of religion stands in contrast with philosophical materialism, the original target of critique in modern Turkish theology.

Materialism's main error is its replacement of the cosmology of eternal religious truth with the inherently limited conclusions of positive science. Religion more broadly, and Islam in particular, is distinguished from other ways of knowing because it concerns humanity's existential significance and the demands placed on humanity by this significance. Because humans are creations of God, their significance is rooted in the divine: though they are existentially distinct from their Creator, they are distinguished from the rest of creation by their capacity and need to fulfil God's moral and spiritual expectations of them.

Modern and contemporary Turkish theologians argue that philosophical materialism is a fundamentally unreliable guide to knowing the world because it restricts human knowledge of the truth by drastically overestimating unfettered reason's capacity to understand the world.[11] By arguing that the world can be explained purely by rational or material causes, this approach actually restricts the interpreter to their cultural context and social structures, causing them to mistake these for absolute truth. Because every human individual exists in, and therefore approaches the world through, a specific cultural and social context, the argument that individual human reason or empirical perception can fully explain the world merely has the effect of conforming our own assumptions and biases. Materialism therefore restricts, rather than expands, our access to the truth of things. As we will see below, the proper use of human reason is a necessary component of knowledge of the truth, but its unrestricted speculative use simply leads us back to our own limitations, and not to knowledge of our transcendent significance or the transcendent significance of the world around us.

Study of the physical world on its own material terms does not, in and of itself, lead to error. Religiously neutral by nature, empirical science morphs into dangerous materialism only when it argues that there is no place for the divine in the universe, that all phenomena in the cosmos can and must be explained solely as a function of natural laws and material causes. The materialist denial of the divine is both an epistemological error and a moral threat. In the first place, materialism makes claims that cannot be verified by its own methods: the positive and empirical sciences are excellent sources of knowledge on physical causes and occurrences, but by definition cannot comment on their ultimate significance. Thus, by denying that physical phenomena can possess any kind of transcendental significance at all, materialism steps beyond the bounds of its own data and makes claims for which it cannot provide evidence. Secondly, denying the transcendental significance of the physical world means denying the transcendental significance of humanity as a whole and humans as individual persons. Materialist anthropology is at best fragmentary and partial, and therefore risks devaluing human life itself by ignoring the ways in which human individuals interact with the world as a realm of ultimate significance, transcendence, and value beyond our own horizons.

İzmirli, for example, makes it clear that empirical sciences are valuable and necessary parts of human knowing. He means this in their speculative sense as well: they are not valuable only insofar as they can be marshalled to support existing religious conviction, but rather their value lies precisely in their ability to uncover new knowledge about the world. Empirical science is therefore a way of deepening our knowledge of God's creation.[12] Moreover, because the conclusions of the empirical sciences are ever changing, theology must be constantly willing and able to incorporate their newest insights. Theology must have no fear of incorporating the most recent advances in science and philosophy into its own reflections and arguments.

İzmirli argues that theology does not need to be protected from, or hostile to, scientific disciplines, because the truths of theology are the truths of religion. As such, these truths are universal and unchanging, and can actually be better understood by skilful appreciation of other ways of knowing.[13] It is in fact the existential certainty of religious knowledge that should render the Muslim theologian entirely unafraid of other disciplines of thought, as these can only add more depth and functionality to the eternal truths of Islam. Theology must adapt to changing circumstances if it is going to be able to fulfil its mission, which is to clearly express the eternal truths of religion through intellectual inquiry and compelling evidence. In short, İzmirli makes a crucial distinction between the content and the methods of theology. The content (the truths of the existence, the revelation and the final judgement of the One God) cannot change; but its methods can and must change as human knowledge in other spheres of learning advances throughout history.[14]

Thus, one important undertaking of modern systematic theology in Turkey is the attempt to re-sacralise modern ways of knowing, not an attempt to reject them. This theological tradition does not intend to seal religion off from modern advances in science and philosophy, or even from all types of modern social change. On the contrary, it has evolved as a way to discuss and define the spheres of (eternal, unchangeable) religious and (contingent, changeable) non-religious ways of knowing precisely so that they can enter into productive dialogue with one another, on the assumption that both can contribute to a holistic understanding of the human person.

How can we express the transcendent significance of created existence? İzmirli uses the term *saadet*, literally 'felicity', to express the dimension of ultimate significance communicated by religion alone. Humanity's transcendent significance lies in its duty to achieve well-being and ultimate fulfilment, *saadet*, in both this life and the next.[15] In her study of classical Islamic ethical treatises and discourses, Zahra Ayubi translates this term as 'happiness/flourishing', and demonstrates that it is understood in the classical sources as the outcome of a process of spiritually and ethically cultivating the self.[16] For İzmirli, ultimate fulfilment and well-being in this life means the establishment of justice and harmony between human beings in this life; in the next life, this means the eternal bliss promised to those individuals who exert their efforts on earth to worship the One God and to create a just and harmonious society.[17] This is precisely why İzmirli describes religious knowledge as the peak of all human knowing: it leads to certain knowledge of how to achieve that which is truly the most significant to all of humanity.[18]

As Alper's work shows, another way to express the transcendent significance of the created order is by focusing on the world as the sphere of ethical action, created to be such by God. The world is the place where we work to achieve *saadet*, and this means that the world is a place for moral striving and ethical exertion. The basic content of the message of Islam orients the believer towards the sacredness of God and the sacred duty that each person has to act out God's moral commands in the created world. The message of Islam is rooted in the main principles of the Qur'an, which consist of the call to believe in the One God, the need to obey and worship the One God alone, the moral responsibility to address injustice in human society and the awareness of the Day of Judgement.[19] This message addresses humans' capacity to reflect reasonably and critically on the world around them. Thus, God gives human beings the necessary tools to come to know and love God, and then to reflect that knowledge and love back towards God's creation. Alper stresses the ethical consequences of the theological awareness of the Divine love and mercy for creation.

Humanity has been created with the unique capability of moral decision and striving, something no other part of creation can claim. Human beings possess a choice that reflects the transcendent significance of their nature: they can either reflect God's loving mercy and justice in the world through their own actions and in accordance with their own created nature, or they can choose to ignore this divine imperative and risk divine judgement. To reflect God's loving mercy in the world means to help other people attain *saadet*, to support and care for them as God does. As will be seen at the end of this chapter, God's attribute of loving mercy plays a key role in establishing the existence of God, in addition to its role in grounding human ethical action and responsibility. God desires both that humanity fulfils this transcendent mission to manifest justice and mercy, and that it does so willingly and sincerely. Thus, God bestows humanity with the faculty of reason and gifts it with access to the Divine Wisdom through revelation, desiring that it makes use of both in its striving to worship God and establish mercy and justice in the world around it. Moreover, cleaving to justice and rejecting oppression is the key rational principle Muslims must adhere to when deriving the specific rules of social practice from the commands of revelation.[20]

Knowing the Truth: Reason, Revelation and Tradition

Given that the basic task of modern Turkish theology has been to describe and defend the transcendent significance of the created world and the sacred role that human beings play in the created order, how exactly can we come to know what this transcendence means? In other words, how can we discuss and elaborate what religion itself means, including its main precepts and the tasks that it sets before us in this life? Modern Turkish theologians describe theological knowledge as a holistic endeavour that integrates human knowledge and experience in order to direct the mind towards God. This integration of human experiences and ways of knowing re-orients human knowledge towards awareness of the transcendent significance of existence, and the consequences of absolute truth for human individuals and human social life. The central method of this integration of human experience is the contact and relationship between human reason (*akıl*) and divine revelation (*vahiy*). The combination of human reason and divine revelation in theological method is that which renders theology the only intellectual discipline capable of producing certain knowledge of the absolute truth of things.[21]

How can we describe theology or religious knowledge itself? What makes it distinct from other ways of knowing the world? What makes theology distinct from, for example, speculative philosophy or empirical science, is the way it relates to questions of ultimate meaning. The great Sunni theologian and scholar Abu Hamid al-Ghazali (d. 1111) made this point by arguing that reflection on the created world, in the context of theology, means reflecting on the world specifically as the work of the Creator. To reflect theologically also means to reflect on the meaning of revelation, God's own communication through the Prophet. Theology is distinct from all other forms of knowing because while it considers a wide variety of possible subject matters, such as the physical world, history and morality, it analyses all of these topics with a view towards how they relate to the consideration of God's essence, attributes and acts.[22]

İzmirli's work follows in the Sunni tradition on these points, specifically through his utilisation of the canonical theological texts of the Ottoman period. İzmirli therefore begins with al-Jurjani's definition, and asserts that Islamic theology is concerned with two main topics: the nature of God and the nature of the created order in relationship to God. These two topics consist of: 1) proving the necessary existence of God and understanding God's attributes on the one hand; and 2) discussing the ultimate origins and ultimate fate of creation on the other.[23] Theology can only take place within this horizon of ultimate meaning, that is, within the framework of Islam itself, which is the message and path of the revealed truth of God. İzmirli uses al-Jurjani's term, 'the law' or 'fundamental principle' of Islam (*qānūn al-Islām*) to refer to this horizon of ultimate meaning. The term 'law' here is not used by İzmirli in any positive legal sense, but instead carries the same connotation as in the phrase 'law of nature': a basic principle that encloses and grounds a larger system of consequences. This basic principle is *tevhid*, the belief in the One God, the all-encompassing context within which all Islamic intellectual reflection takes place. This belief is the foundation of the entire Islamic intellectual tradition and way of life, and so the elaboration and defence of *tevhid* becomes the main preoccupation of Islamic theology in general.[24]

As Öğük shows, the concept of 'the law of Islam' reveals Islamic theology to be a 'holistic' discipline of rational reflection on the totality of the human condition from within the perspective of the Qur'an and Prophetic tradition.[25] Because human nature is oriented towards this life and the next, theology (which proceeds from human reflection on revealed sources) addresses all aspects of human existence, from the doctrine of God to human rights.[26] Theology therefore takes place within the context of belief in the One God and departs from the data of revelation; it is not exactly the same as speculative reason.[27] In other words, theology is a rational meditation on truth and the principles of revelation, rather than a speculative philosophical endeavour.[28]

Moreover, there is a fundamental harmony between reason and revelation. Topaloğlu notes that in the Qur'an, God directly commands the use of reason.[29] This proves that theology and the knowledge of God's existence must be based on reasoned reflection (*tefekkür*).[30] Topaloğlu asserts that faith in God (*iman*) must therefore be *istidlali*, or rooted in evidence and reasoning.[31] This is in fact how Sunni theology developed in the first place, according to Topaloğlu: successive generations of Muslim thinkers developed various kinds of proofs to defend and understand the first generation of Muslims' direct experience of God's revelation to Muhammad.[32] And like İzmirli, Topaloğlu defines theological reasoning as not purely speculative; reason is used functionally to understand and conform to the will of God.[33]

As Öğük also points out, the basis of theology in the process of reason is also rooted directly in the Qur'an, which describes how Abraham used his own human reason to arrive at the truth of monotheism, such as in 6:76, where Abraham reflects on the order of the heavens, and abandons polytheism for belief in the One God that orders the entire cosmos.[34] Abraham's theological reasoning is thus the prototype of the most important Islamic theological argument in support of God's existence, the argument from design which, as will be discussed in more detail below, is the argument favoured in the Quranic text.[35] Theology is therefore a rational systematisation of the theological discourse of revelation.[36] The entirety of Islamic cosmology proceeds from the basic Quranic distinction between Creator and created, and the Quranic understanding of the existence and order of the cosmos as signs of this ultimate truth.[37]

What exactly is human reason, as it relates to theology? Alper identifies reason's nature with its function (*işlev*), which is to attain knowledge and insight through disciplined reflection on sensory data. Reason has value insofar as it is an instrument.[38] Reason's primary function is to enable human beings to engage in systematic reflection and investigation of the world around them, a capacity that is central to their identity as humans.[39] Rational investigation synthesises the disparate data gathered by the physical senses into general concepts and conclusions about the world.[40] 'Reason' is the name given to the faculty that controls the process of organising sensory data into an interpretable whole that forms the basis of all forms of human knowledge.[41] Following al-Maturidi and other traditional *kalām* schemas of epistemology, Alper argues that direct sensory experience is combined with reported information about events that we have not directly experienced in order to form the raw data that is organised by reason in the process of investigation to produce actual knowledge about the world.[42]

This process, however, also points to the inherent limits of reason. Because it can only produce knowledge based on the data from the physical senses, reason can only produce conclusions derived from our own highly limited experience of the world. Thus, human beings can learn a great deal about the world around them, but can never conceive of existence in its totality. This is the reason why human knowledge must always have recourse to God's wisdom through revelation, as God is the only being capable of truly comprehending the entirety of existence at every moment.[43] Reason can, however, independently arrive at the most crucial piece of knowledge in all of existence: knowledge of, and therefore belief in, the existence of the One God.[44] This is why reason is 'a divine responsibility' or 'charge' (*ilahi bir emanet*), according to Alper.[45] It is gifted to human beings so that they might use it to acquire knowledge about the very truths of existence itself, this knowledge being the foundation of their own moral responsibility.

Reason's primary theological role, therefore, is to apprehend the meaning and significance of revealed truths. While reason can arrive independently at the most basic theological truths, it cannot always independently derive the specific ways that God desires us to implement these truths. For instance, human reason can understand the nature and necessity of ritual worship; but it cannot independently arrive at the conclusion that prayer must be conducted in a certain physical way or at a certain time of day.[46] Reason thus becomes the instrument humans use to understand transcendence and ultimate value as general principles. It is the inborn means by which human beings attain certainty of transcendent religious truth, and the means by which they detect the evidences for this truth in the world around them. But reason cannot reach the specific consequences, or commands implied by, absolute religious truth.

The limitation of human reason leads to the necessity of revelation. While reason is the capacity given by God to humans that enables them to recognise and orient their minds towards the truth of the cosmos, revelation is the specific vehicle of this truth in its complete fullness. Thus, though the basic principles of theological truth (such as the existence of God) can be accessed by reason, the infinite vastness of God's creation is only encompassed by God's wisdom (*hikmet*). Revelation is the means by which human beings can begin to interact with the vastness of God's wisdom; it provides humanity with the specific commands and prohibitions that God has given as a means to achieve closeness to God in this world and the next. This is why revelation is properly described as a consequence of God's loving mercy (*rahmet*) towards humankind.[47]

As will be discussed in detail below, observation of the world establishes the existence of a wise (*hakim*) creator. A wise creator must of necessity provide their creation with specific and complete guidance, because to neglect to do so would mean abandoning creation to its own ignorance and limitation. This would certainly lead to the self-destruction and collapse of creation, and of humanity in particular, which is fundamentally incapable of flourishing based on its own intuitive knowledge alone. Were this to happen, it would render pointless and futile the creation of humanity in the first place, something incompatible with the attribute of wisdom. A creator that is truly wise cannot simply stand aside and watch their creation sink into chaos. Revelation is thus a logical consequence of God's essential nature as a wise and loving creator.[48]

Revelation is therefore the way in which the abstract truths of religion become actual realities in the physical world. As Alper puts it, 'religion's transformation into a way of living and a directionality to human life' is enabled by revelation.[49] Revelation is a necessary part of monotheistic faith because it is the means by which this faith becomes actual in the real world. While the basic principle of monotheism is comprehensible to human reason, the ethical and practical consequences of this principle in the real world are beyond humanity's rational capacity. Thus, God in God's wisdom and loving mercy gifts this knowledge to human beings through revelation, showing them how theological truth is to be practically lived out in the world.

Humanity therefore needs God's explicit guidance via revelation in order to obtain full knowledge of the world and its ultimate significance, and full knowledge of humanity's ritual and ethical responsibilities. But why is this full and holistic knowledge necessary for humanity in the first place? Could not human beings simply choose to remain ignorant of absolute truth? The reason why humanity needs to possess this full knowledge is because God has created them with the ability to choose either good or evil and will judge them on this basis. Human beings need the fullness of revealed knowledge in order to live the kind of life on earth that enables them to earn reward in the hereafter. In other words, human ethical freedom and responsibility are the context that makes divine guidance and human reason absolutely necessary.[50]

According to the Quranic worldview, humanity has been created in order that it may demonstrate virtue and pass the moral 'test' (*imtihan*) of this life. In this context, Alper refers to Qur'an 95:4, which affirms that God created humanity 'in the most beautiful stature'. For Alper, this verse refers to the excellence and inherent goodness of human nature, which is therefore capable, albeit in its own limited way, of reflecting the excellence and goodness of God by following the path set out for humanity in revelation.[51] By affirming the fact that God created human beings as inherently good, the Qur'an emphasises that human beings are capable of living a moral life if they choose to do so. Human nature is not designed by God to be perfectly good as God is, but is designed to strive towards goodness through both its own effort and its reliance on God who is the ultimate source of all strength and success in God's creation.

Alper also cites Qur'an 18:7 in this context, which states that God created human beings so that God 'may try them as to which of them is most virtuous in deed'.[52] God thus expects humanity to relate to one another in the context of moral striving. Human virtue not only implies divine judgement, but also requires interaction with other human beings. In other words, the whole of human existence, both as it relates to God and to the rest of creation, is bound up with the necessity of following God's will in this life. It is thus a very urgent matter how exactly humanity is to use reason in order to understand from revelation how they ought to live in accordance with God's commands. The way in which these two forms of knowledge relate to one another is the heart of the Islamic theological endeavour, and the key to humanity's flourishing in this life and the next.

In addition to Quranic concepts and terminology, Alper's reflections on the relationship between human reason and human morality consciously build on the theology of al-Maturidi. For al-Maturidi, the fact that human beings are created with the ability to use their reason to distinguish good from evil means that God has created them to test whether they will choose to follow the good over the evil. Human reason can, for instance, know that certain acts are harmful and certain acts beneficial, even if the same act may be harmful in one situation and beneficial in another. Human reason is not itself that which designates an act good or evil, however. Rather, God designates acts in this way, but God endows human reason with the capacity to know what God has designated good and what God has designated evil. In other words, the very structure of human knowing as designed by God proves that human beings are created for moral testing and moral striving in this life.[53]

From a basis in Quranic and Maturidi theology, Alper proceeds to answer the question at hand: how exactly should reason and revelation relate to one another? Put simply, reason begins the process of theology and revelation fulfils it – what Alper calls 'the priority of reason and the necessity of revelation'.[54] Specifically in the context of theological method, reason and revelation relate to one another in processes of interaction and balance. With respect to processes of interaction, the continual encounter between reason and revelation within the individual human mind leads to knowledge of God's existence, nature and commands for human beings. Alper calls this the 'circular' (*dairesel*) relationship between reason and revelation, or the 'reason-revelation loop'.[55] This circular relationship is the way in which human knowledge achieves its true transcendent significance. Theological method is the way in which human reason comes to achieve its full potential through its contact with revelation.

The circular interaction between reason and revelation begins with reason's meditation on absolute truth and its significance. As will be seen below, reason leads the human mind to the certainty of the existence of God and the necessity of God's communication with humanity in the form of revelation. Reason thus is rendered ultimately significant because it has directed its attention towards the most important of all human knowledge.[56] Moreover, reason comes to understand that God has directly commanded the use of reason in theological investigation, as is made clear in the Qur'an. Reason thus realises its sacredness, and within the context of these ultimate truths, becomes able to comment on and understand the content of revelation properly.[57] In other words, human reason becomes aware of absolute truth and begins to seek it out. Once reason finds this truth in revelation, in the Qur'an, it fully realises the basic truths of existence – that the cosmos is created by a loving God and is under the care and command of that God. Then reason takes up the task of interpreting these commands in order to understand how to grow closer to God and implement God's will in the world that God created.

This circle of interaction is in fact a relationship designed by God in God's wisdom. The God-given human capacity of reason is our point of access to this relationship, and thus it is described as having 'priority' from our epistemological perspective. But revelation, being grounded in God's wisdom, possesses 'necessity' because it is a consequence of the necessary existent, the One God. Revelation is also necessary because it reflects God's design of the world, as we have seen above; and its necessity is also established by our need of it in order to enact the truths of religion in the real world. These two phenomena exist in a continuous relationship, but it is not the case that one simply acts uni-directionally on the other. This interaction does not imply existential parity between the two: human reason can never approach anything resembling the depth and scope of revelation, which is a consequence of God's wisdom. Moreover, the interaction between reason and revelation has been central to Islamic thought since the time of the Prophet, who himself had to interpret the revelations he was receiving from God.[58] In a sense, the Prophet was the first person in the history of Islam to use their reason to reflect on the Quranic revelation (which is the fundamental task of Islamic theology). The Tradition of the Prophet (*Sünnet*) has also been subjected to reasoned interpretation by successive generations of Muslim thinkers and believers, as will be discussed in more detail below.[59]

Öğük defines theological method as a kind of rational reflection (*nazar*) that constitutes 'a middle way' between pure rationalism and textual literalism and which is based on two principles: 'dependence on the texts' and 'rational functionalism'.[60] The first principle recognises the priority of the Qur'an and the Sunna (the tradition of the Prophet Muhammad) as the fundamental sources of Islamic theology.[61] The second principle recognises that reason both acquires its significance from revelation yet does not have an absolute role outside of revelation.[62] This is 'religio-rational grounding' (*dini-akli temellendirme*),[63] or the establishment of Islamic belief within the sure foundation of rational reflection on revealed truth. Reason cannot independently establish religious truth, but it can 'ground' and 'evaluate' religious judgements that are based on the sources.[64]

Moreover, Öğük's use of the term *nazar* emphasises the role of evidence and rational argumentation in theological method.[65] A balance must be struck between the use of reason and revelation because, as discussed above, human knowledge is based on direct human perception of the world through our senses. Humans know things by using their senses to gather evidence, and then using their reason to interpret that evidence. In the case of theology, evidence for propositions about God and religious practice is gathered from the data of the Qur'an, and this data is then interpreted by human reason into judgements about religious belief and practice. The source of this data, being God, has absolute priority in value, but due to the way in which human knowing operates, theologians must delimit the proper balance and method of reason's activity in the production of theological knowledge. The 'holistic or balanced approach' of Islamic theological method is therefore a way to describe the proper ways in which limited, but necessary, human reason interacts with the unlimited absolute of divine revelation.[66]

Öğük's discussion of *nazar* as theological method draws on the richness of this term in the Sunni theological tradition. This term (*naẓar* in Arabic) has the basic meaning of 'looking', or 'seeing'. When used to refer to theological epistemology, it means the process of active rational reflection that leads to knowledge, and is the foundation for certain knowledge of both God and the world. Al-Maturidi describes *naẓar* as the activity of reason that distinguishes between truth and falsehood, and that organises sensory data into reliable knowledge about the world. It is the activity of the intellect that discerns the 'signs' of creation that lead to knowledge of God.[67] For al-Maturidi, *naẓar* is therefore the faculty of mind where reason and revelation meet. This is because our knowledge of revelation is gathered through our senses, such as seeing or hearing the words of the Qur'an. Our intellect therefore applies rational analysis to this data, leading to theological interpretation that is grounded in the words of God but made accessible to humanity via its God-given capacity for investigation and retrospection.

According to al-Iji, *naẓar* is rational reflection that leads to the answer of a specific question under investigation.[68] He asserts that the majority of the Sunni tradition believes that rational reflection is of great benefit to knowledge, provided that it is undertaken correctly and its scope is properly defined.[69] Al-Iji therefore emphasises the investigatory dimension of this term, showing how theology might be understood as knowledge about God that is discovered through systematic study of revelation. Al-Jurjani's defines *naẓar* as 'the establishment of religious beliefs', emphasising the importance of the attainment of certainty in theological knowledge.[70] As we also find with al-Maturidi's work, these definitions understand theology to be the product of methodologies that put reason and revelation into productive conversation with one another. The over-riding importance of revelation is recognised by defining it as the basis of all theological reflection, but the crucial role of reason is emphasised by defining it as the faculty of the human mind that allows us to understand the import of revelation in the first place.

According to Öğük, there are two primary ways that the balance between reason and revelation in *nazar* can be upset, leading to theological error. The first form of error has been discussed above, the fundamental error of materialism that is the original target of critique in the modern Turkish theological tradition. At the same time, however, the opposite extreme is equally hazardous. Outright rejection of the authority of human reason through the uncritical acceptance of authority is equally liable to lead one into error. The proper use of human reason is frequently contrasted in modern Turkish theology with *taklit* (*taqlīd* in Arabic), or the unthinking and uncritical imitation of authority. God directly forbids this in both theological argument and scriptural interpretation. This is a wholly inappropriate method for theological reflection because it cannot result in objectively certain knowledge.[71] As such, theology cannot be based on the imitation of authority, but must be based on rational proof and evidences.[72] The condemnation of arguments from authority and the exhortation to the use of proof and evidence in theology is rooted in abundant Quranic precedent, such as 31:21, which condemns those who claim to 'follow that which we found our fathers following', that is, polytheism, rather than to accept the abundant evidence in the cosmos for a single creator.[73]

Öğük's critique of *taklit* is also deeply rooted in the Sunni theological tradition, including in the works of al-Maturidi and the canonical works of theology studied in the Ottoman period. Al-Maturidi condemns *taklit* in the strongest possible terms at the very beginning of his *Kitab al-Tawhid* precisely because it cannot produce objective criteria for the certainty of religious belief. Instead, he argues that religious belief must be based on 'evidence' (*dalīl*), 'reasoned proof' (*ḥujjat al-'aql*) and 'rational demonstration' (*burhān*).[74] Theology cannot simply be an analysis or rehearsal of what other people say about God and religion, no matter how authoritative those persons might be. If theology is to provide the certainty of the truth of Islam that it is meant to provide, it must do so by appealing to objective human reason in such a way that anyone might be convinced by its arguments, no matter their preconceptions and predispositions.

Similarly, al-Iji describes one of the benefits of theology as the ascent from *taklit* to 'the summit of certainty'.[75] Knowledge that relies on appeals to authority constitutes a lower form of knowing that in many cases may be useful, but cannot be considered the full apex of human awareness of the truths of religion. Theology is designed to take the human mind on a journey that leads it from lower levels of knowing, such as *taklit*, and to the heights of intellectual apprehension of God's acts and attributes, an achievement that God designed our mind to be able to accomplish. This is another important reason why *taklit* is theologically inadmissible: not only does it restrict our intellectual capacity for certainty, but it also neglects the full use of our capacities as God designed them. Remaining content with *taklit* when one is capable of moving beyond it might, therefore, constitute a denial of God's will by neglecting the natural capacities with which God has endowed us.

The inadmissibility of *taklit* also encompasses the inadmissibility of simple textual literalism when reading the Qur'an. İzmirli, for instance, uses his discussion of the sanctity of human reason to roundly condemn literalistic interpretation of the Qur'an, which he defines as a species of inadmissible and irrational argument from authority (*taklit*). He even argues that God directly forbids this kind of narrow interpretation of God's own words, citing Qur'an 2:78 in this context.[76] Öğük similarly critiques a literalist approach to the interpretation of revelation, which refers to the practice of always adhering to the literal meaning of the text regardless of context or the consequences of reasoned reflection. Öğük makes the point that this method, rather than being faithful to God's meaning and intent, actually restricts the interpreter to humanly forms of meaning and intent because words and language are fundamentally human ways of knowing the world.[77] Though literalists often argue that this method is the only way to keep to God's intent in revelation, Öğük argues that this method actually prevents the interpreter from reaching God's true intent because it restricts the interpreter to semantics, which is a human form of knowledge that cannot wholly encompass God's message.

To use Öğük's illustrative phraseology, theological method can therefore be summed up as 'the grounding and defence of the bases of religion in the light of rational truths'.[78] It begins and ends with Qur'an and Sunna, but occurs through the process of human rational reflection on these basic sources. Most importantly, theological method is the logical consequence of the Quranic command to reflect on God's revelation, and the way in which God created human beings. For instance, Öğük cites in this context Qur'an 4:82, which exhorts believers to 'contemplate' the revelation; and 14:52, which describes the revelation of the Quranic text as 'a proclamation' that addresses the entirety of humanity through the use of human intellect and reason, calling humanity to awareness of the existence and the final judgement of the One God.[79]

Finally, it is important to note that although modern Turkish theologians describe theological methodology as rational, they distinguish it from purely philosophical rationalism.[80] Reason is necessary, but cannot be used as simply an end in itself. As shown above, they lay great stress on the need for the use of human reason in theological reflection due simply to the fact that this is how human beings know things. God created us this way, able to understand basic truths about the universe using the faculties implanted in us without reference to external authorities. Yet at the same time, as described above, humanity needs revelation in order to complete its knowledge with all of the information and insights that it needs to achieve ultimate fulfilment in both this life and the next. Pure reason cannot lead to complete knowledge.

Therefore, consideration of the historicity, and thus historical context, of revelation is a crucial component of how modern Turkish theologians define theological method. Because revelation occurs in history, communicated to certain human beings during a certain period of time, consideration of the context and historical form of revelation is crucial to theological method. This is particularly true for theological interpretation of the Qur'an, understood to be the final revelation to humankind. Therefore, both the Qur'an and Prophetic tradition – the Sunna – (the latter being composed primarily of hadith, that is, the sayings and actions of the Prophet as recorded in Sunni tradition) are divine sources of theology and religious practice that require human interpretation. The Qur'an possesses a natural theological priority because it is composed of the exact words of God spoken to Muhammad. At the same time, however, the very concept of revelation itself necessitates Prophetic tradition because an understanding of how the Prophet lived out the revelation he transmitted is central to our proper understanding of the revelation.[81] The revelation of the Qur'an occurred at a certain point in history, and was transmitted by a certain person; therefore, the life and words of the Prophet are the most immediate and the most crucial part of the context within which the words of God were revealed.

As Öğük's argues, with respect to its 'linguistic and contextual structures' the Qur'an is an historical (*tarihsel*) document, but with respect to its 'message and values' it is universal (*evrensel*).[82] In other words, the main message of the Qur'an is the single most important truth of religion (*din*), that is, the existence of the One God. The plurality of religious practice and interpretation, however, is due to 'the intermeshing of fixed and changing, universal and historical, absolute and relative elements' within the text of the Quranic revelation.[83] The Qur'an is therefore indeed the exact words of God, but these words were spoken in a particular time and place, and in order for them to be intelligible to human beings at all they acquire the framing of that time and place. The distinction between their universal import and their contextual framework is therefore essential. In other words, part of the necessary task of theological method is not only identifying the distinction between absolute truth and changeable human circumstance in human history writ large but also within the revelation of the Qur'an itself, precisely because this revelation occurs within history.

Öğük sums up this crucial point by advocating for a theological hermeneutics that 'distinguishes between address and message' within the Quranic text.[84] She extends this point to the proper interpretation of the hadith as well. She distinguishes between authentic Prophetic tradition and the literal wording of the hadith texts. Simply determining the latter is emphatically not the same thing as the former.[85] The body of the hadith is a form of detailed guidance whose proper interpretation is not simplistic or literalistic. As she points out, the Qur'an itself emphasised the humanity of the Prophet, meaning that his immense sanctity was after all possessed by a complex human being who must be understood as such.[86]

Modern Turkish theological methodology insists on not only the historical but also the theological importance of revelation and Prophetic tradition together.[87] As Öğük in particular points out, all monotheistic religions depend on a concept of *haber*, or reported knowledge such as revelation and tradition.[88] Monotheism is fundamentally scriptural and traditional, meaning that its most basic units from a theological perspective are not abstract ideas but actual historical events and the textual sources that record and describe these events. For monotheists, these textual sources are the final source of ultimate truth because they are the record of both the words of God and the context within which these words were revealed. This is yet another reason why theology is not a speculative discipline: if it is to access eternal and universal truths in any way at all, it must be grounded in these specific textual traditions.[89]

At the same time, as Öğük's work makes abundantly clear, simplistic readings of tradition put genuine knowledge of God at risk. Adhering to tradition for its own sake distorts the complexity of tradition itself, and thus distorts the context within which theology must take place. Tradition possesses eternal significance, but by its very nature possesses a temporal structure. Thus, connection with tradition is the necessary foundation of theological reflection, but this connection must always remain open to critique and renewal. Öğük critiques such a 'traditionalist-conservative' approach because it adheres to past interpretive practices without recognising their limitations or cultural context. It accepts no innovation or change in interpretive methodology whatsoever, based on the fear that doing so would risk misinterpreting God's intent in the original revelation.[90] The problem with this approach is the same as with the errors of literalism and materialism, but in an even more severe form: not only does it restrict the interpreter's viewpoint to a human level of understanding, it also has the effect of 'sacralising' the past, demanding therefore that all of the social, political, legal and moral structures of past societies be reproduced in the present.[91] It is noteworthy that Öğük is so critical of this mindset that she describes it as a 'severe and fanatical religiosity' that results in 'dogmatism', 'exclusionism' and the absolute intolerance of divergent viewpoints within religion.[92]

The Content of Truth: God's Existence, Wisdom and Loving Care

As has been discussed above, for modern Turkish theologians, religion is the only system of values and practices that encompasses and dignifies the entirety of the human person. A crucial part of this claim is that religious knowledge is also holistic: it is not merely rational, and instead of competing with scientific truth, it is based on *a priori* truths of human experience that are deeper than, but not discordant with, sensory perceptions of the physical world. Religion unites the entirety of human experience in consideration of the absolute truth of the cosmos. As we have seen above, this truth is approached through a theological methodology that combines human reason with divine revelation to create accurate theological judgements. But what exactly is the content of this theological reflection? What is the specific, absolute and unchangeable truth towards which modern Turkish theology is oriented? This truth is *tevhid*, the truth of the existence and nature of the One God.

As described above, theology is distinct from other modern ways of knowing because it concerns questions of absolute truth and importance. As İzmirli puts it, theology is 'dogmatic' (*ikani*).[93] This means that theology holds that things in the world do possess objective truths about them that humans can come to know, and that these objective truths have universal import regardless of one's position in a certain historical circumstance. Once the truth of things is apprehended by the intellect, certainty of the truth comes from the individual person's continual contemplation of these truths; while it is reason that establishes the factuality of religious belief, it is inner experience of these facts through contemplation that inculcates certainty in the individual person.[94] Reason and sense perception provide objective data about the world, while theological contemplation of this data reveals the world's ultimate significance and transcendent meaning. The source of the world's transcendent significance is the truth of its ultimate origin and destiny, and this truth is the reality of the existence of the One God.

From its earliest beginnings in the late Ottoman period, modern Turkish theology has been founded on the imperative to prove and contemplate the existence of the One God in the face of materialist and secularist doubt. This theological task is termed 'establishing the necessary existent', or 'establishing the creator', and according to İzmirli it is the fundamental task of the *New Theology*.[95] Since İzmirli's work, it has become the core of modern Turkish theological discourse and intellectual output. This crucial task means proving the objective existence of the One God, not merely furnishing rational interpretations of its possibility. Theology must show conclusively that God is real, and that philosophical materialism is therefore false. In order to do this, İzmirli explains that any number of methods is acceptable. As detailed above, because the truth of the One God encompasses all of human experience, a variety of human ways of knowing, proofs and evidences may be used to demonstrate God's existence and help to understand God's attributes. In one of the most memorable phrases of the entire text, İzmirli summarises this point by saying: 'The ways of God are boundless and countless'.[96]

Two primary methods of proving and contemplating the existence of the One God are commonly found throughout modern Turkish theology. These are proofs from rational examination of the created world, and proofs from rational examination of inner human experience of the self. In other words, God's existence can be known, and God's nature can be contemplated, by meditating upon both external and internal human experience. The world outside of us and the world within us both evince clear and convincing signs of the author of their existence. In both cases, what these realms of experience show us is that one all-powerful creator exists, and that this one all-powerful creator possesses infinitely loving compassion, care and concern for this creation.

The first of these arguments is conventionally known as the argument from design: the cosmos is so irreducibly complex that in order to function it must have been consciously designed. Given the infinite magnitude and complexity of the universe, this creator must be infinitely great in order to create and maintain such a creation. Thus, this creator must possess all possible perfections, such as power and goodness. Reasoning in this way, the teleological argument endeavours to show that this creator is identified with the omnipotent, omniscient and infinitely loving and merciful God of monotheism. As mentioned above, in Qur'an 6:76 this is how Abraham, the father of the monotheistic traditions, reasons to the existence of the One God and concludes the falsity of belief in polytheism.

In their formulations of this argument, both İzmirli and Topaloğlu focus on God's attributes of wisdom (*hikmet*) and loving care and concern (*inayet*).[97] These specific foci of argumentation are derived from the twelfth-century philosopher and theologian Ibn Rushd (d. 1198), who argued that the design of the universe proves the existence of God precisely because it proves the existence of a creator that possesses loving care and concern (*'ināya*; the Arabic original of the Turkish term *inayet*). This is evident because the cosmos is clearly designed to sustain human life, a task of immense complexity. That the cosmos should be constructed in such a way as to ultimately allow human life to flourish demonstrates an intentional, willing, loving care for humankind, thus demonstrating the existence of the One God.[98]

God's *inayet* is considered an effective proof for God's existence not only for its logical connection to God's actions in the world, but also because it refers to an absolutely fundamental attribute of God: God's loving mercy and compassion (*rahmet* in Turkish, *raḥma* in Arabic). The two most common names for God in the Qur'an are *al-Raḥmān and al-Raḥīm*, both derived from *raḥma*, or 'loving-mercy'. As Topaloğlu notes, the concept of *rahmet* is explicitly attributed to the divine essence around three hundred times in the Qur'an alone.[99] All of these terms are etymologically related to the Arabic word *raḥim/riḥm*, or 'womb'. God's loving compassion and mercy towards humanity is therefore described in the Qur'an as an infinite intensification of our own conception of loving concern for another, most especially maternal love. This is the sense that is meant when referring to God's loving mercy and compassion, rather than simply a mode of divine condescension or pity. The fact that these terms are, aside from God's Oneness, by far the most frequent way that God chooses to describe God's self in revelation is highly significant. These attributes are central to the Islamic conception of God's nature and actions, and thus are central to every description of God in Islamic theology. They are central to modern Turkish theology in particular because they establish the world as a manifestation of love and intentional concern, rather than as a product of purely material forces and elements.

With respect to the first divine attribute under consideration here, God's infinite wisdom is revealed to us in our contemplation of the origin and transcendent significance of physical reality. Because the universe exhibits structures of order and universal predictability (such as the laws of nature discovered by modern science), these structures attest to the existence of a designer powerful and wise enough to be responsible for their existence. Because these ordered laws of nature produce reliable and predictable outcomes, this means that they also each contain an ultimate end (*gaye*; or, a telos) towards which each of these processes is always moving.[100] The 'goal-oriented', or teleological, processes of natural law require that there must be a will that designs them, because a goal can only be envisioned by a will. Furthermore, this will must possess the infinite power and wisdom required to conceive of, and bring into being, the infinite expanse of the cosmos, because the whole of the cosmos is characterised by natural law. Thus, argues İzmirli, the modern conception of natural law actually proves the existence of God rather than threatens it.

Materialism, by contrast, denies that the cosmos evinces any telos or goal at all, which according to İzmirli is a profound misunderstanding of natural law itself.[101] Philosophical materialism is not the natural outcome of modern scientific investigation; it is the betrayal of it, according to İzmirli. The evidence for divine wisdom is everywhere in the cosmos as it is understood by modern science. The sheer predictability of natural law, and the continual research into the nature of these laws, ceaselessly demonstrates not God's absence but God's wisdom and ordering of the cosmos (*tertib*).[102] In fact, according to İzmirli, all of God's acts proceed from God's wisdom, which encompasses God's love, perfection, power and justice.[103] Furthermore, scientific progress continually strengthens the case for an omnipotent creator. The continual discovery of new natural laws only further reinforces the contention that these laws are universal and furnishes ever more examples of their incredible precision and predictability, thus continually strengthening the case for the presence of an omniscient designer responsible for them. The natural laws discovered by modern science are in fact the signs that lead to the certainty of God's existence because they reveal how the divine will interacts with creation.[104]

İzmirli argues that the primary characteristics of the cosmos that repeatedly present themselves to our senses and our reason are its 'harmony and order' (*ahenk ve nizam*).[105] These characteristics imply orientation towards an end or a goal, and thus an active will that designed them. Topaloğlu orders the argument in a particularly compact and compelling form that is worth quoting in full: 'The cosmos exhibits a system of reasons (*sebepler*) and goals (*gayeler*) congruent to one another. Everything that constitutes a complex of reasons and goals is the work of a knowing and reasoning cause (*illet*). Therefore, the cosmos is the work of a knowing and reasoning author, and this is God the Most High'.[106] The assertion that the cosmos possesses order is a direct refutation of materialist metaphysics, which according to Topaloğlu attributes the operation of the world to mere coincidence (*tesadüf*), which is entirely unable to explain the order of the cosmos.[107]

Revelation also continually calls humanity to contemplation of this central truth of religion. The Qur'an is replete with dozens of allusions to God's ordering of the natural world and God's commands to humanity to direct its contemplation to these signs of God's existence and loving mercy, such as in 36:38.[108] Contemplation of the divine wisdom leads to precisely the objective certainty of God's existence that İzmirli's whole theological system is designed to produce. In this contemplation the theologian immerses their intellect in the majesty that directs the gaze of the mind's eye towards the Infinite, towards the Divine that is the beginning, the end, and the ultimate fulfilment of our existence.

With respect to God's infinite love and care for creation (*inayet* and *rahmet*), these fundamental acts and attributes of God are not only rationally perceived in the order and harmony of creation described above, but also in the inner perception of one's own individual self. Modern Turkish theologians such as İzmirli and Topaloğlu emphasise that certainty about the existence of God is not only achievable by rationally reflecting on the world outside of us, but is also attainable by introspection into the deepest parts of our inner life. This is because God implanted in human nature an inborn awareness of the existence of God.[109] In other words, the essence of absolute truth, the truth of *tevhid*, the existence of the One God, is universally accessible by human beings via meditation on the experience of their own self and existence.

Topaloğlu describes the inner realm of human experience within which we can attain knowledge of God as 'deep inner experience' (*deruni tecrübe*).[110] In fact, this inner awareness is the essence of certainty itself. Topaloğlu argues that rational contemplation of the world only produces certainty about the existence of God when it leads us back into our hearts, where we feel and directly experience this knowledge inside of ourselves. This is because our own experience of our own inner state (*ruhi hal*) is undeniable and *a priori* knowledge: if we feel love, or hate, or wonder, we cannot for a moment doubt that we do feel these things. Topaloğlu seeks to establish our knowledge of God on this level of human experience.[111] Thus, rather than assert that the teleological proof yields certain knowledge of God because it appeals to pure reason, Topaloğlu argues that the teleological proof yields certain knowledge of God because it appeals to existential awareness: it accords with our deepest individual experiences of the world around us.[112] Topaloğlu's main point is that real certainty of God's existence can only come from our own inner perception of ourselves, not from rationally assenting to a given argument made by another person.

Topaloğlu describes this deepening process of inner awareness in striking and beautiful terms, again worth quoting in full: 'In the same way that the eye gradually grows accustomed to seeing weaker, then stronger, light, the human spirit slowly and by degrees becomes able to perceive the existences of the divine realm'.[113] Elsewhere, Topaloğlu describes the process as 'intuiting' (*sezmek*) – a highly evocative term in Turkish.[114] It is interesting to note here that Mehmed Şerefettin Yaltkaya decades before used the very same verb to describe inner perception of God: 'God is not known, God is intuited (*sezilir*)'.[115] Our personal inner experience of divine wisdom and love is always stronger than our reasoned analysis of it.[116] Knowledge of God for İzmirli began in inner experience and ended in rational proofs based on the created world. For Topaloğlu, our reasoned analysis of the world leads us back to our own selves, where the truest knowledge of God resides.

It is important to note here that Topaloğlu's argument that knowledge of God occurs as *a priori* knowledge within the self is based on a highly interesting re-purposing of certain basic principles of pre-modern *kalām* theological epistemology. Many key texts of this tradition affirm that knowledge of our own inner states is necessary knowledge that we as individuals cannot doubt. This kind of knowledge refers to our perception of our own emotional states, for instance, such as love or hate (just as Topaloğlu asserts). Yet in direct contrast with Topaloğlu, pre-modern Sunni *kalām* theologians argue that this kind of knowledge is entirely unfit for theology. In their view, knowledge of one's self is wholly inadmissible for the kinds of investigation demanded by theology because these states cannot be objectively verified. They can only be claimed to exist by someone claiming to experience them. Thus, because specific emotional states experienced by a specific individual are by definition subjective and cannot be independently verified, they cannot be useful to theology.

Both al-Iji and al-Jurjani make this point rather forcefully. Al-Iji refers to inner knowledge of the self as knowledge of 'the states of individual consciousness' (*al-wijdāniyāt*), and affirms that they are forms of necessary knowledge for the individual, but argues that they are useless to theology because of their inherent subjectivity.[117] Al-Jurjani also stresses the individually subjective nature of *wijdānīyāt* because these states can only be described by the one who experiences them. This means that this knowledge occurs through the use of data and processes of reasoning that are entirely closed off from the direct perception of other people, making it unsuitable for theological reflection.[118] These definitions of inner self-knowledge therefore presume that reasoned knowledge functions exactly the same way in every human being, while emotive knowledge is composed of subjective experiences that are always entirely individualised. These arguments are therefore also striking for their implication of the genuine universality of human reason, and its strict differentiation from human emotion.

Topaloğlu uses the exact same definition of inner knowledge of the self as it is found in the *kalām* tradition, but he completely reverses its value. Rather than seeing it as essentially useless to theological reflection, he argues that inner knowledge is in fact the most authentic form of theological reflection and religious certainty. Certainty can only take place as a result of intellectual and spiritual processes in the mind that are inherently subjective. In other words, for Topaloğlu, we may be able to rationally conceive of the objective truth of God's existence, but we can only attain certainty of this conception through subjective experience at the deepest individual level of the self.

Topaloğlu's use of the pre-modern Sunni *kalām* tradition here is worth noting, as it is a particularly striking example of how modern Turkish theologians root their work in the pre-modern *kalām* theological tradition, but in a way that is creative and dynamic. To put it in terms used by these theologians themselves, their use of this tradition does not fall into *taklit*, or mere recitation of the arguments of the pre-modern Sunni theological tradition. Instead, they find new value and meaning in these pre-modern philosophical and theological concepts that give them new power and utility in the modern intellectual context. This particular example exemplifies the historical dynamics discussed in the previous chapters, whereby pre-modern (particularly Ottoman) *kalām* is not rejected, but rather becomes the basis for creative appropriations and reinterpretations of traditional Sunni theology in modern Turkey.

Like Topalolğlu, İzmirli also argues that certainty of God's existence occurs at the level of deep, internal intuition. Quite notably, İzmirli describes this process of achieving inner certainty of God's existence by comparing his theology with Descartes. İzmirli notes that his theological epistemology proceeds just as Descartes' does: it begins with the *a priori* knowledge of one's own existence secured by contemplation of the self, then reaches upwards and outwards to analyse and establish the truth of other existent things in the universe, and leads ultimately to the greatest of all existents, God.[119] Human certainty about God begins with certainty of existence itself, which is the most basic and unassailable truth given *a priori* to all human beings in the act of their own self-contemplation.[120] Once the knowing subject can be certain of existence itself, it is then able to explore the features of existence through rational and scientific investigation of the world around it. Our awareness of, and faith in, the absolute truth of God's existence is based on the harmony of our experience of the world with our experience of our own selves.

İzmirli's comparison of his own theological epistemology with Descartes' is highly noteworthy, given that İzmirli describes his entire theological project as being motivated by a desire to engage with Western philosophy. İzmirli does the interpreter of his theology a great service by this comparison, as it provides the key to İzmirli's theological epistemology. The same inborn faculty of reasoning that guides us to God's existence guides our exploration of the natural world. As Descartes writes in his *Discourse on Method*, knowledge of God begins with 'certain seeds of truths that are naturally in our souls'.[121] Just as in Sunni Muslim theology, God provides humanity with certain inborn capabilities and insights that, when utilised properly, lead naturally to awareness of the existence and nature of their Creator. For both İzmirli and Descartes, theology emerges from the actualisation of the human mind as God intended it to be.

Faith in God (*iman*) is thus, in the final analysis, a subjective experience of objective truth. It is a 'personal experience' that requires 'the establishment of a correlation between reason and heart'.[122] In other words, certain faith in God is not simply assent to a reasoned proof. It can only be produced by the interaction of reason and heartfelt intuition, and the specific dynamics of this interaction are unique to each individual. The teleological proof is valuable precisely because it appeals to each individual human being on this level: it harmonises their experience of the outer world with their own inner intuition. According to these theologians, the argument from God's wisdom and loving mercy is so effective because it allows each individual person to contemplate the specific and entirely individual ways in which they experience God. God's wisdom and love are available as immediate experiences to all human beings. We become certain of these attributes of God in the innermost reaches of ourselves, and the longer we contemplate the world around us, the more certain we become of their reality.

The Qur'an emphasises this point as well, particularly in 41:53, where God declares that God's signs are revealed to humanity 'upon the horizons and within themselves'.[123] This verse aptly summarises the most fundamental theological argument made in the modern Turkish tradition: the world and the human being are signs of the sacred and the transcendent, not mere matter in thrall to the mechanistic operations of the laws of nature. This is the absolute and unchanging truth upon which modern Turkish theology is founded, over and against the prevailing secularist materialism of the late Ottoman and early Republican periods: that the world and humanity are significant because they are creations of, and signs pointing towards, the One God. To deny God's existence means denying the divine love and wisdom that explain and give meaning to the origin and eternal destiny of humanity.

Notes

1. Strong versions of mid-nineteenth century Western European materialism, most especially the work of Louis Büchner, became popular among Ottoman intelligentsia because they saw these ideas as key to scientific progress, and thus social progress and reform. Materialist philosophies such as Büchner's were seen as particularly threatening to Islamic belief in the One God because they explicitly argued that the coming into being and the perpetuation of the universe were solely a result of matter and physical forces, entirely ruling out the possibility of a Creator. See on this point Bulğen, 'The Criticism of Materialism'.
2. See the previous chapter for a brief summary of the main themes in İzmirli's work. İzmirli was one of the most prominent Muslim theologians and scholars whose career spanned the end of the Ottoman Empire and the beginning of the Turkish Republic. He received extensive education in the traditional Islamic religious disciplines and spent most of his career as a scholar, teacher and administrator, specialising in Islamic theology and philosophy. Born and raised in İzmir, from the 1890s to the end of his life he served in a wide variety of prestigious faculty and administrative roles, including in the *Darülfünun*. By the time his work

The New Theology was first published in 1923–4, he had already taught theology and philosophy at both the *Darülfünun* and the Süleymaniye Medrese, in addition to having published numerous well-regarded scholarly and theological publications. Before retiring in 1935, he also worked on national education reform in Ankara, and continued his career as a professor of theology and administrator in Istanbul. He died in Ankara in 1946. For an up to date summary of his life and work, see Birinci and Özervarlı, 'İzmirli, İsmail Hakkı'.

3. Born in the village of Fotogene (now Taşçılar) near the town of Dernekpazarı in the region of Trabzon in 1932, Topaloğlu received traditional training in Islamic fields of learning from his paternal grandfather. He went to Istanbul in 1952 to study and graduated from the İmam-Hatip school there in 1959, and from the Advanced Islamic Institute in Istanbul in 1963. After his retirement, Topaloğlu produced and contributed to some of the most important monuments of theological scholarship in modern Turkey. He and Muhammad Aruçı produced the most recent and reliable scholarly edition of al-Maturidi's *Kitab al-Tawhid* (Ankara 2003; Beirut 2007). He also translated al-Maturidi's text into Turkish (Ankara 2002; Istanbul 2013) and led the production of the most recent scholarly edition of al-Maturidi's monumental Quranic commentary, *Ta'wilat al-Qur'an* in 16 volumes (Istanbul 2005–11). He authored other works on theology and theological history that are considered classics in their own right. Topaloğlu's scholarship revolutionised theology in modern Turkish, and he was widely revered and beloved as a mentor and teacher.

4. Alper is currently Professor in the Faculty of Theology at Marmara University in Istanbul. She received her BA, MA and PhD in Theology from Marmara University in 1991, 1993 and 2000 respectively. Her book on al-Maturidi's theology that is under consideration in this chapter is widely recognised in Turkey as essential reading on this topic, and her work in general is among the most well-regarded in all of contemporary Turkish theological academia.

5. Öğük received her BA, MA and PhD in theology from Marmara University in 1998, 2000 and 2007 respectively. She is currently Assistant Professor of Theology at Tokat Gaziosmanpaşa University. Her work is a particularly important example of the kind of systematic theological projects conducted in Turkish academia today.

6. İzmirli's text was published in Istanbul in two volumes, the first in 1923 and the second in 1924. The version published was actually only meant to be the first half of a larger work. The work that was published deals with questions of theological method, history and philosophy, and focuses on discussion of God's

essence and attributes. İzmirli did not complete the second half, which was to have dealt with revelation and prophecy. Sabri Hizmetli (who wrote his doctoral thesis on İzmirli's text at the Sorbonne in 1979) edited and published the text in the modern Turkish alphabet in 1983. Hizmetli also published a version of the text in modern Turkish (Ankara Okulu Yayınları, 2018). This latest version of the text is a very exact rendering of the Ottoman original into modern Turkish, and deserves a wide readership in Turkish studies given its faithfulness to the original version, and the text's overall importance in modern Turkish intellectual history. For citations from the text in this book, the Ottoman original will be cited, with Hizmetli's modern Turkish version cited in parentheses. Direct quotes and terms, however, are from the Ottoman text only.

7. *İslam Kelamcıları ve Fılozoflarına göre Allah'ın Varlığı (İsbat-ı Vacib)*. This text, completed in 1970, was presented as a research thesis in 1971 in order to secure Topaloğlu's faculty position in the *kalām* section of the Advanced Islamic Institute in Istanbul (İstanbul Yüksek İslam Enstitüsü), which later became the Theology Faculty of Marmara University, where he held a faculty position until his retirement in 2002.
8. Topaloğlu, *Allah'ın Varlığı*, 11.
9. Topaloğlu, *Allah'ın Varlığı*, 11, 16.
10. On this point see also Altıntaş, 'Akıl Nakıl İlişkisi', 234; Bağçeci, 'Māturīdī'nin Kelam Metodu', 25; Bardakoğlu, 'Hüsn ve Kubh Konusunda Aklın Rölü', 42.
11. Öğük, *İstifade Yöntemleri*, 311.
12. İzmirli, *Yeni İlm-i Kelam*, 1:13–14 (17).
13. İzmirli, *Yeni İlm-i Kelam*, 1:11 (16–17).
14. İzmirli, *Yeni İlm-i Kelam*, 1:7 (14).
15. İzmirli, *Yeni İlm-i Kelam*, 1:9 (15). See al-Ghazali, *Moderation in Belief*, 7: 'The most important of affairs for all mankind is the attainment of eternal happiness and the avoidance of everlasting misery'. Note that al-Ghazali uses the same term for 'happiness' or felicity as İzmirli (*sa'āda* in Arabic/*saadet* in Turkish). Note also the subtle difference in emphasis between al-Ghazali and İzmirli: the former stresses the over-riding need to attain eternal reward in the next life, while the latter stresses this need equally with the imperative to improve human society in this life. This subtle shift in emphasis that balances the concerns of eternal reward in the next life with the need to reform social life in the present is indicative of the concern for human rights and social reform that emerges in late Ottoman theological discourse and remains a key feature of modern and contemporary Turkish theology.

16. Ayubi, *Gendered Morality*, 241–2. Ayubi's study illuminates the gendered dimension of these classical ethical discourses, where the fundamental human use of 'rationality' in ethical cultivation is 'explicitly associated with elite masculinity' (242). Though İzmirli's use of this term is clearly drawn from the classical sources, he does not explicitly associate it with a particular gender identity. His usage seems more concerned with elaborating the universal value of religion and concepts of transcendence in response to modern mechanistic worldviews. İzmirli, in other words, attempts to identify human flourishing with a concept of universal human nature – which of course itself is not uncritically free from gendered conceptions of normativity.
17. İzmirli, *Yeni İlm-i Kelam*, 1:9 (15).
18. İzmirli, *Yeni İlm-i Kelam*, 1:9 (15).
19. H. Alper, *Akıl-Vahıy İlişkisi*, 18.
20. H. Alper, *Akıl-Vahıy İlişkisi*, 205–10.
21. Öğük, *İstifade Yöntemleri*, 22. Öğük cites al-Maturidi's term directly here (see *Kitab al-Tawhid*, 480).
22. Al-Ghazali, *Moderation in Belief*, 5–6.
23. İzmirli, *Yeni İlm-i Kelam*, 1:2–3 (11); Al-Jurjani's definition is quoted in Topaloğlu, *Kelam İlmine Giriş*, 50.
24. Öğük, *İstifade Yöntemleri*, 76, 130, 132
25. Öğük, *İstifade Yöntemleri*, 124.
26. Öğük, *İstifade Yöntemleri*, 124, 79, 46.
27. Öğük, *İstifade Yöntemleri*, 293, 45, 59.
28. Topaloğlu, *Kelam İlmine Giriş*, 51.
29. Topaloğlu, *Allah'ın Varlığı*, 37, 135.
30. Topaloğlu, *Allah'ın Varlığı*, 37, 130.
31. Topaloğlu, *Allah'ın Varlığı*, 37, 130; Topaloğlu, *Kelam İlmine Giriş*, 74.
32. Topaloğlu, *Allah'ın Varlığı*, 44.
33. Topaloğlu, *Allah'ın Varlığı*, 44.
34. Öğük, *İstifade Yöntemleri*, 63.
35. Öğük, *İstifade Yöntemleri*, 83.
36. Öğük, *İstifade Yöntemleri*, 83.
37. Öğük, *İstifade Yöntemleri*, 115–16.
38. H. Alper, *Akıl-Vahıy İlişkisi*, 17–18, 58–9.
39. H. Alper, *Akıl-Vahıy İlişkisi*, 68, 94.
40. H. Alper, *Akıl-Vahıy İlişkisi*, 69.
41. H. Alper, *Akıl-Vahıy İlişkisi*, 80.

42. H. Alper, *Akıl-Vahıy İlişkisi*, 77–80.
43. H. Alper, *Akıl-Vahıy İlişkisi*, 82.
44. H. Alper, *Akıl-Vahıy İlişkisi*, 85–6.
45. H. Alper, *Akıl-Vahıy İlişkisi*, 50.
46. H. Alper, *Akıl-Vahıy İlişkisi*, 87.
47. H. Alper, *Akıl-Vahıy İlişkisi*, 116–17.
48. H. Alper, *Akıl-Vahıy İlişkisi*, 123. See *Kitāb al-Tawḥīd*, 247–53.
49. H. Alper, *Akıl-Vahıy İlişkisi*, 146.
50. H. Alper, *Akıl-Vahıy İlişkisi*, 151.
51. H. Alper, *Akıl-Vahıy İlişkisi*, 152.
52. H Alper, *Akıl-Vahıy İlişkisi*, 153.
53. Al-Maturidi, *Kitab al-Tawhid*, 252, 301–4.
54. H. Alper, 'Matüridi'nin Akıl ve Vahiy Algısı', 177; H. Alper, *Akıl-Vahiy İlişkisi*, 57.
55. This quote is from the text of a lecture on al-Maturidi's epistemology, delivered at an international conference and workshop in Ankara on 26 October 2018 (İmam Matürdi'nin Türk İslam Medeniyetine Katkılarının Araştırılması Çalıştayı).
56. H. Alper, 'Matüridi'nin Akıl ve Vahiy Algısı', 179.
57. H. Alper, *Akıl-Vahıy İlişkisi*, 160. See also H. Alper, 'Matüridi'nin Akıl ve Vahiy Algısı', 179.
58. H. Alper, *Akıl-Vahıy İlişkisi*, 19.
59. H. Alper, *Akıl-Vahıy İlişkisi*, 20.
60. Öğük, *İstifade Yöntemleri*, 317.
61. Öğük, *İstifade Yöntemleri*, 317–18.
62. Öğük, *İstifade Yöntemleri*, 319–23.
63. Öğük, *İstifade Yöntemleri*, 316.
64. Öğük, *İstifade Yöntemleri*, 323.
65. Öğük, *İstifade Yöntemleri*, 108.
66. Öğük, *İstifade Yöntemleri*, 332.
67. Al-Maturidi, *Kitab al-Tawhid*, 72–3.
68. Al-Iji, *Al-Mawaqif*, 1:5.
69. Al-Iji, *Al-Mawaqif*, 1:5:3.
70. Al-Jurjani, *Sharh al-Mawaqif*, 1:5.
71. Öğük, *İstifade Yöntemleri*, 308. Like İzmirli, she also here makes the point that theological reasoning can and should update itself in accordance with contemporary scientific and philosophical insights (335).

72. Öğük, *İstifade Yöntemleri*, 21, 290.
73. Öğük, *İstifade Yöntemleri*, 63.
74. Al-Maturidi, *Kitab al-Tawhid*, 65–6.
75. Al-Iji, *Al-Mawaqif*, 1:1:3.
76. İzmirli, *Yeni İlm-i Kelam*, 1:51–3 (50–1).
77. Öğük, *İstifade Yöntemleri*, 310.
78. Öğük, *İstifade Yöntemleri*, 293.
79. Öğük, *İstifade Yöntemleri*, 60.
80. Öğük, *İstifade Yöntemleri*, 332.
81. Öğük, *İstifade Yöntemleri*, 243–4.
82. Öğük, *İstifade Yöntemleri*, 68–9.
83. Öğük, *İstifade Yöntemleri*, 68.
84. Öğük, *İstifade Yöntemleri*, 69.
85. Öğük, *İstifade Yöntemleri*, 286.
86. Öğük, *İstifade Yöntemleri*, 287.
87. Öğük, *İstifade Yöntemleri*, 276.
88. Öğük, *İstifade Yöntemleri*, 276.
89. Öğük, *İstifade Yöntemleri*, 113–14.
90. Öğük, *İstifade Yöntemleri*, 314–15.
91. Öğük, *İstifade Yöntemleri*, 315.
92. Öğük, *İstifade Yöntemleri*, 315–16.
93. İzmirli, *Yeni İlm-i Kelam*, 1:62–3 (61).
94. İzmirli, *Yeni İlm-i Kelam*, 1:67 (66).
95. İzmirli, *Yeni İlm-i Kelam*, 2:3–5 (273–5). A popular genre of theology in the Ottoman period was explicitly devoted to this topic (see Özervarlı, 'Theology in the Ottoman Lands', 573). İzmirli's work asks the same questions investigated in this Ottoman theological genre, but develops innovative answers to them within the context of his examination of modern science and philosophy.
96. İzmirli, *Yeni İlm-i Kelam*, 2:4 (274).
97. Topaloğlu, *Allah'ın Varlığı*, 25–6.
98. Ibn Rushd, *al-Kashf*, 118.
99. Topaloğlu, Allah İnancı, 112.
100. İzmirli, *Yeni İlm-i Kelam*, 2:7–8 (278).
101. İzmirli, *Yeni İlm-i Kelam*, 2:59 (319).
102. İzmirli, *Yeni İlm-i Kelam*, 2:131 (379).
103. İzmirli, *Yeni İlm-i Kelam*, 2:130 (378).
104. İzmirli, *Yeni İlm-i Kelam*, 2:75 (331).

105. Topaloğlu, *Allah'ın Varlığı*, 134.
106. Topaloğlu, *Allah'ın Varlığı*, 144.
107. Topaloğlu, *Allah'ın Varlığı*, 28, 146.
108. İzmirli, *Yeni İlm-i Kelam*, 2:131–2 (379–80).
109. Topaloğlu, *Allah'ın Varlığı*, 21.
110. Topaloğlu, *Allah'ın Varlığı*, 150.
111. Topaloğlu, *Allah'ın Varlığı*, 134.
112. Topaloğlu, *Allah'ın Varlığı*, 28, 143, 133–4, 150.
113. Topaloğlu, *Allah'ın Varlığı*, 134.
114. Topaloğlu, *Allah'ın Varlığı*, 143.
115. Yaltkaya, *Dini Makalelerim*, 11–13.
116. Topaloğlu, *Allah'ın Varlığı*, 143.
117. Al-Iji, *Al-Mawaqif*, 1:4.
118. Al-Jurjani, *Sharh al-Mawaqif*, 1:4.
119. İzmirli, *Yeni İlm-i Kelam*, 1:69–70, 253 (67, 231).
120. İzmirli, *Yeni İlm-i Kelam*, 1:253 (231).
121. Descartes, *Discourse on Method*, 36.
122. Topaloğlu, *Allah'ın Varlığı*, 150.
123. Topaloğlu, *Allah'ın Varlığı*, 150.

4

HUMANITY

As mentioned in the previous chapters, this book argues that modern Turkish theology is an extended and diverse tradition of meditation on the Islamic doctrine of God's Oneness in the context of modernity. The first side of this doctrine of *tevhid* was taken up in Chapter 3, as it discussed how modern Turkish theology defines what is stable and unchanging about the world, and how human beings come to know this truth. The essential truth about the world upon which modern Turkish theology converges is the truth of the existence of the single, omnipotent and infinitely loving and compassionate God. The world and humanity possess transcendent significance, despite the suggestions of modern materialism to the contrary, because they are signs that point to this God, their Creator. Human life and the cosmos obtain ultimate meaning through their relationship with their Creator, and modern Turkish theologians argue that the existence of God and the necessity of a relationship with, and submission to, God constitute the eternal and absolute truth about the world that must be defended in the context of modern doubt.

This chapter concerns the necessary corollary of this truth, the second side of the Creator/created distinction: the changeable nature of the created world and the relationship of this changeability with unchangeable, absolute truth. This chapter argues that modern Turkish theology discusses the created world as a constantly changing sphere of ethical action within which humans are commanded by God to live out God's eternal will. In this way, modern Turkish theologians have attempted to define the relationship between the changeable nature of human society and history, and unchangeable theological truth. These theologians have elaborated a wide variety of methods to analyse this distinction in order to conceptualise exactly how human beings should live out God's eternal will in the context of this contingent and changeable created existence.

Human life is the life of creation; it is by nature totally distinct from the Creator. God's creation is characterised by ceaseless change and contingency. It is always in motion, always in need of something to sustain it, always subject to alteration. This is of course in diametrical contrast with the nature of God, which is changeless, in need of nothing, and omnipotent. At the same time, the world of change that we live in is the sphere of ethical action where we are expected to live out God's will. It is the realm in which eternal values and truths are actualised by human beings. Modern Turkish theologians, in emphasising the dynamism of historical change via their appropriation of late Ottoman sociology, stress the need for theological reflection on the challenges of living out the commands of God's eternal will in the context of a world whose very nature is ceaseless change and instability. This demand in turns implies human freedom, meaning here the freedom human beings have to choose to follow God's will or to reject it. This freedom is not only one of the bases of the changeability of the social world, it is also an ethical responsibility given to human beings by God.

Modern Turkish theologians have therefore elaborated the ways in which the dynamism of human action relates to the eternal truths of God's nature. Modern Turkish theology suggests that if it is the case that we are commanded by God to fulfil God's commands within a context that God deliberately created to be ever changing and dynamic, surely God must also desire that we acknowledge the dynamism within religion itself. As will be discussed in this chapter, modern Turkish theologians have elaborated a wide variety of ways to conceptualise this dynamism, beginning with considerations of human freedom and the potential historicity of religious practice, with applications in contexts such as political organisation and gender relations.

Human Freedom

Human freedom is one of the main reasons the world is ever changing, as human beings continually alter their politics, social structures and attitudes towards the world and towards each other. Drawing on its roots in late Ottoman discourses on political reform and human rights, modern Turkish theology has explored the nature of human freedom as the basis for the ethical responsibility placed on us by God. One of the most influential theologians in the modern Turkish tradition, Hüseyin Atay (b. 1930),[1] has made this theme central to his work, and his discussions of human freedom have continued to impact the entire spectrum of modern Turkish theological reflection on the nature of human beings and the relationship between religion and social change.

Considered to be one of the founding thinkers of the modern Turkish academic tradition of theology, Atay is often described as a theological rationalist with a heavy focus on Quranic discourse.[2] Atay himself often distinguishes his work from that of other theologians who eschew an historicist approach to revelation, and argues for the use of independent reason connected with revealed religious principles as the key to elaborating a modern Islamic theological framework in Turkey. Given their lasting influence, Atay's arguments are therefore a helpful way to introduce this chapter's consideration of the wide variety of ways in which modern Turkish theologians conceive of the changeableness and dynamism of humanity and the world.

Freedom (*özgürlük*) is a pivotal concept in Atay's theology. Freedom means the ability to choose from among different courses of action with different consequences.[3] We are able to know what is good and what is evil through our own rational reflection, and thus we can be sure that we will be held to account by God for choosing one or the other.[4] According to Atay, the central dynamic of religious life is that human beings enter into a conscious and uncoerced relationship with their Creator. Atay notes that the Quranic term for religion, *din*, has the literal sense of binding together: religion is therefore not a static object of contemplation, but an active relationship with the Creator.[5] Atay's reading of the Qur'an thus heavily emphasises human freedom and its ethical consequences. His work emphasises verses such as 2:233 and 286, which emphasise that God does not burden human beings with demands that exceed their individual wills and capacities; and 2:256, which famously and unambiguously states that 'There is no coercion in religion'.[6]

The term 'Islam' itself is interpreted here as a rational acknowledgement of the truth of the existence of the One God and then the conscious placing of one's self in a relationship with God.[7] This action, this submission to God, constitutes the very essence and eternal destiny of the entire existence of the human individual. According to Atay, Islam as a religious tradition has two sources: reason and the Qur'an.[8] These two sources are utilised by the human individual in the context of their own personal freedom in order to follow God's will and fully actualise their human destiny to enter into a relationship with God. They are both 'indicators of the way' that is the religious journey towards full happiness and fulfilment in this life and the next.[9]

For Atay, consideration of the nature of human reason and the nature of revelation lead to the conclusion that human beings are fundamentally free. God has designed human beings in such a way that they are able to freely know God and God's ethical demands of them. God designed human beings to be both intellectually free to discover what is good and evil, and free to choose one or the other, so that God may judge their choices with fairness and justice. The freedom of human reason is so crucial because this is the method that God has given humanity to establish a relationship with God and to fulfil God's will in this life. Atay's theological (rather than purely philosophical) rationalism is thus based on a central argument about God's nature, namely that God desires a direct relationship with human beings. God's will that all of humanity freely and consciously enter into a relationship with God and follow God's will is the basis for the structure of human nature itself, and is also the basis for human happiness in this life and the next.

Consideration of the structure of the created world reinforces the importance of the free exercise of human reason. There are two kinds of existents in the cosmos, physical and metaphysical. The former comprises phenomena that are made up of substances and their qualities, and that therefore have some kind of physical existence that we can perceive with our senses. The latter comprises phenomena that have no features that can be directly detected with our sense perception, such as God and the afterlife. This is why reason (*akıl*) is important: it is the one tool we have that is capable of detecting and describing metaphysical phenomena, because it itself is a metaphysical existent.[10]

Human reason is thus not simply a deductive faculty, but also constitutes the deepest and most intimate ways in which humans come to know basic truths about themselves and the universe through the exercise of their freedom. It is more than simple mental processes, and is in fact the way that God has chosen to communicate truth directly to human individuals: in Atay's words, 'Reason is God's non-read (wordless) revelation'.[11] Through its free rational reflection, humanity can come with certainty to know God's existence. By reflecting on the continuous rise and fall, the ceaseless coming into being and passing out of being, of things in the cosmos, human beings come to an awareness that there exists something directing these processes that is beyond themselves, something that is omnipotent and omniscient.[12] Because reason is a universal feature of all individual human beings, given by God so that all human individuals may come to know God, every human culture over time has come to the conclusion that God exists. All human cultures have given a name to this ultimate being that directs the cosmos.[13]

Theology is thus an activity of intellectual freedom that leads to rational knowledge about God. For Atay, it is utterly necessary to emphasise the free nature of this activity because theology that irrationally restricts itself by blind imitation of authority or tradition cannot lead to the kind of knowledge that God wants human beings to acquire. In other words, theology should be free because God created us to think freely. Numerous contemporary Turkish theologians have made arguments similar to Atay's on these points. Sönmez Kutlu, for instance, frequently contrasts theological rationalism with more conservative strains in modern Turkish Islamic thought. He criticises what he calls a 'closed frame of reference mentality'.[14] This refers to a religious epistemology that does not appeal to any category of knowledge universally accessible to all people, such as reason or empirical experience. Instead, these irrational theologies appeal to the singular authority of a charismatic leader or authority figure. In doing so, they stifle the ability of their members to think freely and to rationally interpret Islamic doctrine.

Kutlu argues instead for a 'rationalist-civilisational mentality' (*akılcı-hadari zihniyet*).[15] This approach refers to a theological method that explicitly takes into account the dynamism of human action and human societies. Moreover, this theological method interprets the dynamism of historical change as part of God's design of the universe: God wants us to freely apply our reason in order to build better societies on the bedrock of the eternal truths of God's will, such as the principles of justice and equality. Religion is an active process of civilisation-building that God calls us to undertake. Along similar lines, Hanifi Özcan calls for 'a religion indexed to knowledge' that opposes traditionalist approaches to religion that do not take into account the advances and changes brought by modernity.[16] Özcan's work emphasises heavily emphasises the point that change in religious practices (isolated from the sphere of eternal religious truth) brought about by changing individual and social circumstances is an undeniable fact that theologians must always take into account.[17]

In the same way that God has designed human reason to affirm human freedom, God has also sent down revelation in such a way that affirms human freedom. As described in the previous chapters, the Qur'an is the basis of the universality of the Islamic message.[18] The eternal principles elaborated therein are the surest guide to the eternal truths of religion and human nature. Furthermore, humans' use of their God-given reason is often in competition with human delusion, desire and ignorance, all of which can interfere with a person's ability to use reason correctly.[19]

At the same time, revelation affirms human freedom: one of the unchangeable truths that revelation establishes is in fact the changeability and freedom inherent in human nature. Revelation is the way that God ensures that human beings are able to freely access the complete truth about themselves and the universe. Revelation is sent to clarify the essential truths about the universe, and to enlighten human beings as to their own nature, which leads them to actualise their own powers of independent reasoning and reflection on the cosmos.[20] By communicating through revelation, God has begun a relationship with creation that human beings are expected to freely reciprocate.

Moreover, by choosing to communicate with human beings in their own linguistic medium, God chooses to dignify human freedom. God desires that human beings enter freely into a relationship with God, and this means that they must have the ability to do so using their own innate capacities, such as the capacity for language.[21] God addresses humanity in ways that both preserve the integrity of the way God created them, and also call them to use their created nature to reach out to their Creator. For Atay in particular, reason then becomes the primary means by which human beings interpret revelation, because reason is the way in which human beings come to know all things in the universe, exactly in accordance with the way God created them.[22]

Through its heavy emphasis on human freedom, Atay's theology of revelation thus features a notable theological humanism that has had a wide influence on modern Turkish theological discussions of human nature and the created world. When describing the reason why God sent revelation in the first place, Atay declares rather strikingly: 'Human beings are the goal! The Qur'an is for human beings, human beings are not for the Qur'an. The Qur'an is not to use human beings, human beings are to use the Qur'an'.[23] This means that God's revelation to humankind is meant to actualise human nature: it is meant to encourage and enable human beings to live up to the potential that God created in them. Atay's theocentric conception of human nature leads to his distinctly humanist religious vision: human nature and human reason are so crucial because they are direct creations of God, and God made them to be what they are. As Özcan puts it, 'Religion exists for the person, not the person for the religion'.[24]

In contrast to the humanist theological rationalism of Atay, Kutlu or Özcan, other theologians such as Emine Öğük (whose work is discussed in more detail in the previous chapter) rely on more explicitly traditional theological discourses to discuss the reality of human freedom. While the importance of human freedom as a theological argument is widely accepted in modern Turkish theology, how exactly to conceive of this freedom is subject to variance and debate. The explicit humanism of Atay and similar theologians is oftentimes critiqued by those who feel that this approach is too far removed from the explicit terms and concepts used in the classical Sunni dogmatic tradition.[25]

In her discussion of human freedom, for example, Öğük analyses al-Maturidi's discussion of the example of the classical *kalām* problem of *kader* (*qadar* in Arabic), or God's determination of events.[26] This is the classic theistic dilemma posed by divine omnipotence and human free will: genuine monotheism requires the former for its definition of God, but the latter is also required if it is to be believed that God judges the actions of individual human beings. But how can both of these propositions be true at the same time? If God is omnipotent, that means that God controls everything that happens in the universe; and if that is so, how can human beings be said to freely choose any course of action? Moreover, if human beings are not truly in charge of their individual decisions, then how can a just God judge them for these decisions?

Öğük points specifically to al-Maturidi's answer to this question as a guide for contemporary theologians.[27] Al-Maturidi begins by grounding his theological reflections in Quranic principles, noting that both of these claims are emphatically asserted in the text. The Qur'an repeatedly makes clear that humans are both morally responsible for all of their actions and that God has power over and knowledge of every occurrence in the cosmos. Human beings do indeed choose and perform their own actions.[28] Based on these two Quranic principles, al-Maturidi then constructs a theory of theological 'realism' which asserts that human actions have multiple 'aspects' to them from the divine and human perspectives. In other words, while both of these claims must be true, the truth of each claim can only be rationally apprehended one at a time. Human actions must therefore be multi-dimensional in a way that cannot be totally comprehended all at once, but must be true on the whole.[29] Thus, we learn from revelation that human freedom is real; but our reason cannot entirely comprehend how this can be so. As Öğük points out, affirming the reality of human freedom does not necessarily require a thorough-going theological humanism or rationalism. Reasoned reflection on revelation guided by self-conscious fidelity to tradition may also lead to this important theological conclusion.

Eternal Truth, Changeable Human Life

The fact of human freedom is the basis of the variability of religious experience through time. Human beings, as the trustees of the absolute truths of the universe and those expected by God to defend and live out those truths in this life, are uniquely responsible for preserving authentic religious truth and tradition in the real world. The fact that the created world, which is by its nature changeable and unstable, is the context in which human beings must undertake this responsibility makes the need to distinguish between unchangeable absolute truth and changeable historical context absolutely crucial. The nature of the created world thus mandates reflection on which aspects of religious tradition must be understood as eternally valid, and which may be regarded as historically contingent and thus liable to modification. Meditation on this distinction thus emerges as one of the most important ways in which modern Turkish theology approaches the problem of the Creator/created distinction, and the consequences this distinction has from the perspective of humankind.

One of the most common motifs used in modern Turkish theology to talk about the distinction between the changeable and the unchangeable aspects of religion is discussion of the relationship between 'religion'/'religious belief' (*din*) and '*Shari'ah*'/'religious practice' (*şeriat*).[30] This particular theological motif distinguishes between the essential beliefs and practices of Islam and the specific ways in which these essential beliefs and practices are interpreted and implemented in the real world. Otherwise put, this motif is employed as a method of clarifying the relationship between religious belief and practice. This distinction therefore becomes a way to help understand whether a certain belief or practice within Islamic tradition should be considered essential and unchangeable, or historically contingent and thus potentially changeable.[31] A close analysis of this particular theological motif in modern Turkish theology reveals the significant nuances in how various theologians navigate the distinction between absolute, unchangeable religious truth and contingent, changeable human life. Though this particular theological motif is phrased in multiple and even contradictory ways in modern Turkish theology, it runs as a clear thread though all the various methods this tradition uses to discuss the theological problematic of the nature of the created world.

This distinction is in fact an ancient and common feature of Hanafi-Maturidi theological tradition, having developed long before the Ottoman Empire or the modern Turkish Republic. The ninth-century text *Kitab al-'Alim wa-l-Muta'allim*,[32] attributed to the great Sunni theologian and scholar Abu Hanifa, includes a famous discussion of the difference between *din* (religion) and *Shari'ah* (Islamic ritual practice) and argues that all of the prophets sent by God shared one *din* but each brought their own *shari'ah*.[33] This argument occurred in the context of a wider debate about the nature of religious faith itself: is it a unitary act of the heart and mind, or is it something that is composed of both faith and works? This particular text deploys this distinction to support the principle that works are separate from faith.[34]

Medieval Hanafi-Maturidi theology developed the position that faith is an internal act of assent whose authenticity cannot be judged based on a person's actions alone. In other words, the distinction between 'religion' and 'Shari'ah' developed in this particular strain of medieval Sunni theology as a way to talk about the difference between internal faith and external religious observance. Al-Maturidi also utilises this distinction in his works, where he for instance argues that 'matters of religion (*diyānāt*) are matters of belief (*'itiqādāt*)'.[35] Al-Maturidi thus emphasises that adherence to religion and religious belief is properly located in the heart (*qalb*) and cannot be subject to any outside coercion or influence.[36] This theological position became standard dogma in the Hanafi-Maturidi tradition, maintaining influence among theologians of this school through the Ottoman period.

Modern Turkish theologians quickly noticed the implications of this distinction for modern discussions of religious identity and religious practice. As with their creative reappropriation of Hanafi-Maturidi tradition more broadly (the history of which is outlined in Chapter 2), these thinkers recognised that the texts of Sunni dogmatic theological tradition could take on a new relevance in the modern period. This distinction provided an ideal way to use traditional discourse to conceptualise a distinctly modern question; indeed, the most urgent question asked in the modern Turkish theological tradition: what is the difference between absolute truth and contingent human life? In this moment of modern change and instability, what constitutes the changeable and the unchangeable in religion?

İsmail Hakkı İzmirli, the pre-eminent late Ottoman theologian, took up this question himself. As discussed in the previous chapter, for İzmirli theology is a rational and disciplined meditation on deep truths of human experience and existential awareness that point with utter certainty to the existence of God. In order to better organise this process of meditation and analysis, İzmirli organised theological knowledge into three different types of 'religious judgements': creedal judgements, *Shari'ah* judgements and moral judgements.[37] All of these aim at the 'reforming', or the 'transformation' (*ıslah*) of the human person in accordance with the eternal truths of religion that lead to the achievement of ultimate fulfilment (*saadet*).[38]

İzmirli argues that the first and third categories in their entirety are part of the unchangeable elements of religion because they concern eternally true dogmas of the faith and eternally valid ethical principles. The first category, creedal judgements, aims at the transformation of human reason in accordance with eternal truths, such as the proposition that there exists one God who sends revelation to human beings instructing them to worship the One God and to institute justice and loving kindness among one another. These essential truths are summarised in the Islamic profession of belief that there exists only one God and that Muhammad is the Prophet of God – the first Pillar of Islam.[39] Islamic theological propositions therefore possess the following characteristics: they are rooted in sound evidence; they are in accord with and elucidated by human reason; and they are not subject to change (though the intellectual methods that express them may change).[40] Theological truth is in accord with both reason and human nature, and elevates both of them to the higher levels of transcendence that constitute their ultimate significance.

The third category of religious judgements, moral judgements, aims at the transformation of the heart. These propositions foster togetherness, love, harmony and support among individuals.[41] They might simply be called morals or ethics, and are the inner basis and principle of all human interactions. These propositions train and condition the soul and inner person to learn to treat other persons with the love that God shows humanity. The basis of Islamic morality is here what İzmirli calls 'loving kindness towards all of God's creation', that is, an individual and social mirroring of God's infinite attributes of loving kindness and mercy.[42] Like the theological dogmatic judgements that are their basis, these ethical principles cannot be subject to change over time: God will never command us not to be loving and merciful, because God will never cease to be loving and merciful.

By contrast, the second category, *Shariʿah* judgements, does contain elements of religion that are changeable over time, according to İzmirli. *Shariʿah* judgements aim at the transformation of human deeds and are oriented towards the establishment of civilisation, moderation, justice, goodness, freedom and equality.[43] *Fiqh*, or the discipline of deriving the rulings of the *Shariʿah*, is based on the principle of the general welfare and the fostering of both the individual and social good.[44] In other words, the *Shariʿah* is understood here as the ideal path leading to *saadet* that God sets out for individuals and societies. Its basis is the universal good of human flourishing, which lends it flexibility in practice due to change in social conditions.

This consideration leads to the crucial distinction at issue here. Within the *Shariʻah* category of religious judgements, there are two types of judgement that need to be distinguished from one another: those that concern rituals of worship (such as prayer), and those that concern 'worldly interactions', that is, relationships between people and societies. The rules of worship are the means of establishing a sincere and devoted relationship between the individual and God. The rules of worldly interactions are the means of establishing justice between human individuals in worldly social life.[45] This is a conventional distinction in *Shariʻah* practice: the former concerns the ritual duties of Islam, most particularly the Five Pillars in the Sunni tradition, while the latter concerns civil legislation and social practice.[46]

But İzmirli takes this traditional distinction one step further. He argues that, within *Shariʻah* propositions, those that have to do with worship are never subject to change, but those that have to do with worldly interactions can change precisely because human social conditions are ever changing.[47] This distinction effectively delimits the bounds of religious practice that are not subject to modern social reform, while clarifying where such reform can take place: the ritual duties of the faith must remain constant, but social policies (such as forms of government, civil legislation and even gender relations) become open to change and reinterpretation.

İzmirli's argument here is a key moment in the development of modern Turkish theology. Using terminology taken from Sunni dogmatic theology, he lays out a structure for how to talk about the central issue in modern Turkish theological development, the relationship between absolute truth and contingent human life. That so influential a figure as İzmirli would consider this distinction viable allowed it to become a common feature of theological argument in the modern Turkish tradition. İzmirli found in this distinction a key insight into the future of religion in the modern period: in order to ensure the survival of religion in the turbulence of modernity, it is necessary to isolate what is essential to the faith and what is liable to reinterpretation. Given the threats to religious belief and practice from philosophical materialism and from the sheer disorientation that comes from modern social change, it becomes necessary to decide what must be defended without compromise and what can safely be reimagined in the light of modern concerns.

Twentieth-century Turkish theologians since İzmirli have elaborated on this distinction in great detail in order to continue the theological task of defending absolute truth and reinterpreting how this absolute truth can best be actualised in the ever-changing realm of human life in this world. The first step in determining what can be changed is determining what cannot be changed. Following İzmirli, these theologians have defined the essence of religion with theological truth about God's nature, essential ethical precepts and the basic ritual requirements of Islam. This definition is necessary from both a theological and sociological perspective, as it divides human life into realms of experience with different kinds of religious value. It is in fact this sociological distinction that enables the perpetuation rather than diminution of religious values in the modern world. By properly delimiting the spheres over which religious values have sway, Turkish theologians ensure that these values have a space to thrive in the modern context. This defining of the nature of religion proper then allows for a definition of what is changeable in religious practice.

İlyas Çelebi, for example, describes religion in general as 'the totality of rules (*kurallar*) that give direction and meaning to the life of the human being' and that therefore constitute the foundation of the relationship the individual human being has with God, the world and other people.[48] More specifically, Islam is the truest religion in this sense because it is revealed through prophecy, addressed to human reason, and through its ethical commands ensures happiness and felicity in this life and the next; in its essence, it is composed of divine rules that are not subject to change.[49] The 'fixed elements' (*sabitler*) of true religion include the belief in the One God and the creation of the world; the fundamental freedom, equality and moral responsibility of human beings; belief in the afterlife; and many other basic ethical and theological propositions that flow from these key principles.[50] These essential elements of religious faith are, moreover, consonant with human nature and universal human experience, as Hanifi Özcan has also argued. Religious belief and eternal truth represent the most interior spiritual experience of a human being, a true gift from God.[51]

Similarly, İlhami Güler defines the essence of religion as a person's submission to God, the imputation of authority to God, right belief about God and the moral imperatives that follow from this submission.[52] He roots his definition of religion in the Qur'an, where religion's content is described as a direct relationship between God and humankind comprising 'the totality of moral decrees from God to humankind' and the 'submission, gratefulness, respect and worship' that is due to God.[53] 'Islam', as a theological term, refers to religion in its truest sense.[54] For Güler, the essence of religion is above all a moral and theological concept that constitutes a direct relationship between human beings and God, and is thus conceptually distinct from external factors such as social organisation. Religion is a moral stance and a set of moral commands, to be sure, but these are distinct from the specificities of concrete social relations.

To give one final example, the prominent Turkish scholar and theorist of *fiqh* Saffet Köse uses traditional Islamic legal theory to delimit the sphere of unchanging and absolute religious truth from areas of religious practice that can be reinterpreted. He mentions the higher ethical objectives of *Shari'ah* as a key example of the basic principles that can never be violated when undertaking interpretation of Islamic belief and practice. These goals, or *maqāṣid*, are a common feature of traditional Islamic legal theory. They are based on the fundamental principle that the *Shari'ah* is meant to 'facilitate improvement and perfection of the conditions of human life on earth'.[55] In other words, the *Shari'ah* is designed to enact God's will on earth through the protection of certain key values and goals that maximise human welfare. The specific historical forms that *Shari'ah* takes in the world are theoretically designed to conform to God's loving mercy towards human beings and God's will that justice be enacted on earth. Concrete rulings in *Shari'ah* are thus evaluated with respect to the higher goals that God has for humankind. These have been variously defined over the centuries and up to the present day, but include such goals as the safeguarding of religion, life, property and the exercise of human reason.

Given the eternal significance of these aspects of religion, the essence of religion itself, what specific relevance does absolute religious truth have in the ever-changing context of human life? This relevance is precisely the capacity of eternal truth to inform and transform the natural process of change in human life. As İzmirli suggested, the theological dogmas, the basic ritual duties and the ethical principles of Islam are non-negotiable and cannot be subject to reform over time. However, the precise manner in which these values and truths are lived out in the real world, that is, their 'practical' manifestation, can change over time.[56] Religious rulings and guidelines having to do with human interactions do not exhibit the same fixity that theological dogma, worship or ethical principles do. Religious rulings having to do with human interactions are subject to change in accordance with social and political change, precisely because they are the concrete manifestation of abstract ethical principles (such as justice and the protection of individual rights), the application of which will necessarily vary from time to time and place to place.[57]

This point is absolutely crucial, Çelebi for example insists, because it is at the core of the Islamic duty to advance human rights throughout history. While revelation itself and its theological, ritual and ethical messages are perfect, the exact manner in which the truths of revelation are implemented in the real world are subject to change simply due to the changeable nature of the world itself. Religion is perfect, but 'religiosity' is a process.[58] This process is the ongoing 'harmonising' between revelation and real life, a process that the Prophet himself undertook. Çelebi argues that this evolution of religiosity over time is the process of further improving human rights in this world. Muslims are called to complete the always ongoing process of human rights advancement that the Prophet began in his own life. Establishing justice in this world is a continual process that requires constant struggle to harmonise social practices with the eternal religious ideals of Islam.[59] This struggle is never-ending due not only to the always changing nature of human society itself, but also due to the inherently imperfect nature of human beings. Nevertheless, for Muslims the ceaseless striving for improvement and justice is itself an eternal part of the Islamic religious message.

This argument also implies that the essential theological and ethical teachings of Islam contain within themselves consequences that can only be realised in the future. The abolition of slavery or the defence of universal human rights may not have been conceivable by human beings in the seventh century, as Çelebi points out, but the seeds of these concrete ethical projects lay nestled within the Islamic ideals of justice and the Oneness of God from the beginning of revelation.[60] They flower at the right moment in history, and they require the cultivation of believing Muslims in the present. Islam is eternal, and the human ability to actualise its message must continue to progress until God calls the entirety of humanity to account at the end of history.

The sphere of human life exhibits this component of changeablity and progress because human life is inherently social (recalling the importance of Durkheim's and Gökalp's sociology, as discussed in previous chapters). Because human beings are both free to choose their actions and must live together in order to advance their collective and individual interests, human life exhibits a constantly changing and dynamic structure as human societies constantly endeavour to harmonise the needs of the individual with the needs of the group. Importantly, this application of a sociological understanding to human religious experience can result in a highly historicist reading of Islamic tradition as part and parcel of the effort to distinguish between eternal religious truth and changeable human circumstance.

As Hanifi Özcan points out, human religious practice via the *Shari'ah* reflects the historical variability of human experience itself. Religious practice has an 'aggregational' character, meaning that it is often composed of accumulations of concepts and practices rooted in historical contexts that no longer persist.[61] It is precisely this historical character of the *Shari'ah* that places it within the realm of changeable human experience. The essence of religion itself is revelation, which because it occurred once and in a perfect form is not itself subject to historical variability. Insofar as our interpretation of this event of revelation is implicated in our own social circumstance, which is always historically conditioned, religious practice itself is subject to historicist analysis and understanding. Özcan's distinction between religion and *Shari'ah* is so strong that it historicises the entire notion of *Shari'ah* by arguing that change is always possible within it.

The radically critical potential of this historicism is brought to its fullest expression by Güler. Güler in fact argues that the term '*Shari'ah*' is used as a kind of figure of speech in the Qur'an, as the practical manifestation or 'way' (the term's literal meaning) of enacting religion in a particular time and place. For this reason, *Shari'ah* is most akin to the concept of 'religiosity'.[62] It is in fact a kind of historical 'reification' of the essential truths of religion, and the multiplicity of these reifications over time reveals their connection to changing social conditions, politics and other properly extra-religious factors.[63] *Shari'ah* is the institutionalisation of religious truth.[64] In other words, Güler argues that religious practice, *Shari'ah*, is thoroughly conditioned by human social structures and considerations; not only does it contain the potential for change or dynamism over time, but is itself a largely human interpretation and construction.

The radicalism of Güler's approach is evident in his discussion of the history of religious practice in Muslim societies. Having established his theological argument on the definition of religion and *Shari'ah*, Güler goes on to make a crucial critique of how these concepts have traditionally been understood in Islamic jurisprudence. Güler argues that traditional *fiqh* scholars followed the eminent scholar Muhammad ibn Idris al-Shafi'i (d. 820)[65] in conflating religion and *Shari'ah*. Güler thus criticises the great majority of *fiqh* texts by pointing out that they have deviated from the Quranic understanding of the nature of religion itself, and thus have inadvertently sacralised social and political institutions rather than enabled their continual reform and critique by holding them accountable to Quranic ethics. Güler even goes so far as to claim that this conflation of religion with its concrete historical expression has prevented Muslim societies from developing a successful native vision of modernity.[66]

While he criticises Islamic tradition for its deviation from Quranic roots, Güler also criticises Western conceptions of religion embodied in Western secularism. According to Güler, secularism has 'imprisoned' religion within the conscience, the afterlife and worship spaces, thus robbing religion of its naturally dynamic and morally transformative relationship with changing social conditions. At the same time, however, modern religious thought is also afflicted with a severe conservatism that has confused a series of historical and interpretive developments with the universal essence of religion itself, thus attributing parts of religious tradition with absolute value that does not properly belong to them.[67]

Güler's theology of the relationship between absolute religious truth and changeable human life represents the most radically critical potential of this line of thinking. Köse's work, more closely grounded in the *fiqh* tradition of which Güler is so thoroughly critical, offers a useful counterpoint. Köse argues that *Shari'ah* exhibits a 'dynamic structure' due to the fact that social life is organic and therefore ever changing and developing.[68] This dynamic structure is known specifically as *ictihat*,[69] the term used in *fiqh* to refer to the reinterpretation of a *Shari'ah* ruling or to the derivation of a new *Shari'ah* ruling (*hüküm* in Turkish, *ḥukm* in Arabic). Ictihat (*ijtihād* in Arabic) in its most basic sense is the principle that allows the *fiqh* tradition to be subject to continual clarification and reinterpretation. Köse argues that the large majority of Islamic legal rulings actually fall into this category, meaning that the large majority of traditional Islamic *Shari'ah* practice can be reinterpreted in the contemporary period. The types of *Shari'ah* rulings that are not subject to reinterpretation are a small number of rulings that possess a clear and explicit basis in the Quranic text and the *Sunna* of the Prophet, and whose general applicability and universal benefit is fixed and not subject to change.[70] The need for *ictihat* is particularly acute in the modern period due to the massive social changes that have resulted from the global shift from agricultural to industrial societies.[71]

Köse stresses the need for *ictihat* on the basis of two theological principles, one relating to the nature of God and one relating to the nature of humanity, and emphasises the moral responsibility that God places on each human individual. God's role as judge of humanity requires that every human being who can be held morally liable for their individual actions[72] expend every reasonable effort to find the correct action to take in any given situation. At the same time, the everyday, worldly context within which individual human beings take these individual actions is constantly changing. Thus, continuous interpretation and reinterpretation of the specifics of Islamic legal practice through the use of *ictihat* is a direct consequence of both God's nature as eternal judge and of humanity's nature as conditioned by continuous social change. As with the theologians discussed above, therefore, Köse's argument is based ultimately on the theological distinction between the nature of the Creator and the nature of creation.

İctihat can be understood as a middle way between the twin errors of strong historicism, such as that advocated by Güler and Özcan, and traditional conservatism. The former attempts to historicise every legal ruling in the Qur'an, thus rendering all of them subject to change or abandonment. The latter error of traditional conservatism is excessively focused on staying within the boundaries of the historical *fiqh* tradition, which is a denial of the necessary dynamism of *fiqh*.[73] Unthinking reliance on a particular school of thought or a particular historical figure can replace the focus on basic religious principles themselves, thus undermining the necessary dynamism of Islamic religious practice. The basic principles of the Islamic faith are by nature broader than any particular historical movement or personage.[74] As Köse puts it, 'in Islam it is not persons but principles that come to the forefront'.[75]

Theologians such as Köse stress a balance between extreme historicism and extreme conservatism because this balance enables human beings to remain obedient to God's eternal commands and at the same time advance the cause of justice in the world, a cause that itself is a command of God that can be variously carried out. On the one hand, Muslims have a duty to follow the revealed commands of God that God fixes for all eternity, such as the commands of ritual worship. On the other hand, the moral commands of God, such as the command to act justly and with loving mercy in the world, will require continual flexibility and even creativity on the part of human interpreters in order to make them a reality in human society.

It is crucial to note here that with respect to the imperative to follow God's eternal commands, *ictihat* cannot be used to justify moral or dogmatic relativism, or to excuse fundamentally immoral behaviour. While *ictihat* can apply to questions of ritual and legal practice, it cannot apply to questions of theological belief or questions of morality.[76] For instance, *ictihat* cannot be used to declare permitted what the Qur'an has explicitly forbidden, nor can it invalidate the basic ritual duties of the faith.[77] In other words, while dynamism is an inherent feature of Islamic *Shari'ah* practice, this dynamism cannot be construed to undermine the integrity of the faith or the revelation itself.[78]

With respect to the imperative to advance justice in the world, however, *ictihat* must be free of methodological barriers to this goal, such as formalism and literalism. With respect to formalism, an act may be construed to be formally acceptable, but is in reality totally inadmissible from the broader moral perspective of Islam. Islamic *Shari'ah* rulings that adhere to the letter of the law, as it were, but violate its fundamental moral spirit, cannot be understood as actually following the will of God in the world. For instance, a marriage may take place that meets the formal requirements of Islamic ritual practice, but if it occurs under coercion, it cannot be said to be Islamically valid. Using a phrase from Ottoman legal texts, Köse describes such situations as 'accidentally, but not religiously, valid'.[79] In other words, the tendency to focus on the formal requirements of the *Shari'ah* to the detriment of its fundamental moral and spiritual principles results in legal rulings that are contrary to God's will, even if they appear to be acceptable under the formal terms of the *Shari'ah*.

The error of textual literalism functions in a similar fashion. Literalistic interpretations of Islamic scriptural and traditional texts are fundamentally ineffective because the texts are based on broad principles and general goals designed for use within the complexities of the real world.[80] Any form of textual interpretation, therefore, must never lose sight of the general goals of the *Shari'ah* itself, and must retain a holistic structure that takes the entirety of relevant texts into account. As Köse explains in a particularly useful analogy, the text's literal wording and its actual intention are analogous to a person's body and spirit: they are formally inseparable but conceptually distinct, and it is possible to prioritise the former to the detriment of the latter.[81] Scriptural interpretation must also retain its focus on the overall meaning and goal of a given textual source when attempting to evaluate its literal meaning.[82]

Overall, wherever they stand on the exact theoretical lines drawn in this debate, modern Turkish theologians have all stressed the necessity of taking the dynamism of religious life and practice into account in the modern period. This imperative is vital to the survival of religion itself in the modern period, and is in fact a simple reality of the human experience. As Özcan points out, the variability that people show towards religious practice is, quite simply, 'a fact of history'.[83] The distinction between Creator and created simply necessitates an acknowledgement of the variability of human life, and this acknowledgement has critical implications for religious practice if we are to take seriously the task of preserving religious values within the vicissitudes of modernity.

Put another way, the neglect of the dynamism of *Shari'ah* threatens the continuing viability of religion itself in the modern period. Köse suggests that the reason Western Europe went through a process of social secularisation that marginalised the church was the Western church's insufficient response to the changes of modernity. Likewise, he argues that '*ictihat* is a vital imperative and a religious duty' because if Muslims refuse to nurture the dynamism inherent in their own tradition, they are giving people a compelling reason to discard religion altogether.[84] Modern Turkish theology has converged on the need to emphasise the dynamism of religious practice not out of a desire to submit religion to modernity, but out of a desire to allow religion to thrive within modernity. In other words, if we are to fulfil God's commands within a context that God deliberately created to be ever changing and dynamic, surely God must also desire that we acknowledge the dynamism within religion itself.

Applications I: Politics and Democracy

Given the fact that the theological distinction between the changeable and the unchangeable in religious practice is meant to have concrete ramifications for the social world, it is important to consider areas of potential application of this argument. By far the most common example of the influence of this theological distinction in contemporary Turkey is the very widespread argument for the compatibility of Islam and representative democracy. The notion that Islam and democratic governance are compatible is so common among Turkish theologians as to be taken for granted.[85] To state the argument more specifically, in modern Turkish theology it has become commonplace to assert that novel modern political systems, such as representative democracy, are entirely acceptable within an Islamic worldview so long as they result in justice and equanimity. In short, Islam is concerned with the implementation of God's demand for justice and mercy between human beings, but leaves the specifics of how to do this to human beings.[86] As discussed in the second chapter, the ethical values of liberal democratic governance such as freedom, equality and social justice, were promoted by prominent late Ottoman theologians as central to the values of Islam. Accordingly, the goal of establishing a democratic and republican state was seen as harmonious with the vision of Islam by Turkish theologians in the early Republic.[87]

Though this assertion is so common in modern Turkish theology as to be seen as merely common sense, it is important to emphasise its rootedness in the particular theological argument about the need to distinguish between the changeable and the unchangeable in religious practice. In modern Turkey, the sheer mundanity of the claim that Islam and representative government are compatible is precisely what makes the claim so interesting. Given that representative democratic systems were almost universally rejected by theologians of all three major monotheistic faiths in the pre-modern period, the presence of widespread support for democracy on Islamic theological grounds deserves some sustained analysis in order to uncover its specific conceptual bases.[88]

Modern Turkish theological arguments in support of the implementation of novel modern political systems (such as representative democracy) are based on a theological distinction between the 'political' and the 'religious'. As described in previous chapters, this distinction has been inherited from late Ottoman and early Republican theologians. According to this distinction, political affairs are by their very nature related to the worldly needs of human beings and how to secure these needs in the present life. Thus, these affairs are fundamentally connected with the changeableness of the created world, and cannot be placed in the same category as theological truth, which by definition concerns the nature of God and is therefore unchanging. Thus, Islamic thought and culture explicitly provides space for continuing innovation in political organisation so long as a given political system fulfils the divine command to implement justice in the world. In other words, the moral values of politics are reflective of God's attributes and manifest as God's commands, and are thus unchanging. Freedom, justice, equality and service to others can never be dispensed with because they are rooted in theological truth. However, the specific ways in which these values are manifested from one place and one time to the next may be subject to change.

Köse's work provides a particularly clear example of this line of thinking. He distinguishes between three realms of human life that each have their own relationship with religion: 1) the realm whose entirety is determined by religion; the 2) realm whose basic principles are determined by religion; and 3) the realm that religion itself indicates should be left to human reason alone. The first of these categories encompasses actions that are entirely dictated by revelation itself and as such cannot change with time or place. Köse offers the example of worship and ritual duties as the primary example of this category.[89] Because these actions (such as prayer and fasting) are duties that are owed to God, they are not subject to change over time. The third category concerns the natural sciences, which the Qur'an and Islamic tradition both indicate should be left to unhindered rational and empirical investigation.

The second realm includes parts of human life which must be based on religious principles, but the specific implementation of which is left to human choice and design. The examples Köse gives here include politics, economics and law. Köse stresses, however, that though the specifics of these systems may change over time, these areas are inextricably connected to religious principles because they involve areas of individual and social moral action.[90] The underlying principles of these areas of life (such as justice) are based on religious precepts and are thus unchangeable, while the specific social forms that these principles may take in their application can change according to time and place.

Köse provides two clear examples of this second realm of human life: clothing and the form of the state. Clothing is a natural, physical requirement for human beings. Religion specifies some requirements for clothing, such as covering certain parts of the body on account of modesty, but leaves the overall style and form of clothing to the variability of individual taste and social custom.[91] Likewise, the organisation of a state is a natural, social requirement for human beings. Religion establishes certain universal principles that must form the basis of every legitimate state, such as justice, popular supervision and election, and respect for basic human rights, but because social conditions change over time, it leaves open what particular form a government may take in order to fulfil these principles (and he notes that in this particular day and age, the countries that best fulfil these requirements are those with democratic systems of government).[92]

Ali Bardakoğlu similarly describes political and social organisation as tools with which to implement the immutable principles of revelation. Governance is intimately tied with the changeability of social context and historical experience. Islam's universality, as a reflection of the basic truths of the universe, means that it possesses the authority to judge the outcomes of specific governance structures, but it leaves the job of designing and implementing these structures to 'human initiative'.[93] Moreover, as Süleyman Uludağ notes, no particular political system or state system is specifically recommended by the Qur'an or Sunna.[94] Thus it is neither correct to say that Islam rejects democracy, nor to claim that Islam mandates it. While Islam does not remain neutral towards the value of justice in governance, it does remain neutral towards the specific form that governance may take.

What makes democratic governance compelling is its ability to secure certain outcomes, such as the protection of human rights or individual liberty. However, because political systems are evaluated from an Islamic perspective based on their efficacy in securing moral outcomes, and not on the presumption that one is inherently more Islamic than another, it is entirely conceivable that multiple and even mutually contradictory forms of governance might be Islamically acceptable from one place and historical time period to the next. In other words, while there is nothing inherently Islamic about any political system, democracy must currently be upheld because it is the system that at present is best able to secure justice and the protection of human rights.[95]

This distinction between universal and unchangeable religious moral values, and concrete, changeable political systems, can also be understood with respect to the distinction between reason and revelation.[96] As Şaban Ali Düzgün notes, it is logically impossible that a specific form of the state should be mandated by religion, because as pointed out above no specific guidance on this topic exists in revelation or Prophetic tradition. If the form of the state were subject to divine command, it is simply inconceivable that God would not provide absolute clarity on this matter. Thus, the form of the state falls under the activity of human reason, and is distinguished from the category of divine revelation.[97] As with natural science, because politics concerns observable phenomena in the physical world, its specific structures are subject to human rational analysis and argument, and are to be categorically distinguished from the universality of revelation. As Wilkinson notes in her thorough analysis of Düzgün's theology, his thought on this point and in general combines Western Enlightenment moral categories with Islamic theological anthropology and offers a vigorous defence of human initiative in the social sphere anchored in the universal commands and values of Islamic theology.[98] Thus, historical variability in political systems can be seen as a natural outcome of the way that God designed human nature, meaning that political reform is always a possibility within an Islamic ethical worldview.

Applications II: Gender Justice

The distinction between the changeable and the unchangeable has obvious implications for questions of gender justice and gender relations. Do relations between men and women fall properly into the sphere of changeable or unchangeable religious truth? What is their relationship with theological questions of eternal significance, and contingent social questions that have to do with universal values but are also dependent on changing social circumstances? In other words, what is the proper theological status of gendered distinctions in Islamic thought? These questions are frequently approached in modern Turkish theology by proceeding from a consideration of the changeable/unchangeable distinction in religion discussed in detail throughout this chapter.

Moreover, it is precisely within the realm of gendered practice that many contemporary Muslim thinkers worldwide have sought to delineate the boundaries between normative and deviant religious practice. As Kecia Ali's work powerfully demonstrates, the realm of gendered practices is very often the battleground for determining the boundaries of 'authentic' Islam itself.[99] This crucial dynamic of modern and contemporary Muslim thought is no less important in modern Turkish theology. The work of Hidayet Şefkatli Tuksal explores these questions with the most theological depth of any other contemporary Turkish Muslim thinker, and her theology clearly illuminates that importance of the changeable/unchangeable distinction in the current development of Turkish theology on the topic of gender justice.

Hidayet Şefkatli Tuksal's systematic critique of patriarchal discourse within Islamic tradition is a pioneering example of theological reflections on gender in contemporary Turkish.[100] Her work is based on a distinction between the unchangeable truths of Quranic theology and the influence of changeable human social systems, such as patriarchy, that are detectable throughout Islamic tradition. Her main argument is that key genres of traditional Islamic texts, most particularly the hadith, include examples of misogynistic discourse (*kadın karşıtı söylemi*), but that these discourses are contrary to the spirit of the Quranic revelation and thus need to be re-examined in the light of the Quranic message of fundamental human equality. Furthermore, this task of re-examination and reinterpretation is particularly urgent because the uncritical acceptance of these misogynistic discourses has led to detrimental consequences for the social status of women in Muslim societies.

Tuksal describes patriarchy or the patriarchal social system (*ataerkillik/ ataerkil sistem*) as a social order that is historically extremely widespread, but that is at the same time emphatically not a 'universal or inevitable phenomenon'.[101] Tuksal's theological analysis begins, therefore, with the kind of insights anticipated in the late Ottoman reception of sociology described in the first chapter of this book. Her first methodological point is to acknowledge the changeability of human social organisation and institutions, a point that is founded both on sociological theory and the distinction between the unchanging nature of God the Creator and the ever-changing nature of the created order.

The misogynistic discourse she critiques can be found in both the Qur'an and the hadith, in her view. Indeed, she puts her critique rather starkly. She argues that though the material in question is 'marginal' when considered against the backdrop of the entirety of the Quranic text and the hadith tradition as a whole, the extremely widespread usage of this material in traditional Islamic thought makes it actually more difficult to claim that misogynistic attitudes are not Islamic than to claim that they are.[102] The most immediately striking characteristic of Tuksal's theology is in fact her frank assessment of Islamic tradition on this score: that it, like any other religious tradition, is always influenced by its historical context and thus will inevitably contain misogynistic discourses and practices simply due to how historically widespread these discourses and practices are.

Tuksal's main claim, however, is that these misogynistic discourses are real, but not indicative of the basic and unchanging message of the Quranic text. On the contrary, misogyny and patriarchy are diametrically opposed to the 'essence and basic principles' of Islam.[103] The most fundamental Quranic principle with respect to human nature is the 'ontological quality of value' between human beings.[104] The main task of her theological analysis therefore becomes 'identifying the traces of patriarchal tradition that have influenced the anti-woman narrations' in the hadith tradition.[105] Tuksal focuses on the hadith tradition because of their wide influence in religious practice throughout the history of Islam.[106]

The foundation of her critique is her analysis of the Quranic view of human nature. She focuses on the Qur'an for two reasons. First of all, it is composed of the revealed words of God to Muhammad, the final Prophet to humankind, and so its worldview takes ultimate precedence in a moral and theological sense. Secondly, it is the earliest document we have that is a contemporary witness to the practice of the earliest Muslim community, and thus preserves a record of the most essential parts of Muslim religious practice before they became subject to historical development.[107] Thus, Tuksal's direct critique of the extant text of certain hadith reports proceeds by comparing them with the basic Quranic message.[108]

The Qur'an constitutes divine guidance for humanity during its life in this world. It has been revealed in order to allow humanity to reach its full potential in the light of divine truth. This attainment of righteousness is the goal of human existence itself, and is achieved by harmonising our individual human nature with God's wisdom.[109] The words of God in the Qur'an are directed towards the perfection of human nature as it manifests uniquely in each individual. As the Qur'an repeatedly emphasises, God only distinguishes between human beings based on their actions in this life, that is, whether or not they fulfil their spiritual obligations to God and their ethical obligations to other human beings.[110] The requirements that each individual person must meet in the eyes of God are requirements of faith and action, not requirements that have anything to do with one's gender.[111] Among dozens of other Quranic verses to this effect, Tuksal cites 33:35 in this context, which famously declares that men and women are equal in the reward they receive from God for their individual moral actions, individual ritual practices and individual belief in God.[112]

As Tuksal notes, however, the Qur'an itself bears traces of the misogynistic cultural mindset of the society within which it was revealed. Because the text was revealed to address a specific audience within human history, the discourse of the text includes elements of the 'patriarchal codes' embedded in that society.[113] Tuksal argues, however, that the task of the interpreter is to disentangle these codes from the elements of the text that constitute its eternal message. Thus, Tuksal acknowledges the existence of misogynistic discourse within the specific phraseology and social mores within the text of the revelation itself, but points out that these are theologically distinct from the universal message of the text that is meant to address all times and places, which is clearly a message that stresses the equal dignity of men and women.

Having established the basic message of the Qur'an on the topic of gender, Tuksal then compares this message to the misogynistic discourses present in the hadith literature. Tuksal notes that one of the key features of the hadith literature is the presence of contradictory material within the massive corpus of hadith transmissions. Muslim scholars have over the centuries therefore attempted to resolve these contradictions when attempting to interpret the hadith as a guide for Muslim religious ethics and practice. However, because most Muslim scholars across Muslim history have lived in patriarchal societies (as is the case with every other great religious tradition), they did not identify the existence of misogynistic discourse in the hadith literature as in evident tension with the Quranic message, and thus as an interpretive problem that needed to be solved.[114]

The basis of Tuksal's critique of traditional hadith scholarship therefore combines both sociological and theological insights. Because traditional hadith scholars, like any other human being, were influenced by the social structures within which they found themselves, they were liable to read their own social situations back into the text as normative, thus seeing patriarchy as a natural condition of human societies that elicits no theological or ethical dilemma. But the basic theological anthropology of the Qur'an poses a clear problem for the existence of any misogynistic discourse in Islamic tradition. Because social conditions in our own time have shifted such that scholars living now are able to perceive this problem, it becomes the responsibility of contemporary Muslim scholars to address it.[115] Tuksal thus levels a sharp critique at Islamic tradition and its acceptance of misogyny, but she accuses it of a failing that is universal to human nature and thus to all human religious practice and belief the world over.

Tuksal examines five types of hadith reports that contain misogynistic discourse: 1) reports that describe the creation of Eve from Adam's rib; 2) reports that claim that the majority of the denizens of hell are women; 3) reports that women are 'deficient in reason' and corrupters of the morals of men; 4) reports that describe women as 'inauspicious'; 5) and reports that mention women alongside animals such as donkeys and dogs.[116] Though these reports constitute a tiny fraction of the many hundreds of thousands of reports that make up the overall hadith literature, they have been seized upon by scholars in pre-modern societies as justifications for preventing women from serving in positions of power or in granting women equal social status with men.[117] Tuksal's analysis of these hadith is designed to show that they not only contravene the spirit of the Qur'an, but contravene the spirit of other hadith reports that are much more likely to be reflective of what the Prophet himself actually said. In other words, Tuksal argues that not only did pre-modern Muslim scholars ignore the fundamental message of the Qur'an when evaluating whether or not the Prophet actually said what is contained in the hadith reports, but they also ignored other hadith reports that are explicitly anti-misogynist.

The hadith in the last of these categories of reports provides the clearest example of her historical and theological argument. These hadith have to do with how to perform the daily ritual prayer correctly (*namaz* in Turkish/*ṣalāt* in Arabic). One of the key requirements for each session of *ṣalāt* to be valid is that the participant must be in a sound and focused state of mind such that they are performing the prayer with proper intention (rather than as a merely mechanistic exercise). Hadith that speak to the issue of how to maintain one's proper state of mind are therefore very common.[118]

One subset of the large number of hadith on this issue has to do with the question of a person or animal passing in front of a person performing the prayer. Does the fact that someone or something passes in front of a person performing the prayer invalidate the prayer because it constitutes a significant distraction? These hadith are sometimes referred to as the '*sutra*' ('prayer screen'; *sütre* in Turkish) hadith because a possible solution to this dilemma mentioned in these hadith is the imposition of an item to serve as a screen or barrier between the front of the worshipper and anything passing in front of them. Thus, any hadith that mention deeds or sayings of the Prophet that might have relevance to this issue are grouped in the traditional hadith collections under the category of the *sutra*.

Tuksal outlines two possible answers within this hadith category to the question of whether or not something passing front of the worshipper constitutes a distraction. These views are diametrically opposed: one group of hadith indicates that something passing in front of a worshipper poses no problem or distraction whatsoever, and the second group indicates that something passing in front does constitute a distraction that could invalidate the prayer, thus necessitating the imposition of a *sutra*.[119]

What does this hadith subset have to do with the question of misogyny? One group of hadith that argue that something passing in front invalidates the prayer claim that three situations are particularly distracting for the worshipper: when a woman, an ass, or a dog pass in front of a worshipper.[120] Take for instance a report narrated by Abu Dharr: 'The Messenger of God said: When any one of you stands for prayer ... [and if] there is not before him (a thing) equal in size to the back of a saddle, his prayer would be cut off by (the passing of an) ass, woman, and black dog'.[121] Or put more simply by the narrator Abu Hurayra: 'The Messenger of God said: A woman, an ass, and a dog disrupt the prayer, but something like the back of a saddle guards against that'.[122]

Tuksal argues that these hadith have clearly misogynistic overtones. They associate female nature with animality, including animals like the dog that were considered particularly repellent in the culture of seventh-century Arabia. Moreover, these hadith imply the common patriarchal trope that women's mere presence constitutes a sensual distraction for men, rendering men incapable of controlling their minds and thoughts around them.[123] Yet, as mentioned above, a subset of hadith within the category on the *sutra* argues that someone or something passing in front of a worshipper in fact does not constitute a distraction for the worshipper. As it turns out, this subset of hadith makes this argument precisely by responding to the above hadith that associates women with these animals. These reports are narrated by 'A'isha bint Abi Bakr, one of the Prophet's wives and one of the most widely respected social, political and intellectual leaders of the early Muslim community. Reports attributed to 'A'isha were considered particularly trustworthy by traditional Islamic scholars.[124]

In these reports, 'A'isha vociferously objects to the very premise implied in the reports that associate women with animals.[125] In multiple versions of these reports, 'A'isha hears other Muslims relate the claim that the Prophet said that women, asses and dogs disrupt the prayer. Upon hearing this, she reacts with astonishment: 'Is the woman an ugly animal? I lay in front of the Messenger of God like the bier of a corpse and he said prayer'.[126] In another version, she says: 'You likened us to the dogs and the asses. By God! I saw the Messenger of God saying prayer while I lay interposed between him and the *qibla* [i.e., the direction of prayer towards Mecca]'.[127]

These narrations from 'A'isha are striking indeed. They are a dramatic illustration of just what makes interpreting the hadith material so difficult: even the Muslims who lived during the lifetime of the Prophet disagreed on what he said with respect to key matters of Islamic practice. This is why the hadith do not exist in any single fixed version; there is contradictory, confusing and simply mysterious material related in countless specific reports. Tuksal's analysis then proceeds to the question of how the Muslim interpretive tradition dealt with this specific contrast which is, as she notes, a very clear example of disagreement over Prophetic practice within the early Muslim community.[128]

As Tuksal and other hadith scholars note, there is every reason to accept 'A'isha's version of events as authoritative. Her reports are considered by the early hadith scholars to be at least as historically plausible as the other reports, and she had much closer access to the Prophet's behaviour than anyone else mentioned in the reports. In fact, as Asma Sayeed points out, 'A'isha's authority as a transmitter and interpreter of Prophetic tradition was often considered to be superior to that of her male contemporaries: traditional accounts of her life conclude that her transmission of Prophetic tradition was superior to others because she had an extraordinary ability to interpret the inner meaning and practical significance of incidents in Muhammad's life.[129]

Moreover, her version of events seems to accord with what we know from other sources about public congregational prayer during the life of the Prophet. The earliest sources of hadith scholarship in fact adopted this viewpoint. As Tuksal shows, highly authoritative early scholars such as Abu Dawud (d. 889)[130] and Malik ibn Anas (d. 795)[131] preferred the opinion that passing in front of a worshipper does not invalidate the prayer.[132] It is also noteworthy that the scholar Muslim ibn al-Hajjaj (d. 875)[133] records 'A'isha's hadith at the very end of his section on the *sutra*, thus indicating that he felt she should have the last word on the matter.

The solution to the problem of the misogynistic discourses in these hadith seems clear enough, then. More reliable contemporaneous reports should rule out the claims that the Prophet associated women with animals and that he considered them to be sensual distractions for men. But as Tuksal points out, the medieval tradition of hadith scholarship could not allow 'A'isha's version of events to simply cancel out the claims of male hadith reporters. Rather than accept her version of events as authoritative, many medieval scholars instead preferred to try to 'aggregate' or harmonise these two clearly mutually incompatible versions of events.[134] The opinion became widespread that while the passing in front of a worshipper does not invalidate the prayer, it is nevertheless to be strongly discouraged and severely condemned.[135] These medieval scholars therefore often turned to one particular report to this effect: 'Abu Juhaym reported that the Messenger of God said: 'If anyone who passes in front of a man who is praying knew the responsibility he incurs, he would stand still forty [days, months, or years] rather than to pass in front of him'.[136]

As Tuksal insightfully points out, while this position may at first glance seem like a sensible middle ground between conflicting reports, it actually reveals the patriarchal bias of the medieval hadith scholars. The argument to aggregate, or harmonise, these contradictory reports only makes sense if one refuses to recognise 'A'isha's clear authority on this particular issue. If one recognises 'A'isha's authority here, then there is no need at all to so severely condemn one who passes in front of a worshipper, because according to 'A'isha's version of events the Prophet saw no issue with someone being directly in front of him during his prayer. These medieval interpreters also went to great lengths to try to explain away 'A'isha's version of events, rather than accept their veracity based on her clear authority on the matter.[137]

Tuksal's analysis of this well-known debate in the hadith epitomises her theological and historiographical critique of traditional Islamic scholarship and hermeneutics. Her analysis of the reception of the hadith reports on the *sutra* indicate just how the 'seepage' of patriarchal and misogynistic cultural impulses occurred throughout Islamic history, from the earliest generations of Muslims through the tradition of medieval commentary on these early reports.[138] Subtle but monumental shifts in interpretive methods used by traditional scholars can be driven by their unconscious social biases. The consequences of these biases may in some cases be negligible. But in the cases that Tuksal documents above, these biases result in the perpetuation of misogynistic discourse across Muslim societies by wrongly imputing it to the Prophet, and in clear contradiction with the fundamentals of God's own speech in the revelation itself.

The main argument of Tuksal's work is that contemporary Muslim theologians have a sacred duty to critically analyse their tradition by comparing it with the unchanging message of the Qur'an and the wider context of the entirety of the Prophet's life. In Tuksal's estimation, the life of the Prophet when considered as a whole is the living embodiment of the basic Quranic message of human dignity and freedom. One of the key lessons of Muhammad's Prophetic mission is that human beings are called to self-sacrifice for each other, but they live in subservience to no-one except God.[139] According to Tuksal, contemporary Muslim theologians must undertake the 'difficult, daring, and even risky' work of re-evaluating their own historically bound tradition from the perspective of eternal Quranic and Prophetic truth. Yet as Tuksal makes strikingly clear, 'despite all these difficulties, those who are in search of truth will get the reward of their search, sooner or later'.[140]

Tuksal's theology therefore epitomises the broader dynamics of modern Turkish theology's approach to understanding the created world. Tuksal's work is a call to action based on a firm commitment to God's command to establish justice between people in this life. Her theological arguments reflect her own moral striving to do God's will, even if this means risking critical engagement with one's own tradition. God's judgement of our own ethical striving is more urgent, and more final, than the judgement of tradition. In other words, though her conclusions might be seen as controversial in modern Turkish theological academia, they are in fact rooted in the same historical and intellectual dynamics that produced the modern Turkish theological tradition. As we have seen, though the answers to how we are to live out the truth of *tevhid* in the modern world are highly variable and even contradictory in modern Turkish theology, the same theological argument underpins them all. Because the created world is fundamentally distinct from the Creator, it is ever changing, and this requires that we reconsider theological tradition in the light of new modern realities.

As this chapter argues, therefore, the ethical imperative of modern Turkish theology is grounded in the Creator/created distinction. God makes ethical demands of us because God is perfect and eternal. Universal and eternal ethical principles, such as mercy and justice, are possible because they are commanded by the One God who is eternal and unchangeable. Yet at the same time, we are to undertake these commands freely and sincerely because God has created the changeable world as a place of moral striving among human beings. The very changeability of the world implies and necessitates ethical action and commitment, specifically to live out God's command to reflect, in our own small way, the justice and loving mercy of our Creator.

Notes

1. Atay was born in 1930 in the small village of Hacı Şeyh Köyü near Güneyce in the region of Rize. He learned to memorise the Qur'an from his father and uncle at an early age, and learned Arabic and studied the traditional Islamic religious disciplines from *medrese*-trained instructors in Istanbul. He travelled to Baghdad and finished high school there in 1948, and also received a degree in theology there in 1954. He received his doctorate in theology from the Ankara University Faculty of Theology in 1961. Until he retired in 1997, he researched and

published on Arabic and Hebrew philosophy and nearly every area within traditional Islamic religious thought. He taught theology, specifically in the *kalām* tradition, in Konya, Ankara and Saudi Arabia; was appointed the dean of the Ankara University Faculty of Theology from 1980 to 1982; and in 1989 became the director of the *kalām* course of study at Ankara.

2. Sinanoğlu, 'Gelenek ve Modernite Arasında Bir Arayış', 117.
3. Atay, *Ben*, 51–2.
4. Atay, *Ben*, 61.
5. Atay, *Ben*, 92.
6. Atay, *Ben*, 52, 55.
7. Atay, *Ben*, 90.
8. Atay, *Ben*, 63.
9. Atay, *Ben*, 87, 46. Atay's description of the ultimate goal of religion as the attainment of complete happiness in this life and the next recalls İzmirli's use of the term *saadet* as described in the previous chapter.
10. Hüseyin Atay, 37, 49.
11. Atay, *Ben*, 63.
12. Atay, *Ben*, 63.
13. It is worth noting that Atay here uses the Turkish term for God, '*Tanrı*', rather than the term borrowed from Arabic, *Allah*.
14. Kutlu, 'Matüridi Akılcılığı', 8.
15. Kutlu, 'Matüridi Akılcılığı', 8–9.
16. Özcan, 'Dinin Birey ve Toplum için Anlamı', 134.
17. Özcan, 'Dinin Birey ve Toplum için Anlamı', 139.
18. Atay, *Ben*, 38–9, 87.
19. Atay, *Ben*, 62.
20. Atay, *Ben*, 61–2.
21. Atay, *Ben*, 65.
22. Atay, *Ben*, 67.
23. Atay, *Ben*, 58.
24. Özcan, 'Dinin Birey ve Toplum için Anlamı', 134.
25. On this point see Dorroll, 'The Turkish Understanding of Religion', 1059–60.
26. The issue of *qadar* (*kader* in Turkish) is one of the oldest and most widely debated theological questions in the *kalām* tradition. The term has the literal meaning of 'determining' and refers in theology to 'God's eternal knowledge and determination of all objects and outcomes' in the entirety of the cosmos (Topaloğlu and Çelebi, *Kelam Terimleri Sözlüğü*, 73). For an overview of the various positions in

this debate, see Yaman, 'Small Theological Differences, Profound Philosophical Implications', 187–93.
27. Öğük, *İstifade Yöntemleri*, 149–50.
28. Öğük, *İstifade Yöntemleri*, 150; in Maturidi's terms, this means that human beings possess both choice (*ikhtiyār*) and are the 'doers' of their own actions (*fāʿil*), that is, they are not mere passive vessels for God's actions. See *Kitāb al-Tawḥīd*, 307, 349.
29. Öğük, *İstifade Yöntemleri*, 150–2. See *Kitāb al-Tawḥīd*, 310, 321, 323.
30. Recep Şentürk mentions the use of this distinction in what he calls 'reformist discourses' in modern Turkish Islamic thought. While his analysis identifies the importance of this strain of thinking to modern Turkish Islamic theology, he suggests that its influence is marginal and compromised by its association with the political project of the Turkish state. This chapter hopefully demonstrates that the opposite is true: that these discourses are both organic developments within Islamic theology and integral to the development of Islamic theology in modern Turkey overall. See Şentürk, 'Islamic Reformist Discourses and Intellectuals in Turkey'.
31. As mentioned in the first chapter, this theological distinction is a crucial feature of all Islamic modernist theology. Fazlur Rahman, for instance, frames this as the distinction between 'normative Islam and historical Islam' (Rahman, *Islam and Modernity*, 141).
32. The distinction between religion and the *Shariʿah* in Islamic theology first appears in this text, which Joseph Schacht convincingly shows to have been written sometime in the middle of the ninth century and thus could not have been composed by Abu Hanifa himself (Schacht, 'An Early Murji'ite Treatise'). The work systematically expands on theological principles reliably attributed in a simpler form to Abu Hanifa. This text enjoyed extraordinary popularity throughout the history of Hanafi theology. It is mentioned in the *Fihrist* of al-Nadim and in the works studied by a prominent Hanafi Bukharan scholar of the twelfth century. See 'Abd al-Qadir ibn Abi al-Wafa' al-Qurashi, *al-Jawahir al-Mudiyya fi Tabaqat al-Hanafiyya*, Vol. 1, entry 11. The famous Bukharan Maturidi theologian Nur al-Din al-Sabuni (d. 1184) also refers to this treatise by name (see *al-Bidayah fi Usul al-Din*, 87–8). Al-Maturidi himself seems to have been familiar with it or at least with some its major teachings, as his discussion of dogmatic belief draws on many of the same arguments made in the text.
33. *Kitab al-ʿAlim wa-l-Mutaʿallim*, 14.

34. In classical Hanafi theology this is termed '*taṣdīq bi al-qalb*', or the affirmation of faith in a person's heart, which is distinct from their external actions in the world. In other words, the theological tradition founded by Abu Hanifa and followed by al-Maturidi made a clear distinction between faith (*īmān*) and works ('*āmāl*); for an effective summary of this point, see Watt, *The Formative Period of Islamic Thought*, 128–34. The notion that a person's profession of religious faith is something that cannot be doubted by any other person, because it is an action that is taken inside a person's heart and is therefore inaccessible to any outside observer, is therefore a basic principle of the Hanafi understanding of religious belief. See for instance *Kitab al-ʿAlim wa-l-Mutaʿallim*, 16.
35. Al-Maturidi, *Kitab al-Tawhid*, 467.
36. Al-Maturidi, *Kitab al-Tawhid*, 471–7. Later Ottoman theologians developed this point into an explanation of how human beings can be said to freely choose acts for which they can be held morally liable by God: God judges human beings for their acts because these are the results of their free, inner deliberations. See on this point Dorroll, 'Māturīdī Theology in the Ottoman Empire' and Öçal, 'Osmanlı Kelamcıları Eş'ari miydi?'
37. İzmirli, *Yeni İlm-i Kelam*, 1:21–7 (23–8).
38. İzmirli's use of the term *ıslah* is illuminating. At this point in Ottoman history, this term could be used to refer to a wide range of social and political reforms. It was also used to refer to the creative 'revitalisation' of traditional Islamic thought in the modern context (Özervarlı, *Kelamda Yenilik Arayışları*, 55). The Arabic term from which it was derived (*iṣlāḥ*) is also used in the Qur'an in the sense of 'setting aright', as in 11:88, where the Prophet Shuʿayb says to his people, 'I desire naught but to set matters aright [*iṣlāḥ*] so far as I am able'. İzmirli's use of this term invokes this entire range of meaning, encompassing both sacred and secular dimensions and uniting the language of individual spiritual progress and broader social change.
39. İzmirli, *Yeni İlm-i Kelam*, 1:21–2 (23–4).
40. İzmirli, *Yeni İlm-i Kelam*, 1:22 (24).
41. İzmirli, *Yeni İlm-i Kelam*, 1:21–2 (23).
42. İzmirli, *Yeni İlm-i Kelam*, 1:26 (28).
43. İzmirli, *Yeni İlm-i Kelam*, 1:21 (23). Note how İzmirli here combines pre-modern Islamic ethical terminologies such as justice, moderation and goodness with strikingly modern human rights language, such as the concepts of freedom and equality.
44. İzmirli, *Yeni İlm-i Kelam*, 1:43, 2:151–2 (43, 397).

45. İzmirli, *Yeni İlm-i Kelam*, 1:23–4 (25).
46. For a concise exposition of this point see Kamali, *Shariah Law: Questions and Answers*, 11.
47. İzmirli, *Yeni İlm-i Kelam*, 1:23–4 (25–6).
48. Çelebi, 'Din ve Mahiyeti', 9.
49. Çelebi, 'Din ve Mahiyeti', 11. It is worthwhile to note that Çelebi uses İzmirli's term here, *saadet*.
50. Çelebi, 'Din ve Mahiyeti', 19–20.
51. Özcan, 'Dinin Birey ve Toplum için Anlamı', 135–7.
52. Güler, *Sabit Din, Dinamik Şeriat*, 11.
53. Güler, *Sabit Din, Dinamik Şeriat*, 14.
54. Güler, *Sabit Din, Dinamik Şeriat*, 17.
55. Kamali, 'The Objectives of Islamic Law', 193.
56. Çelebi, *İslam'ın İnanç Esasları*, 17–18.
57. Çelebi, *İslam'ın İnanç Esasları*, 17–18. Note again here that this distinction is very analogous with arguments made by İzmirli in his *New Theology*, as discussed in the previous chapter.
58. Çelebi, *Dini Düşüncede İ'tıdal ve Hoşgörü*, 39.
59. Çelebi, *Dini Düşüncede İ'tıdal ve Hoşgörü*, 39.
60. Çelebi, *Dini Düşüncede İ'tıdal ve Hoşgörü*, 39.
61. Özcan, *Maturidi'de Dini Çoğulculuk*, 33–4.
62. Güler, *Sabit Din, Dinamik Şeriat*, 23. On this point in Güler, see also Aktay, 'Historicist Dispute', 74–5.
63. Güler, *Sabit Din, Dinamik Şeriat*, 26.
64. Güler, *Sabit Din, Dinamik Şeriat*, 27.
65. One of the earliest and most influential *fiqh* theorists and scholars, and founder of a Sunni school of *fiqh*. He is usually credited with the formation of the basic methodology of nearly all subsequent Sunni *fiqh*, and so Güler's critique of his ideas represents an extremely wide-ranging critique of the entirety of the Sunni Islamic legal tradition. As Ahmed El Shamsy's recent study argues, Shafi'i was responsible for the creation of the basic format of Sunni Islamic legal thought by canonising a conception of Sunni tradition and applying a synthesis of rationalist and textualist interpretive approaches to that canon in order to systematically develop Sunni *fiqh*. See *The Canonization of Islamic Law*, 70–7.
66. Güler, *Sabit Din, Dinamik Şeriat*, 32–6.
67. Güler, *Sabit Din, Dinamik Şeriat*, 38–9.
68. Köse, *Çağdaş İhtiyaçlar ve İslam Hukuku*, 43.

69. As Bernard Weiss notes, the *Shari'ah* 'is not given to man ready-made, to be passively received and applied; rather, it is to be actively constructed on the basis of those sacred texts which are its acknowledged sources'. See Weiss, 'Interpretation in Islamic Law', 199. The ongoing process of actively interpreting and deriving the details of Islamic religious practice from the revelation is termed in Arabic *ijtihād*.
70. Köse, *Çağdaş İhtiyaçlar ve İslam Hukuku*, 43.
71. Köse, *Çağdaş İhtiyaçlar ve İslam Hukuku*, 45.
72. According to traditional Islamic ritual and ethical practice, in order for a human being to be held accountable by God for their actions they must be of mature age, be of sound mind, and possessing the requisite bodily and/or financial requirements to satisfy the ritual duties. Much of *fiqh* is devoted to discussing the specifics and nuances of these issues.
73. Köse, 'Kuran Hükümlerini Doğru Anlamak'.
74. Köse, *Çağdaş İhtiyaçlar ve İslam Hukuku*, 52, 62.
75. Köse, *Çağdaş İhtiyaçlar ve İslam Hukuku*, 62.
76. Köse, *İslam Hukukuna Giriş*, 209.
77. Köse, *Çağdaş İhtiyaçlar ve İslam Hukuku*, 67.
78. The question of which pre-modern *fiqh* rulings are subject to change over time invariably brings up the issue of punishments mentioned in the Qur'an for moral offences such as adultery. It is worth noting here that the idea of implementing pre-modern *fiqh* punishments (such as lashing, stoning, and so on) has been extremely unpopular with the Turkish populace, devout and secular alike, for decades. Surveys conducted in Turkey from the 1970s to the 2000s have consistently shown less than 10% support for government based on *Shari'ah* law (which is, for instance, far lower than average American support for the use of the Bible as a source of law, or for a constitutional amendment declaring Christianity the official religion of the state). Moreover, even conservative Muslim movements in Turkey that have referred to *Shari'ah* almost never argue for the instatement of *Shari'ah* as a civil code, but have instead referred to it as a programme for conservative social values (Dorroll, 'Shari'a and the Secular in Modern Turkey', 131–2). Köse himself notes that the decision of whether or how to implement these Quranic punishments is, as a general rule of *fiqh*, left to the discretion of the civil authorities, as has been the case throughout Islamic history (*Çağdaş İhtiyaçlar ve İslam Hukuku*, 85, 250, 381). Discussion of the validity of these Quranic rulings emerges from a desire to protect the integrity of the

revelation as a whole, rather than to suggest ways to implement such rulings in the present day.

79. Köse, *Çağdaş İhtiyaçlar ve İslam Hukuku*, 66.
80. Köse, *Çağdaş İhtiyaçlar ve İslam Hukuku*, 67.
81. Köse, *Çağdaş İhtiyaçlar ve İslam Hukuku*, 71.
82. Köse, *Çağdaş İhtiyaçlar ve İslam Hukuku*, 71.
83. Özcan, 'Dinin Birey ve Toplum için Anlamı', 139.
84. Köse, *Çağdaş İhtiyaçlar ve İslam Hukuku*, 52.
85. This does not of course mean that Turkish theologians agree on what exactly a democracy should look like in practice, as demonstrated in Chapter 2 and as will be discussed in Chapter 5. The appeal to democracy, freedom and equality is nearly universal in modern Turkish political discourse – but what these terms mean is subject to extreme differences in political opinion.
86. The arguments in this section are reminiscent of the main themes of Egyptian theologian and political philosopher 'Ali 'Abd al-Raziq's 1925 work, *Islam and the Foundations of Political Power*.
87. Interestingly, Muhammad Iqbal noted the rise of Turkish Muslim theological and cultural support for representative government as it happened at the beginning of the Turkish Republic (Iqbal, *Reconstruction of Religious Thought*, 124–5).
88. See on this point Hashemi, *Islam, Secularism and Liberal Democracy*.
89. Köse, *Çağdaş İhtiyaçlar ve İslam Hukuku*, 246.
90. Köse, *Çağdaş İhtiyaçlar ve İslam Hukuku*, 246–7.
91. Köse, *Çağdaş İhtiyaçlar ve İslam Hukuku*, 250.
92. Köse, *Çağdaş İhtiyaçlar ve İslam Hukuku*, 251.
93. Bardakoğlu, 'Teorik Açıdan İslam ve Demokrasi: Yasama', 362.
94. Uludağ, 'Teorik Açıdan İslam ve Demokrasi: Yargı', 399. 'Abd al-Raziq made the same point in 1925 (see *Islam and the Foundations of Political Power*, 92).
95. Uludağ, 'Teorik Açıdan İslam ve Demokrasi: Yargı', 400. For other useful summaries of the kinds of pro-democracy arguments made in modern Turkish Islamic thought, see Koyuncu, 'İslami Yönetimde Demokrasi var mıdır?'
96. Yıldırım, 'Din-Devlet İlişkisine Bakışı', 156.
97. Düzgün, 'Matüridi'de Din, Siyaset Kültürü ve Yönetim Erki', 351. Wilkinson's *Dialectical Encounters* includes a thorough and authoritative analysis of Düzgün's theology.
98. Wilkinson, *Dialectical Encounters*, 129.
99. Kecia Ali, *Sexual Ethics and Islam*, xxi.

100. Tuksal received her doctorate in theology from the Ankara University Faculty of Theology and her work is likely the first systematic utilisation of feminist theory in modern Turkish theology. She has long been a prominent activist for social and gender justice, particularly in the struggle against the Turkish state's discrimination against pious headscarf-wearing Muslim women in Turkey in the 1980s and 1990s. She has also publicly opposed bans on abortion, spoken out against homophobia and toxic masculinity in Turkish culture, and against Turkish racism against Syrian refugees, and has been a strong critic of human rights abuses under the AKP government. For discussions of her work, see Aksoy, 'Invigorating Democracy in Turkey', 159–66; Arat, 'Islamist Women and Feminist Concerns', 128, 140–2; Jelen, 'Educated, Independent, and Covered', 316–17; Korteweg and Yurdakul, *The Headscarf Debates*, 92; and Tajali, 'Islamic Women's Groups', 573.
101. Tuksal, *Kadın Karşıtı Söylemi*, 20–1. This landmark work, *Projections of Misogynistic Discourse in Islamic Tradition*, was first published in 2001.
102. Tuksal, *Kadın Karşıtı Söylemi*, 27; Tuksal, 'Misogynistic Reports', 154.
103. Tuksal, *Kadın Karşıtı Söylemi*, 27.
104. Tuksal, *Kadın Karşıtı Söylemi*, 275.
105. Tuksal, *Kadın Karşıtı Söylemi*, 31.
106. Tuksal, 'Misogynistic Reports', 134–5.
107. Tuksal, *Kadın Karşıtı Söylemi*, 31.
108. Tuksal, *Kadın Karşıtı Söylemi*, 46.
109. Tuksal, *Kadın Karşıtı Söylemi*, 48.
110. Tuksal, *Kadın Karşıtı Söylemi*, 48–50. This is one of the theses of amina wadud's classic study. According to wadud, in the Quranic worldview, men and women 'have the same rights and obligations on the ethico-religious level' (see *Qur'an and Woman*, 102).
111. Tuksal, *Kadın Karşıtı Söylemi*, 49.
112. Tuksal, *Kadın Karşıtı Söylemi*, 51.
113. Tuksal, *Kadın Karşıtı Söylemi*, 71.
114. Tuksal, 'Misogynistic Reports', 151–2.
115. Tuksal, *Kadın Karşıtı Söylemi*, 275.
116. Tuksal, 'Misogynistic Reports', 135.
117. Tuksal, 'Misogynistic Reports', 134.
118. Tuksal, *Kadın Karşıtı Söylemi*, 262. The Islamic tradition unanimously asserts that conscious intent and engagement is a necessary precondition for valid ritual prayer. As Marion Holmes Katz puts it in her important study on Islamic

prayer, 'the basic function of [intention] is to distinguish the ritual of prayer from other, merely routine activities', denoting its status as worship rather than a worldly activity. See *Prayer in Islamic Thought and Practice*, 5.
119. Tuksal, *Kadın Karşıtı Söylemi*, 262–5.
120. Tuksal, *Kadın Karşıtı Söylemi*, 265–9.
121. Tuksal, *Kadın Karşıtı Söylemi*, 266; Tuksal, 'Misogynistic Reports', 150–1; *Sahih Muslim:* Kitab al-Salat,1032. Here and in citations below I have slightly modified Siddiqui's translations for clarity where necessary.
122. *Sahih Muslim*: Kitab al-Salat, 1034.
123. Tuksal, *Kadın Karşıtı Söylemi*, 274.
124. Tuksal, *Kadın Karşıtı Söylemi*, 269; Spellberg, *Politics, Gender, and the Islamic Past*, 9–17. See Spellberg's landmark study for a comprehensive discussion of the complexity of 'A'isha's reception and legacy in the pre-modern Islamic intellectual tradition.
125. Tuksal, *Kadın Karşıtı Söylemi*, 270.
126. *Sahih Muslim*: Kitab al-Salat, 1037; Tuksal, *Kadın Karşıtı Söylemi*, 270.
127. *Sahih Muslim*: Kitab al-Salat, 1038.
128. Tuksal, *Kadın Karşıtı Söylemi*, 269–70.
129. Sayeed, *Women and the Transmission of Knowledge in Islam*, 26.
130. Collector of one of the six canonical books of Sunni hadith.
131. One of the most influential early Muslim *fiqh* scholars and founder of the Maliki school of Sunni *fiqh*.
132. Tuksal, *Kadın Karşıtı Söylemi*, 271–2.
133. Collector of one of the six canonical books of Sunni hadith, the *Sahih Muslim* referenced above.
134. Tuksal, *Kadın Karşıtı Söylemi*, 272–4; Tuksal, 'Misogynistic Reports', 150–2.
135. Tuksal, *Kadın Karşıtı Söylemi*, 272.
136. *Sahih Muslim*: Kitab al-Salat, 1027. As a subsequent narrator notes, it is unclear in this particular report what length of time is meant. The main point is of course that passing in front of someone during prayer is a grave sin.
137. Tuksal, *Kadın Karşıtı Söylemi*, 274.
138. Tuksal, *Kadın Karşıtı Söylemi*, 274.
139. Tuksal, 'Kadın Gözüyle Hz. Peygamber', 74
140. Tuksal, 'Misogynistic Reports', 154.

5

FUTURES

Having outlined the basic contours of the history and main themes of modern Turkish theology, this chapter turns to a discussion of the possible future directions Turkish theology might take. As the previous chapters have demonstrated, modern Turkish theology is both deeply rooted in Islamic tradition and highly creative in the ways it interprets this tradition in the light of modern social change. Its development and sophistication rival any other modern theological tradition. The challenges that lie before it are not, therefore, related to any particular intellectual shortcoming within its modern tradition. Instead, this chapter argues that the primary challenge that lies before Turkish theology, and the main factor that will influence its future development, is the impact of the Turkish state. This chapter will show that the politicisation of theology by the Turkish state throughout the history of the Republic remains the most influential factor in the range of possible future directions of Turkish theology.

More specifically, this chapter will explore the consequences that the modern Turkish statist tradition has had on theology, arguing that the Turkish government's statist approach to religion throughout the twentieth and twenty-first century has meant that the government maintains the power to nurture or to stifle the organic development of theological discourse in the country. The centralised statist supervision of religion in Turkey means that the widespread success of any given theological school of thought or particular theological argument is contingent on its acceptance by the Turkish government's central ministry for religious affairs, or *Diyanet İşleri Başkanlığı* – known simply as the Diyanet. Established in 1924, this institution was given legal jurisdiction over all Muslim religious institutions in the country, requiring all mosques and their personnel to be officially registered with and authorised by this department of the central government.[1]

As we will see below, this means that the degree to which the state chooses to assert jurisdiction over theology in Turkey is the most crucial social and political factor in the future of its development. If the Turkish government chooses to support a given theological school of thought or specific theological argument, that school or argument has the possibility of attaining wide acceptance. If, however, the Turkish government chooses to direct its power towards the suppression of a given school or argument, this makes the widespread acceptance of that argument much more difficult.

This chapter will distinguish two phases in the history of the modern Turkish state's intervention into the development of Turkish theology. The first is the way in which secular Kemalist discourses from the founding of the Republic to the rise of the AKP have suppressed conservative religious thought and practice through a secularist form of Kemalist statism. The second phase is the way the AKP has carried on this statist tradition in ways that have both benefitted the development of theology in Turkey and at the same time limited its possibilities.

Specifically, the AKP administration has revolutionised the future of Turkish theology through its patronage of theology faculties and its encouragement of women's participation in theological studies and positions of religious authority in the Diyanet. At the same time, AKP theological discourses have stifled theological arguments that contradict their vision of social morality, in particular the voices of LGBTI+ affirming Muslim theologians and activists. Given the power the Turkish state has to influence the direction of theology in the Republic, this chapter argues overall that the future of Turkish theology will be deeply influenced by the way the Turkish state chooses to engage with it.

Statism and Politics in Modern Turkey

In her landmark study of the Diyanet, İştar Gözaydın argues that the relationship between the Turkish state and religion is based on a strong conception of the role of the state that has underpinned Turkish politics and governance since the founding of the Republic.[2] This strong notion of statism (*devletçilik*) has played a central role in the modern Turkish Republic in governing the relationship between social forces and the government itself. The Turkish state has frequently seen its administrative legitimacy as constantly under siege by hostile social forces outside of its ranks. Modern Turkish statism has therefore seen politics and culture as legitimate only insofar as they do not threaten the legitimacy of the state, rather than as realms of social practice that have the moral authority to challenge and alter the governmental practices of the state.

Since the founding of the Turkish Republic, dissident forms of religion have been seen by the Turkish state as among the most potentially dangerous of all social forces because they have the capability to challenge the state itself for legitimate control of society. Religion represents such a serious potential threat to the state's monopolistic control of social morality because it can easily present an alternative vision of morality that is immediately compelling to millions of citizens of every social class and background. In other words, religion has a mobilising power that can match and outstrip that of the state. For this reason, in the Turkish Republic religion has always been subject to close state supervision under the principle of *laiklik*, or Turkish laicism.

Laiklik refers to the particularly strong version of secularism practised by the modern Turkish Republic whereby the state retains the right to approve and supervise all formal religious institutions and organisations in the country. *Laiklik* can be defined as a highly statist form of governmental secularism. This statist control is distinguished from individual freedom of religious expression, which is considered a fundamental right. *Laiklik* dictates that the state itself may not be based on any specific religious principle or reference, but that the state reserves the right to supervise religious institutions. Thus, the Turkish state's administration of religious institutions can have a dramatic influence over the intellectual discourses available in the public sphere, as this chapter will argue in detail. Religious discourses such as theology are therefore seen by the Turkish state as legitimate objects of control. This means that throughout the history of the Turkish Republic, the state has wielded its coercive power to influence the direction that theological reflection takes in Turkey.[3]

Ironically, this statist approach to religion is reinforced by the unintended consequences of late Ottoman and early Republican theological discussions. As noted in previous chapters, one of the key features of modern Turkish theology from the late Ottoman period to the present is the pervasive influence of universal human rights discourses and an Islamic modernist conception of religion that distinguishes it from the political. As detailed above, this does not mean that Turkish theologians do not consider religion to be a social phenomenon; quite the contrary. At the same time, the theological language of universal human rights, and the distinction between the changeable and unchangeable that figures prominently in modern Turkish theology, have been easily co-opted by the laicist Turkish state for its own purposes.

For instance, the act passed in 1924 by the Turkish parliament that established the Diyanet granted it authority over the administration of all Islamic religious affairs, institutions and practices in Turkey, which it defines as *itikadat* and *ibadat* (belief and worship).[4] These are, it will be recalled, the exact categories of Islamic religion that modern Turkish theological discourse customarily defines as the unchanging essence of Islam, in explicit contrast to political systems (which are subject to change over time). It is highly unlikely that late Ottoman theologians such as İzmirli had French laicism in mind when they developed their thinking on the necessary conceptual distinction between the unchangeable essence of religious truth and the changeable realities of human social life. This distinction, however, came to be considered useful by the Kemalist state as it developed its policy of statist control over religious affairs.

In other words, once religion became theologically distinct from politics in modern Turkish theological discourse, this meant that the essence of religion was understood to exist naturally outside the boundaries of the state. From the perspective of Turkish statism, however, this meant that religion constituted a social power (to use Gözaydın's phrase) that could threaten the state, thus necessitating its supervision. The key point here is not that the theological discourse of late Ottoman Islamic modernism itself argued for state control of religion, but that the late Ottoman and early Turkish Republican theological arguments that defined religion as ultimately transcendent in nature, but at the same time socially significant, were taken up by the Turkish state as justification for its assertion of jurisdiction over religious affairs. The statist politics of theology in Turkey are therefore the key to understanding the possible futures that Turkish theology might embrace.

Having defined modern Turkish statism, we now look at exactly what constitutes 'politics' in the modern Turkish context. As with other aspects of human existence, such as aesthetics, ethics or religion, the political has its own distinctive definition.[5] Carl Schmitt defines 'the political' as the social actualisation of 'concrete antagonism' between groups of people.[6] 'The political' expresses an existential reality that is fundamental to human life, a reality that cannot be simply reduced to other realms of human existence such as the economic, the ethical, the aesthetic, the religious or the ethnic. 'Politics' is the term used to refer to the dynamics of social conflict; it is the realm of human experience that has to do with social conflict, contest and competition.[7] The political is based on the most fundamental motivation of separation in human existence – the distinction 'between friend and enemy'.[8]

The political therefore refers to the natural experience of conflict that is a basic element of human existence. Schmitt asserts that the friend-enemy distinction is an unavoidable component of human relationships, and therefore he is highly critical of what he views as liberalism's attempt to efface this reality by striving for a social state that eliminates the possibility of armed conflict. Otherness in human relations, in a negative sense, is inevitable and may even be the key to group solidarity. In this sense 'the political enemy' does not have to correspond to moral conflict or even economic competition. Its mere otherness is enough for a threat to be perceived, and for conflict to be possible.[9]

Schmitt's analysis of the political includes a number of dimensions that are particularly germane to a discussion of Turkish statism. In the situation of social conflict (that is, in a political situation in Schmitt's sense of the term), the mutual antagonism between two parties is based on the perception of threat to one's existence and way of life.[10] Each party fears and opposes the other because it fears the possibility that the other might take away its own ability to live as it chooses, or even to live at all. Schmitt's analysis of the political implies that even though the experience of the political is itself an irreducible phenomenon, what causes the political to emerge has to do with a perceived threat to one's own existence. This accounts for the existential dimension of the political in the first place. In other words, the most urgent reason to define another person or group as a political other is if they are perceived as an existential threat. There is no stronger reason to initiate a situation of conflict (that is, a political situation) between two parties.

Schmitt's notion of the political therefore helps us to understand how Turkish statism and laicism conceives of what is at stake in politics. Since the founding of the Republic, the tradition of Turkish statism has understood the legitimacy of state control of religion in terms of the defence of the state from its enemies who seek to undermine it. Turkish statism treats politics exactly in the way defined by Schmitt – as a process of securing one's existence by means of defeating external enemies. According to Turkish statism, theology is capable of producing enemies of the state, thus necessitating state intervention into the development of theology in modern Turkey.

The Politics of Theology I: Mid-century Secular Kemalism

In order to demonstrate the importance of the Turkish state to the future of Islamic theology in the Turkish Republic, this chapter charts how the Turkish state has decisively affected the development of Turkish theology in the past and in the present. The first phase of this history concerns one particular kind of Kemalist politics and ideology, which as a larger political tradition is highly variable. The term 'secular Kemalism' is used here to refer to strains of modern Turkish administration and political ideology that focus on a secular, linguistic ethnicity as the definition of Turkish identity. In secular Kemalism, Turkish language and national culture are key to what it means to be a Turk, whereas Muslim piety is treated as only appropriate in the private sphere and potentially threatening to positivist social values when emphasised in public. This particular type of Kemalist attitude towards religion took hold of Turkish state policy with the consolidation of the authoritarian Kemalist state in the 1930s.[11]

Use of the phrase 'secular Kemalism' is necessary here because the Kemalist political movement throughout Turkish history is highly multi-vocal and ambiguous with respect to religion, and is notoriously difficult to define as a coherent ideology. As Sinan Ciddi points out, 'Kemalism' is best understood as the specific social and political modernisation policies carried out under the government of Turkey's first president, Mustafa Kemal Atatürk. These policies were specifically tailored to the social and cultural context of the new

Turkish nation. Thus, the modern Turkish state, or the Kemalist state, never articulated a universal ideology, leaving the notion of 'Kemalism' difficult to define as a coherent ideological programme.[12] Therefore, this chapter refers to 'secular Kemalism' in order to pinpoint the modern Turkish state's policies and ideologies that sought to restrict the growth of public Muslim piety. Secular Kemalist policies lead to the repression of the individual rights of devout Muslim citizens, most especially in the 1930s and 1940s but lasting in various forms (such as headscarf bans) throughout the twentieth century. Importantly, it was these types of secular Kemalist attitudes towards religion that dominated the Diyanet into the twentieth century, and up until the rise of the AKP. This shift in the Turkish statist management of religion is the shift charted throughout this chapter as a way to show just how important Turkish statism will continue to be to the future development of Islamic theology in the Turkish Republic.

In order to ideologically justify the repression of devout Muslims in the modern Turkish Republic, secular Kemalist policies and ideologues developed a Schmittian conception of the political danger of Muslim religious practice. The term used in early to mid-twentieth-century secular Kemalist discourse to refer to religious political enemies is *irtica*, or 'reactionism', meaning a reaction by backward elements against secular Kemalist progress, in particular the representatives of socially conservative Islamic thought and practice.[13] As Umut Azak points out, for secular Kemalists at the beginning of the Republic, this term signified the consummate enemy of their entire political project, a political project that depended on the state control of religion. At the beginning of the Republic, the Turkish state politicised the positivist social values of laicism in order to depict its most serious religious opponents as dangerous reactionaries bent on arresting the progress of the secular Kemalist modernisation project.[14]

This term became a key component of the secular Kemalist ideological lexicon after the 'Menemen Incident' in 1930, when a young teacher was beheaded by the leader of an Islamic insurrection against the Kemalist regime.[15] Mustafa Fehmi Kubilay, who died at the age of twenty-four, became a martyr for the secular Kemalist cause (then only seven years into its political administration) and the leaders of the republic in Ankara made elaborate arrangements to memorialise his sacrifice. Every year this sacrifice is commemorated in the small city of Menemen north of Izmir on Turkey's Aegean coast, attracting thousands of participants showing their support for the secular Kemalist vision of society.[16] The uprising at Menemen came to symbolise the notion that the secular Kemalist vision faces an ever-present danger from conservative, reactionary Islamic forces who would seek to arrest Turkey's progress towards modernity. These forces are the extreme political enemy of secular Kemalism, its clearest political other.

The notion of a conservative, irrational and religiously authoritarian Islam epitomised in the concept of reactionsim would come to constitute the enemy of some influential strains of Turkish theology that were patronised by the state in the middle of the twentieth century. The term *irtica*, loaded as it is with the concrete politics of the 1920s and 1930s, is by no means a common theological term. Instead, some Turkish theologians during the middle of the twentieth century defined their ideological counterparts in ways that suggest the accusation of *irtica*. This was the primary example of the politicisation of Turkish theology before the rise of the AKP.

Yusuf Ziya Yörükan's work is an example of theological discourses that were strongly influenced by secular Kemalist politics. In his summary of Muslim belief and practice published in 1957, he argued that Islam's fundamental theology of God's Oneness, *tevhid*, is based on a vision of social progress, social order and the 'cleansing [of] society from superstitions'.[17] For Yörükan, the essential meaning of the theology of *tevhid* is that the belief in the rational truth of the One God necessitates belief in the positivistic values of progress, order and the absolute value of scientific knowledge. As in his theology more generally, Yörükan stands as a kind of intermediary between secular Kemalism and the broader tradition of Islamic modernist thought. He adopts his positivistic moral concepts from secular Kemalist discourse.[18] His use of the term 'superstition' echoes the way this term is used in the secular Kemalist definition of *irtica*, and the way it has been used by the Diyanet to control religious practice in Turkey.[19]

As with secular Kemalist political thought, Yörükan is particularly critical of Islamic religious practice that resists the civilising discourse of positivist modernism. During his discussion of *ijtihād*, he argues that this classical Arabic term for independent reasoning in *Shari'ah* refers to the ability of any devout Muslim to make personal choices on how to best practice Islam to suit one's current situation. He alludes by way of contrast to *mutaassıplar*, a rather strong term which can be rendered into English as 'fanatics' or 'bigots'.[20] This is how Yörükan refers to any Muslim who opposes the idea that specific provisions of the *Shari'ah* or other elements of traditional Islamic religious thought can be amended or even abandoned if they no longer prove suitable for current social conditions. For Yörükan, the unwillingness to identify those elements of traditional Islamic religious practice that must be discarded or reformed in the light of modern conditions is a major religious error in the Muslim context.

In his critique of Turkish Sufism, Yörükan presents a summary of the concrete social phenomenon that he sees as the clearest embodiment of these conservative Islamic religious errors: *tarikatçılık*, a term that refers to the institutionalised Sufi religious orders that flourished during the Ottoman period, but is imbued with much deeper ideological significance (no doubt as a consequence of the secular Kemalist assault on the Sufi orders as the quintessential enemy of the enlightened and progressive Turkish state). While acknowledging that many features of traditional Sufism are highly honourable components of Islamic practice (such as the control of worldly appetites and the pursuit of piety), Yörükan attacks institutionalised Sufism as the vehicle for the fanatical and reactionary trends of Islamic thought that he so strongly opposes.

He describes *tarikatçılık* as a direct threat to the future of the Turkish nation that must be distinguished from genuine piety. It can only be defeated by proper religious education, and it must be vigorously combatted in order to save the Turkish nation from backwardness.[21] In his own striking words, conservative Sufi groups 'drag the nation into discord, incite the people to fanaticism and ignorance, and pave the way to indolence'.[22] Yörükan uses this highly politicised terminology to describe a larger religious attitude that he sees as the most serious threat to contemporary Islam: religious conservatism or anti-modernism.

Yörükan's critique of Sufism is closely related to similar arguments made by Islamic modernists from the late nineteenth and early twentieth centuries, such as the critique of Sufism found in Rashid Rida and Muhammad 'Abduh's *Tafsir al-Manar*.[23] Since Yörükan mentions 'Abduh as one of the main sources for his own theology, it is likely that his critique of Sufism was influenced by his reading of works such as *Tafsir al-Manar*, though the critique of Sufism in this particular work most probably belongs more to Rida than 'Abduh.[24] Yörükan's adoption of this argument was probably most influenced by his dislike of the kinds of conservative Sufi opposition to the secular Kemalist state that came to be identified with the term *irtica*.

The critique of Sufi spirituality as a source of irrational superstition also features prominently in the works of later Islamic modernists, most notably Fazlur Rahman, who argued that institutional Sufism in the Muslim world has been responsible for the spread of superstitious attachment to saints and miracles, thus contributing to the debasement of Islamic thought and practice. Such beliefs, in his view, have 'enchained the minds and spirits' of Muslims around the globe, across all education levels.[25] Rahman counts the rooting out of this kind of irrational spirituality to be one of the most urgent goals of Islamic reformism. His continuing critique of Sufi spirituality probably also influenced subsequent generations of Turkish Muslim modernists, who counted him as one of their most important influences in the 1980s and 1990s.[26]

Some Turkish theologians who identified themselves with the revival of al-Maturidi in the mid-twentieth century were also influenced by this secular Kemalist political discourse. Ahmet Vehbi Ecer, for instance, has utilised the same terminology as Yörükan, referring to the ever-present threat of 'fanatical *tarikatçılık*' (*mutaasıp tarikatçılık*).[27] Ecer describes this phenomenon in terms very reminiscent of Yörükan, but focuses to a much greater degree on the need for a revival of Maturidism to counteract this conservative Islamic threat. Ecer argues that al-Maturidi's rational and scientific theology can save the Turkish nation from 'disunity, lethargy, and backwardness'.[28] Ecer's popularised and highly politicised descriptions of al-Maturidi's theology are therefore a particularly arresting example of the intersection of theological discourse with secular Kemalism in the mid-twentieth century.

As will be discussed below, the marginalisation of conservative Muslims by the secular Kemalist state contributed greatly to the rise of the AKP. The intersection of the otherising discourse of *irtica* with some versions of mid-century Turkish theology contributed to this marginalisation by excluding many pious Muslims from academic theological institutions and discourses. In response to this othering, the AKP would revolutionise theology in Turkey by supporting academic theology in ways never imagined under the secular Kemalist regimes of the twentieth century. Over time, however, the AKP's politicisation of theology would come to mirror that of the secular Kemalists of the twentieth century. As we will see, the AKP's unprecedented level of support for diverse theological voices would transform into policies that restricted dissenting theologies in much the same way that the secular Kemalists had done in the previous decades.

The Politics of Theology II: The Early AKP (2002–11)

The second phase of the politicisation of theology in Turkey mirrored the statism of the first phase, but differed in the specific ideology espoused by the state. The current ruling party of Turkey, the AKP (*Adalet ve Kalkınma Partisi*, or the Justice and Development Party), began its early years (from 2002 to 2011)[29] by championing the opposition to the secular Kemalist authoritarianism described above. It pledged to further democratise Turkish politics and society by weakening the power of the state to control individual religious expression. During this period, measures initiated by the AKP resulted in a renaissance of academic theology in Turkey, and the AKP administration took massive strides in addressing the patriarchal gender imbalance in Turkish theological academia and at the Diyanet. These institutional and structural changes in Turkish theology were genuinely salutary and revolutionary: they dramatically raised the profile and quality of theological academia in the country and injected it with a new vitality unseen since the end of the Ottoman Empire.

As will be further described in this section, however, the AKP eventually transformed into the mirror image of the repressive secular Kemalism of which it had been so critical. In the second half of its history (2011 to the present), the politics of the AKP acted as a mechanism to restrict, rather than enable, creative theological expression in the country. As the AKP's governance style became more and more authoritarian, it asserted both discursive and institutional control over Islamic theological discourses in Turkey, resulting in the deliberate marginalisation of theologies deemed contrary to conservative Islam (such as LGBTI+ affirming theology, as will be demonstrated at the end of this chapter).

The AKP came to power in 2002 on a wave of popular resentment due to the economic crisis of 2000–1 and a general opposition to the anti-democratic and anti-liberal policies of the secular Kemalist state that had been developing for decades. The illiberal tendencies of Kemalist secularism in particular were epitomised in the 1990s by the exclusion of pious headscarf-wearing Muslim women from state buildings (such as universities), and the 1997 soft coup initiated by the Turkish military that dissolved the elected civilian government. The AKP was founded by a group of pious conservative Muslim politicians (Recep Tayyip Erdoğan, Abdullah Gül and Bülent Arınç) after the 1997 coup, and their party platform disavowed both Islamism and Kemalist secularism, seeking a third way that recognised the Islamic heritage of Turkish culture while at the same time securing genuine democratic liberties and economic development for every citizen of the Turkish Republic.[30] These twin goals, democratisation development and economic development, are summed up in the name of the party itself: the 'Justice and Development Party'.

This ideological programme appealed to a wide variety of constituencies in Turkey, including secular liberals who had become critical of the Turkish state's infringements of the individual freedoms of both pious Muslims and religious and ethnic minorities; and pious conservatives who had been both culturally marginalised by the state and economically marginalised due to the economic underdevelopment of rural areas of the country. The AKP positioned itself as a party dedicated to fighting for the rights and advancements of anyone previously marginalised by the secular Kemalism that had become the norm since the founding of the Republic.[31] As M. Hakan Yavuz has argued, the political rise of the AKP represented in effect a larger movement away from secular ethnic nationalism towards 'a more multi-cultural understanding of nation'.[32]

The AKP programme, quite notably, did not oppose secularism itself. Instead, it proposed a new definition of secularism that mirrored the American model of protecting individual religious liberties from the state. AKP ideology distinguished this form of secularism from the older Kemalist model of secularism (*laiklik*) that restricted personal religious expression in the name of protecting society and the state from religious influence.[33] Since its founding, the AKP described itself as a 'conservative democratic party', an identity that it stressed was neither Islamist nor anti-religious. While the AKP's early programme stressed the centrality of Islamic tradition to Turkish identity, it also stressed that key to this tradition was a respect for individual freedom and self-expression that the AKP would draw on in its opposition to the homogenous nationalism of the secular Kemalists. Thus, in its early years, the AKP described itself as a political movement that embraced a wide variety of cultural, political, social and religious identities.[34] During its first years in power, its political style was generally pragmatic, as it pursued the goal of broadly improving quality of life in Turkey.[35]

The AKP's official party programme in 2002 therefore heavily stressed universal human rights discourses, arguing that the AKP's combination of cautious and conservative social change with a liberalising economic and democratising political agenda was the ideal way forward for Turkish politics in the new millennium. The programme explicitly aligns the party with international universal human rights standards, and places these principles at the centre of its social vision. Strikingly, the programme even includes the famous dictum that 'unless everyone is free, no one is free'.[36] The use of universal human rights discourses was both a strategic decision by the AKP to defend itself from its secular Kemalist critics and a natural philosophical outgrowth of its belief in the necessity to improve the lives of marginalised peoples in the Turkish Republic.[37]

During the AKP's first years in power, these principles ushered in a host of democratisation initiatives. As part of this climate of encouraging civil society and debate, and consonant with its general interest in shoring up the Islamic identity of Turkish society, the AKP initiated an unprecedented level of support for academic theology in Turkey. At the end of the 1980s, only nine faculties of theology existed in Turkey.[38] In January of 2019, according to the head of the Diyanet Ali Erbaş, there were 105.[39] According to government statistics, the current number of students enrolled in faculties of theology at the vocational and undergraduate level in Turkey exceeds 96,000. Of this number, 60 per cent are women.[40] Erbaş rightly emphasised in the same announcement that this development represented a victory over the unjust repression and marginalisation of religious academic study at various periods throughout the history of the Republic.

It is worth pausing over these simple but extraordinary statistics. The meteoric increase in the number of faculties of theology and the number of theology students, and in particular the predominance of female students in these faculties, represents a turning point in the history of the Turkish

Republic. Professional students and scholars of Islamic theology in Turkey, once relegated to the fringes of academic life and public debate, have emerged as some of the most influential voices in contemporary Turkish culture. It is nearly impossible to calculate the number of theses, dissertations and other academic projects that have emerged over the past decade and a half as a result of this development. Indeed, it is no exaggeration to say that modern Turkish theology has reached its current state of sophistication and maturity thanks to the political and financial support of the AKP government.

Alongside the predominance of female students in the theology faculties, AKP policies within the Diyanet have resulted in an historic increase in the number of female religious authorities in Turkey. As Chiara Maritato's extensive research has shown, women's participation and influence in religious life in Turkey has been dramatically redefined via the AKP's transformation of the Diyanet.[41] The Diyanet's policy of addressing gender inequities in Sunni Islamic institutions in Turkey, initiated by the new AKP administration shortly after its first election to power, has radically improved women's access to religious spaces, education and leadership (including in theology). This effort has been led by prominent female religious leaders and theologians, such as then vice Mufti of Istanbul, Kadriye Avcı Erdemli, who began (in 2012) and then led the programme to improve women's spaces in mosques.[42]

The Diyanet has employed women as religious specialists since the 1960s, but the number of women enrolling in theological education and seeking careers in this field increased dramatically in the 1980s and 1990s.[43] Following the 1997 coup, the ban on wearing religious garb in state institutions began to be rigorously enforced, thus leaving many women who wore headscarves without jobs or career prospects.[44] Women who wished to attend a state university were forced to remove their headscarf in order to do so. The marginalisation of pious Muslim women by the Turkish state even affected duly elected members of parliament. In May of 1999, newly elected MP Merve Kavakçı entered the parliament building while wearing a headscarf to take her oath of office. She was jeered so viciously by other members of parliament that she was forced to leave the building. Merely for wearing a headscarf in the parliament building, she was accused by then President Süleyman Demirel of attempting to undermine the Turkish state and the Turkish nation itself, and she was later stripped of her Turkish citizenship.[45]

The AKP's policy of hiring women to work in the Diyanet as religious experts and the AKP's sponsorship of theological education throughout the country were actions taken to address these injustices, and such measures have dramatically reduced the marginalisation of women that occurred under the secular Kemalist administration of the Diyanet.[46] One of the most notable examples of this change concerned the employment of female preachers, an official profession within the Diyanet system. Because all mosques and their staff must be approved by the Diyanet, the Diyanet has developed specific professional roles to serve in each mosque. One of these is the preacher, who serves as an officially trained and recognised religious expert and educator for the faithful (the Friday sermon is delivered by the leader of the prayers, the imam).[47] When the AKP won election to power in 2002, there were a few dozen professional female preachers in Turkey. The AKP's revitalised Diyanet quickly initiated a policy of 'positive discrimination' to increase the number of women working in this field.[48]

By 2013, there were 727 professional female preachers in Turkey, 48 per cent of the total. In Istanbul, there were 54 female preachers, 44 per cent of the total.[49] Female religious leadership in the Diyanet has increased in other striking ways during this period. In 2005, two women were appointed as deputy muftis, one in Istanbul, by far the largest city in the country; these positions meant oversight of religious guidance and education for millions of people.[50] In March of 2018, the head of the Diyanet announced plans to appoint women as deputy muftis for all provinces in the country.[51] In 2017, Professor Dr Huriye Martı was appointed deputy director of the entire Diyanet.

These women have had an incalculable influence over religious life and theology in contemporary Turkey, directly resulting from the AKP's administration of the Diyanet. At the present moment, women are serving at the highest levels of religious expertise throughout Turkey, and will probably form the majority of academically trained specialists in theology and Islamic religious studies for years to come. Combined with the AKP's patronage of theological academia and education in general, these developments have amounted to a revolution in the history of Turkish Islam.

What is important to note here is that these developments are in fact a result of one particular way in which the AKP has politicised theology in

Turkey. The fact that the AKP used its statist authority over religion in these ways has resulted in previously unthinkable levels of advancement in theological studies and religious practice in Turkey. It is also important to note that these initiatives were a direct result of the AKP's concern for universal human rights during its first years in power. In the cases outlined above, Turkish statism resulted in the flourishing of theological voices that had been previously marginalised and suppressed. These are clear examples of the power of the Turkish state to directly influence the future of theology in the country in ways that expand the scope of theological discourses and the range of its contributors.

The Politics of Theology III: The Later AKP (2011–19)

This same statist power can, however, be used for precisely the opposite effect. Turkish statism grants the Diyanet the power to nurture some voices, and the power to stifle others. The latter part of this chapter will explore the consequences of this form of statist power. Towards the end of its years in power, the AKP under Erdoğan's unchallenged leadership has tended towards authoritarian repression of dissenting voices within Turkish politics and civil society. This desire to control public discourses that do not fit with the AKP's conception of Turkish identity has stifled the growth of dissenting theological voices, such as those of LGBTI+ affirming theology. Just as with the examples outlined in the section above, this type of statist power can decisively affect the future of Turkish theology, in this case by foreclosing the possibility of some theological voices flourishing in the Turkish public sphere and in Turkish theological academia.

As Courtney Dorroll, Hikmet Kocamaner, Ahmet T. Kuru, Necati Polat and many other scholars have pointed out, the period between 2011 and 2013 saw a decisive shift in the governing style of the AKP. This shift did not represent a drift away from secularism, as the AKP's critics have often alleged. Neither Erdoğan nor any other prominent AKP official has taken serious steps to alter the secular character of the state. Instead, the AKP during this period abandoned its initial goal of weakening the power of the Turkish state to control the lifestyles of its citizens, and turned towards policies that sought to promote a socially conservative lifestyle by marginalising and suppressing any other form of religiosity or social expression.

In short, the AKP did not in the end abandon the repressive potential of the Turkish state in order to promote the flourishing of diverse identities, as it had initially promised. Instead, to use Kocamaner's phrase, the AKP has transformed into 'a mirror image' of the Kemalist laicism that had previously repressed devout Muslims in Turkey.[52] Polat has termed this process a form of 'mimesis' of the older version of Kemalist statism, this time favouring pious social conservatism instead of positivism and laicism.[53] In other words, the contemporary AKP has not abandoned the Kemalist principle of statism: instead, it has exchanged one kind of statist moral hegemony for another. Furthermore, as Courtney Dorroll's work has shown, under Erdoğan's leadership the AKP has endeavoured to homogenise Turkish identity and moral discourse in much the same way as did the secular Kemalists. In the case of the AKP under Erdoğan, this means reifying and appealing to the Ottoman Islamic past in such a way as to privilege conservative social morality and social conservative uses of public space. Dorroll effectively describes this complex of social policy and political discourse as 'Erdoğanian Neo-Ottomanism'.[54]

This process began with the AKP's drive to civilianise control of the government and eliminate the power of the military to intervene in democratic elections, which it had done in 1997 (and again attempted to do in 2016). Trials against alleged 'deep state' actors within the Turkish military allowed the AKP government to break the power of an intransigent bureaucracy left over from previous administrations that was genuinely resistant to the agenda of the newly elected AKP. The Turkish judiciary itself had even attempted to shut down the party in 2008. In other words, the transformation of the AKP from a standard-bearer of universal human rights to an authoritarian party was not pre-ordained, but occurred as a result of its struggle with the resistance of the remnants of the old Kemalist order.[55]

In the years that followed, the AKP showed increasing willingness to suppress forms of free expression that it considered threatening to its definition of Turkish identity. Opposition to the AKP came to be understood as a conspiracy against the state itself, and thus against the Turkish nation. In 2013, the Gezi Park protests mobilised some 2.5 million protestors nationwide who were expressing their grievances against the increasing authoritarianism of the government – but these protests were met with police violence and the detainment of some 5,000 individuals.[56] In 2014, the AKP turned against the pious followers of Fethullah Gülen, who had previously been close allies of the AKP, after Gülen-affiliated members of the Turkish police initiated anti-corruption investigations against members of the party.[57] A cascade of national traumas in the subsequent years provided an emergency context within which the AKP continued to consolidate its hold over the Turkish government and bureaucracy. These crises included a series of terrible ISIS attacks in 2015 and 2016, and the failed military coup against the elected AKP government that resulted in the loss of 240 lives after Turkish civilians of all political allegiances bravely stopped rogue members of the military from carrying out the coup plotters' objective.[58] All of these events were followed by further restrictions on free expression, including media bans, media closures, the imprisonment of journalists, the jailing of opposition party leaders and ever more severe attempts by the government to curtail any form of civil opposition to the AKP.[59]

This shift in AKP governance had a serious impact on the possibility of free expression in theological discourse. The suppression of any dissenting Islamic voices meant a restriction in the kinds of theological projects that the state would sponsor or tolerate. In order to provide a clear example of the consequences of this statist authoritarianism on the development of Turkish theology in the present day, the concluding section of this chapter will examine the controversy that erupted after LGBTI+ affirming Islamic theological discourses were first widely discussed in Turkish media. These discussions occurred at the height of the liberalising and democratising period of the early AKP, and their marginalisation by pro-AKP theological discourses and subsequently by the AKP itself coincided with the party's drift towards broader authoritarianism.

LGBTI+ Affirming Theology in Turkish: The Case in Point

On 28 June 2008, Muhsin Hendrix participated in a panel discussion on the subject of LGBTI+ individuals and Muslim societies, held in Istanbul during annual Pride celebrations led by Lambdaistanbul, the city's largest LGBTI+ advocacy organisation.[60] A few months later, Hendrix was interviewed by the Ankara-based LGBTI+ advocacy organisation, Kaos GL, and the interview was printed in Issue 103 (November-December 2008) of Kaos GL's widely read journal of LGBTI+ issues in Turkey. The interview was publicised widely by Kaos GL itself, and was quickly noticed in the Turkish press. From the point of view of the journal's readers and the Turkish media, the most striking element of the interview was Hendrix's discussion of the Quranic story of the Prophet Lot.

In this interview, Hendrix presented his argument that this story, when read and interpreted correctly, does not support the condemnation of homosexuality, as is usually supposed. In Hendrix's view, God did not destroy the people of Lot (*Lut kavmi*), the Biblical Sodom and Gomorrah, because of homosexual sex. Instead, Hendrix contended that God punished the people of Lot because they used sex as a weapon of domination and oppression, rather than as a form of loving intimacy. Hendrix argued that loving and mutualistic forms of homosexual relationships are nowhere considered in the Qur'an, positively or negatively. The sin of the people of Lot was rape and sexual assault (*tecavüz*), not homosexuality.[61]

This interview is very likely the first time this particular theological argument was published in major Turkish media. It was certainly the first time the argument was publicly and widely discussed in Turkish. This particular argument about the Quranic story of Lot has emerged in recent years as a foundational element of LGBTI+ affirming Islamic theology, and its translation into the Turkish context is an extremely significant event in the history of modern Turkish theology. Moreover, as this section will demonstrate, the emergence and reaction to Hendrix's article illustrates the central argument of this chapter: that the future of Islamic theology in Turkish will depend on the degree to which theology is politicised by the Turkish state.

The story emerged in Turkish media during the time of the AKP's openness to human rights development in Turkish politics and social policy, a time of optimism among the LGBTI+ community in Turkey that their rights as individuals would be explicitly acknowledged by the AKP programme of human rights advancement. The precise opposite happened. AKP politicians and pro-AKP social movements and theologians reacted dismissively and with hostility to the LGBTI+ community's requests for recognition, revealing the limit of the AKP's theological and political commitment to human rights advancement.[62] At a moment when LGBTI+ affirming theology was emerging as a possibility in Turkey, the response of the state in the form of the words and actions of AKP politicians and intellectuals foreclosed this possibility. The AKP committed itself to routinely homophobic theological discourse, rather than allow for the emergence of LGBTI+ affirming Islamic theology. This section will analyse this episode in detail in order to illuminate the limits of the AKP-led renaissance of Islamic theology in Turkey, and the role the state in Turkey can play in fostering or hindering organic theological development in the contemporary Turkish Republic.

The History of the LGBTI+ Movement in Turkey

Before delving into the specifics of Hendrix's argument and its reception in Turkey, a brief discussion of the history of the LGBTI+ movement in modern Turkey will provide necessary context. The earliest advocacy on behalf of the LGBTI+ community in Turkey took place in the 1970s and 1980s, particularly in the context of new leftist political parties after the 1980 coup.[63] The movement developed from gatherings in private homes into established advocacy organisations in the early 1990s, after the Istanbul city government cracked down on efforts to begin Pride celebrations in the city.[64] In response, Lambdaistanbul was founded in Istanbul in 1993, and Kaos GL in Ankara in 1994. The 2000s witnessed a proliferation of LGBTI+ advocacy organisations.

After a decade of organising and advocacy, the first Istanbul Pride march was held in 2003, and continued until the city government again shut down the marches in 2015, the 23rd anniversary of Istanbul Pride celebrations. The first commemoration of the International Day Against Homophobia was held in Ankara in 2008, and the first march for the rights of transgender persons in Turkey was held in 2010.[65] The Gezi Park protests in particular marked an important moment in the history of the LGBTI+ movement in Turkey, as the courageous involvement of LGBTI+ activists in the protests galvanised support for the cause of LGBTI+ rights and helped bring these issues to the fore in Turkish political and social debate.[66] After Gezi, the Turkish public began to more openly discuss the many threats facing the LGBTI+ community in the country, ranging from harassment, discrimination in all sectors of society from the workplace to education to government, police brutality against LGBTI+ persons, anti-LGBTI+ violence and hate crimes and the murder and lynching of LGBTI+ persons in Turkey.[67] Anti-transgender violence is particularly horrific in contemporary Turkey. Out of fifty-three hate-motivated murders of transgender people reported in Europe between 2008 and 2011, twenty-three occurred in Turkey alone.[68]

The printing and discussion of Hendrix's LGBTI+ affirming Quranic hermeneutics in Turkish media occurred at a critical point in the history of the relationship between pious Muslims and the LGBTI+ movement in Turkey, as Evren Savcı's and Fuat Muedini's research on this relationship has shown. The summer of 2008, when Hendrix participated in Lambdaistanbul's panel on LGBTI+ persons in Muslim societies, coincided with the full swing of the AKP's 'democratic openings', when the party endeavoured to move its policies and Turkish society more generally in the direction of further liberalisation on sensitive issues, such as Kurdish rights, relations with Armenia and the freedom to wear the headscarf. This was also a period that witnessed discussions on how to reform the Turkish constitution to reinforce civilian control of the government. During this period, LGBTI+ advocacy organisations such as Lambdaistanbul and Kaos GL publicly lobbied the government for the inclusion of anti-discrimination clauses in the new constitution. These calls were quickly and publicly rebuffed by AKP politicians, signalling how the government would treat such issues in the future.[69]

As Savcı demonstrates, these developments foreshadowed the beginning of a tense relationship between pious Muslim advocacy groups, such as headscarf rights groups, and the LGBTI+ advocacy community. In March of 2010, Selma Aliye Kavaf, the AKP minister of state responsible for women and family affairs, declared that homosexuality is a 'sickness', prompting fierce public debate in Turkey.[70] She also claimed that LGBTI+ identities were inherently opposed to Turkish national culture.[71] Her statements were quickly condemned by LGBTI+ advocacy groups, but they received public support from a signed declaration that included many pious Muslim women's advocacy groups, including groups that LGBTI+ organisations had supported in the past in the context of the struggle for the freedom for women to wear the headscarf without being subject to state and social discrimination.[72]

Some prominent figures within these Muslim women's advocacy groups developed ways to articulate their opposition to the mistreatment and marginalisation of LGBTI+ persons in Turkey without affirming the moral permissibility of the LGBTI+ identity. Savcı describes these forms of support as 'opposition against cruelty', in distinguishing them from 'support for abstract, liberal rights'.[73] Savcı also points out that secularist critics of the Muslim women's advocacy groups made hypocritical and opportunistic use of the issue of LGBTI+ rights: they critiqued these groups for their description of LGBTI+ identities as sinful, but they did not expect their own, or any other, ideological constituencies to seriously discuss the issue of LGBTI+ rights. Savcı's work therefore makes the crucial point that Muslim women's rights groups in Turkey have articulated complex and varied positions on the issue of LGBTI+ identities, and thus cannot all be reduced to the category of homophobia. As Savcı argues, viewing women's groups in this way risks reinforcing secular Kemalist justifications for the mistreatment and marginalisation of pious Muslim women in the first place.[74]

At the same time, from the perspective of many LGBTI+ groups, these developments were extremely distressing and signalled that religious advocacy was an ineffective approach for their movement. Savcı contrasts the 2008 Istanbul Pride events, which openly discussed the possibility of LGBTI+ affirming Islamic theology via Hendrix's participation, with the 2010 Istanbul Pride panels on religion, which were dismissive of, and severely disillusioned with, the possibility of partnering with pious Muslims or combining an LGBTI+ identity with a Muslim identity.[75] Muedini's recent study bears this out. His interviews with leaders of the major LGBTI+ advocacy groups in Turkey revealed that they were on the whole reluctant to use theological arguments in support of LGBTI+ activism and identities because they felt they lacked the theological expertise to do so and the general politicisation of Islamic identity under the AKP made such arguments very risky.[76]

Muhsin Hendrix's Quranic Hermeneutics and the Theology of Divine Mercy

A close analysis of Hendrix's theological hermeneutics will reveal the potential theological development that was cut off by the AKP and some of its supporters. Muhsin Hendrix is a well-known imam and theologian from South Africa and a leading figure in the global progressive Muslim movement. He was raised in a devout Muslim family and pursued a traditional Islamic religious education, after having studied the Qur'an and the hadith since he was five.[77] He struggled to reconcile his identity as a gay man with his identity as a pious Muslim, and came to realise that these two identities were compatible through a proper understanding of Quranic revelation and Islamic tradition. He came out in 1996 at the age of twenty-nine, causing him to lose his madrasa teaching positions. He subsequently devoted himself to developing activism and theology that would help other LGBTI+ Muslims see the compatibility of their sexual and gender identities and their faith.[78]

To this end, Hendrix founded the al-Fitra foundation in 1998, the title of which reveals the basis of his theological hermeneutics.[79] Hendrix begins his theological argument from his reading of 30:30, which famously refers to a concept of inborn human nature that is shared by all human beings as a result of their creation by God. Following the terminology used in this verse, this key Islamic theological concept is referred to as *fiṭra*, the innate nature of each human being that naturally inclines towards God. As this verse makes clear, the inborn nature of the human individual cannot be altered, as it is a creation of God as God desires it to be. Hendrix argues that this verse includes an individual's sexuality, given its inherency in a person's individual nature and the possibility of its use in the context of mutualistic and loving relationships. For Hendrix, then, homosexual love is a part of the way God created humanity. It is a form of relationship that, just like heterosexuality, can be used to express love and fidelity to one's self and to God.[80]

Hendrix's conception of God's nature therefore emphasises God's love and mercy for the entirety of creation in all its diverse forms. For Hendrix, the core of *tevhid* is the acknowledgement of the infinite love and acceptance that the One God has for the diversity of God's creation. In another interview given to Kaos GL, this time in 2013, Hendrix emphasised that Islam is based on the principle of God's boundless love for human beings in their diversity of expression. This is the essential message of the Qur'an, in his view. He describes Islam as 'a mercy and a healing for mankind'.[81] Hendrix's theology consistently focuses on God's central attribute of loving mercy (*raḥma*), because (as described in previous chapters) this attribute is indeed the way that God most frequently describes God's self in the Qur'an (along with God's Oneness). Hendrix's theology argues that this fact reveals the capacity to discern the sanctity in a variety of human identities, including gender and sexual identities. 'Mercy and healing' are the cardinal principles, taken from God's description of God's self, that govern his theological hermeneutics and religious vision overall.

It follows, then, that suppression of loving forms of homosexual relationships amounts to injustice. Hendrix's theology is for this reason deeply informed by the liberation theology of the anti-apartheid movement in South Africa, and his and other international LGBTI+ affirming Muslim movements have based their theological approach on a reading of the Qur'an that emphasises its message as 'striving for justice in solidarity with the oppressed'.[82] According to Scott Kugle, this approach is based on verses such as 4:75, which calls upon Muslims to fight for and protect the oppressed.[83] Farid Esack's Islamic liberation theology (though not originally concerned with LGBTI+ liberation) has played a particularly decisive role in Hendrix's hermeneutics.[84]

Hendrix analyses the Quranic story of Lot within the framework of these general Quranic principles. He argues that the Prophet Lot did not condemn same-sex love but instead condemned sexual assault. As Kugle points out in his discussion of this particular theological argument, Lot's condemnation amounts to a divine denunciation of 'the use of sex as coercion against the vulnerable' rather than a divine denunciation of same-sex love.[85] Hendrix's argument about Lot rests on a contextual and holistic theological hermeneutics. First, it is clear that loving and mutualistic forms of homosexual love are not at issue in the Lot story. It therefore cannot be assumed that these are the subject of divine condemnation, because these kinds of homosexual sexual contact do not come up for discussion at all in the text. Secondly, Hendrix's reading of the verses having to do with Lot, which are scattered throughout the Quranic text, recognises that these verses are, to use Kugle's phrase, 'inter-referential'.[86]

This means that if these verses are read in isolation from one another, it becomes easy to assume that homosexual sexual contact itself is the subject of condemnation in the Qur'an. However, reading all of these verses in conjunction with one another reveals that the Qur'an emphasises the violent and unjust nature of these acts. Thus, given the general Quranic principle of solidarity with the injured against the unjust, Hendrix argues that it is clear that what is being condemned in the Qur'an is rape and violence, not homosexual sex itself. As Samar Habib puts it, these verses do not amount to 'a story about all homosexuals that ever were or ever to be', but refer to the actions of these specific men.[87] The men of Lot were not condemned for sex with men in the abstract, but for the manner of this sexual contact, preferring rape over consensual sex.

This was the argument that Hendrix provided to Kaos GL in his 2008 interview, and the argument that was printed in their Winter 2008 journal issue. Given the surprised reaction to this argument in the Turkish press, it seems clear that this was a novel argument in the Turkish context. The prominence it received in Kaos GL's Winter 2008 issue, and the prominent role that Hendrix played in Lambdaistanbul's Summer 2008 discussion of Islamic and LGBTI+ identity, also suggests some measure of optimism for the further development of LGBTI+ affirming theology in Turkey at that time. The response to this argument by the prominent AKP-supporting theologian, Hayrettin Karaman, foreshadowed and likely helped to ensure the rejection of this theological possibility in contemporary Turkish Islamic theological discourse.

Karaman's Response and the Theology of the Family

As discussed in Chapter 2, the theologian Hayrettin Karaman has become one of the most outspoken supporters of AKP social conservatism over the past decade. His favour with the current AKP government is analogous to the favour that Yörükan's work enjoyed under Kemalist secularist governments in the middle of the twentieth century. Karaman's long academic career is well known for his studies of *fiqh* and *ijtihād*, the subject of his 1971 doctoral thesis. Throughout the 2000s, his works on these subjects enjoyed the rare distinction of garnering both academic praise and popular acclaim. His most popular books have sold thousands of copies, and are frequently reprinted.[88] Prior to the rise of the AKP, Karaman had already achieved great renown as a public theologian, and so his vocal support for the AKP over the past decade has meant a great deal to that party and its supporters. He is even said to enjoy a considerable measure of respect from Erdoğan himself.[89]

At the end of May 2009, shortly after Hendrix's interview with Kaos GL was published in the Winter 2008 edition of their journal, Karaman published a series of rebuttals of Hendrix's theological arguments in the conservative newspaper *Yeni Şafak*. That Hendrix's argument received this kind of attention is highly significant. Given Karaman's level of influence in the theological discourse of the AKP, the fact that he was the one to offer the first sustained attack on Hendrix's arguments was devastating. Despite these columns having been published over eleven years ago, they are still readily available online and have been very widely read. Karaman's reaction perfectly epitomises the shift in AKP governance described in the previous sections, and exemplifies the consequences for organic theological development in Turkey should the power of the state be levelled against nascent theological movements.

Karaman tells his readers that he felt compelled to write this series of columns because he heard from a reader who was distressed by Hendrix's Islamic theological arguments for the moral legitimacy of LGBTI+ identities.[90] Karaman asserts in summary that Islam and other monotheistic faiths 'view homosexuality as a kind of degeneracy, immorality, deviance from what is natural, shame, and mortal sin'.[91] He directly critiques Hendrix's reading of the Qur'an. Karaman argues that because all of the sexual relationships that the Qur'an explicitly mentions as licit are examples of heterosexual relationships, this means that the Qur'an only supports heterosexual relationships in general and implicitly rules out the permissibility of any other form of sexual identity.[92] It is important to note here that the difference between Hendrix's and Karaman's theological hermeneutics as applied to the story of Lot rests on the silence of the Qur'an on mutualistic and consensual homosexual relationships. Hendrix's view is that because these relationships can manifest the wider Quranic virtues of love and justice, they can accord with larger concepts of Islamic virtue. Karaman contends that the Qur'an's silence on these kinds of relationships is an implicit condemnation of them.

Karaman condemns LGBTI+ identities in particularly severe terms. He emphasises his view that they constitute 'perversion and ugliness (*sapıklık ve çirkinlik*)'[93] and he rules out the possibility that any part of Islamic tradition can be understood in an LGBTI+ affirming way.[94] Karaman argues that Hendrix's theological hermeneutics is nothing more than a manipulation of the scripture to accord with his own assumptions.[95] He also claims that science rules out the possibility of the naturalness of homosexual relationships and even goes so far as to use antisemitic and racist language when condemning LGBTI+ activism, comparing it to what he calls the 'Jewish and Armenian lobbies'.[96] Karaman's criticism of Hendrix's argument thus evokes highly anxious and otherising discourses. He casts LGBTI+ identity as a threat to not only the integrity of the Islamic faith, but to the integrity of an ethnically Turkish national community, and to the notion of human moral virtue itself.

Given his argument that LGBTI+ identity constitutes a dire threat to the nation of Turkey and the religion of Islam, Karaman takes the step of arguing for deliberate marginalisation and stigmatisation of LGBTI+ persons in Turkish society. He clearly states that this issue is where his theological conception of universal human rights ends: 'Even though Islam is the religion of peace and tolerance (*barış ve müsamaha*), both of these have limits'.[97] He argues that in the case of behaviours that are considered by the majority to be socially unacceptable, the government has the right to consider restricting some individual freedoms of individuals who engage in such behaviour, including their deliberate social stigmatisation. Karaman asserts that these measures must be considered necessary in the case of the LGBTI+ identity and persons in Turkey because these constitute a direct threat to the religion, tradition and culture of the Turkish nation.[98]

The argument that the government has the right to suppress 'sin' would go on to become a key feature of Karaman's theological support of the conservative authoritarian turn of the AKP's governance style. In 2011, he wrote that sin must not be tolerated in public at all; and perhaps not even in private, if the sin in question was threatening to the predominant social order.[99] He also wrote in 2014 that social pluralism must be disallowed if this means the legal and social tolerance of what he deems to be sinful.[100] Karaman's reaction to Hendrix's theology thus represents a significant strand of thinking in his conception of the relationship between the state and theological questions such as sin and wrongdoing.

Karaman's homophobic theological discourse foreshadowed later AKP political discourse on the LGBTI+ movement in Turkey. Kavaf's remarks followed in 2010. In 2012, the AKP mayor of Ankara, Melih Gökçek, described homosexuality as contrary to Turkish national values. In 2013, then Prime Minister Erdoğan referred to homosexuality as 'contrary to the culture of Islam'. In 2015, then Prime Minister Ahmet Davutoğlu criticised an openly gay opposition candidate for parliament, saying that 'gays caused the destruction of the tribe of Lot'.[101] All of these comments were made by the highest-ranking members of the AKP, and thus of the Turkish government in general, after the same sentiments were forcefully expressed by Hayrettin Karaman, the most well-known pro-AKP theologian in Turkey. All of these remarks followed the translation of Hendrix's LGBTI+ affirming Islamic theological argument into Turkish in 2008. It is no coincidence, then, that after Hendrix's theology became known in Turkey, it failed to gain traction within theological debate in Turkish. Given the public stance of the Turkish government on this issue, to adopt this theological position meant risking social and political consequences. This development exemplifies how the intervention of the state can stifle organic theological development and debate in the Turkish context.

It is noteworthy that homophobic theological discourse is still a prominent feature of AKP governance. As with Karaman over a decade ago, official AKP theological discourses still categorise LGBTI+ identities as beyond the limits of their appeals to universal human rights discourses. In a speech delivered in July of 2019, the head of the Diyanet, Ali Erbaş, made this point particularly clear. He emphasised Islam's support for universal human values such as justice, peace and coexistence. He forcefully condemned terrorism and violence in the name of Islam, while also citing extremism and ignorance as two of the severest problems afflicting the Muslim world. He further criticised Islamophobia as a threat not only to Muslims, but to global human rights in general. He drew attention to the roots of Islamophobia in racism, xenophobia and 'social marginalisation' and 'othering'.[102] Erbaş's speech was relentlessly critical of not only political and legal injustice directed against minorities, but also of the individual mentalities and social prejudices that enable these kinds of injustices.

It is therefore all the more striking that he talked about LGBTI+ identities and individuals in the same speech. Erbaş described advocacy for the rights of LGBTI+ persons as dangerous and deceptive propaganda that aims at the destruction of the nuclear family and the erosion of morality itself. He argues that the use of concepts such as freedom, pride and equality are totally inappropriate when describing LGBTI+ rights, as these identities are threatening to a virtuous social order. He further argued that these identities threaten a true understanding of femininity and masculinity, and thus constitute an unacceptable deviance that is 'contrary to creation and our God-given nature'.[103] His remarks made it clear that the AKP's theological appeals to universal values of coexistence, pluralism and respect for the other come to an end with LGBTI+ persons. It is remarkable that Erbaş's impassioned and explicit denunciation of the social exclusion and demonisation of Muslims by non-Muslim majorities should exist side-by-side with otherising rhetoric directed towards the marginalised minority of LGBTI+ persons in Turkey.

The appeal to the integrity of the family as a way to marginalise some gender and sexual identities that features so prominently in Erbaş's statement above has become a key feature of AKP moral and theological discourse in recent years, and is also a cornerstone of Karaman's recent theological works. As Zafer Yılmaz has argued, discourse on the sanctity of the family has been central to AKP political discourse since its founding. The AKP's conception of family has conditioned the whole of its social policy, which is framed as a question of safeguarding and promoting certain conceptions of family life rather than as a general question of citizenship and rights.[104] In other words, over the course of the AKP administration, the securing of individual liberties has gradually become seen as secondary to preserving the integrity of the nuclear, heterosexual family structure.

This has been particularly true since the period 2011–13. In 2013, Erdoğan famously remarked that 'any attack against the family is an attack against humanity', thus casting advocacy work such as secular feminist or LGBTI+ activism as quite literally a threat to humanity itself.[105] Erdoğan's conception of family is backed by a theological conception of the heteronormative family unit as the moral and spiritual backbone of Turkish identity.[106] This is the underlying theological logic of Erdoğan's equation of femininity with motherhood and the AKP's general anxiety about alternative gender and sexual identities. This theological conception allows Erdoğan and the AKP to equate the very spiritual health of the Turkish nation itself with the integrity of the heteronormative family structure.[107]

Karaman's theology is deeply connected with these AKP social policies, and his discussions of the nature of the ideal Islamic family clearly illustrate the theological underpinning of the AKP's conservative social vision. Karaman's conception of Islam itself is very similar to that of many other theologians discussed in this book: it is based on the eternal truth of the universe, the doctrine of the One God (*tevhid*), and as such is the basis for the inherent dignity of human nature and the inherent connection of human nature to the transcendent. As with all of the theologians discussed in this book, from

İzmirli to the present day, Karaman's work emphasises the connection between *tevhid* and the sacred value of humanity as a creation of the One God. For Karaman, Islam is the truth because it is founded on the acknowledgement of the One God and the consequences this has for human life. The distinction between the Creator and the created is the foundation of Karaman's thought as it is with the entirety of the modern Turkish theological tradition.

As described in the previous chapter, the Creator/created distinction can be used to argue for the dynamism of human experience, insofar as the created world stands in contrast to the eternal and unchangeable Creator precisely because it is by nature dynamic and changeable. In this way, consideration of *tevhid* can lead to arguments in favour of changing how human beings have in the past viewed gender relations for instance, as described in the previous chapter. By contrast, Karaman uses the Creator/created distinction to argue for a static, rather than a dynamic, understanding of human nature and social relations.

According to Karaman's theology, the sacred core of human nature becomes a way to argue for the immutable nature of certain social arrangements, in this case the patriarchal family structure. Karaman's work asserts that because human nature is universal, it is static and monolithic, and cannot admit of a diversity of sexual or gender identities. In his conception, God's creation of a single human species means that all members of that species must adhere to certain specific arrangements of gender relations if they are to remain faithful to the human nature that God has given them. For Karaman, Islamic theological anthropology is based on the same theological concept of *fıtra* that Hendrix centres in his own theology. Karaman takes this concept in the opposite social direction to Hendrix, however. He views it as a concept that restricts the possible forms of sexual and family expression, rather than as a concept that expands the possible forms of sexual and family expression by defining them as part of the inherent diversity within human nature (as Hendrix does).

Karaman also appeals to the very same Quranic verse as Hendrix, 30:30. For Karaman, human nature is composed of an inherently spiritual dimension that distinguishes it from the rest of creation.[108] Essential human nature, due to its spiritual grounding and significance, is constituted by not only soul and spirit, but also reason, virtue and moral responsibility.[109] The way that Karaman defines these latter two elements is key to his theological anthropology. As with many other theologians discussed above, Karaman argues that the unchanging moral principles of Islam are meant to allow human beings to achieve happiness and fulfilment in this life and the next.[110] Furthermore, what distinguishes Islam from other value systems is its balance between the individual and the collective. Karaman calls this a 'personalist' (*şahsiyetçi*) approach to human nature, distinguishing it from an 'individualist' or a 'collectivist' approach.[111]

What this means is that Islamic theological anthropology, by nurturing the spiritual essence of the human individual, both guarantees the actualisation of the inner truth of human nature while also realising that this actualisation can only fully take place within the context of a striving for individual virtue within the context of a larger tradition. By virtue of their shared human nature, all human beings are entitled to basic human rights as a core principle of Islamic ethics. At the same time, argues Karaman, because human nature is not infinite, neither are these rights: human nature has certain precise characteristics, and thus human rights are subject to 'balance' and 'measure'.[112] Precisely because human rights are sourced in human nature, rights must be guaranteed in accordance with human nature. The Islamic theological anthropology of human rights cannot, therefore, encompass the right to act in ways deemed contrary to universal human nature.[113]

Karaman thus argues that certain conceptions of the family are contrary to human nature, and thus cannot be considered to have the same moral or legal validity as the patriarchal family structure. As with the AKP theological discourse cited above, Karaman defines the family as the foundation of civilisation and a well-functioning society. It is a spiritual institution whose ultimate significance cannot be measured solely in secular or scientific terms.[114] Moreover, the basic principle of family organisation is that each member has designated rights and responsibilities. Karaman emphatically goes on to state that 'the headship of the family is given to the husband', who is granted by divine right the authority to act as the manager and supervisor of the family.[115]

By defining the family in this way, Karaman rules out the moral possibility of other familial arrangements, including of course LGBTI+ identities. His view of the patriarchal family is underpinned by a theological anthropology that renders only the patriarchal family potentially sacred and thus morally acceptable. Karaman makes it clear that the unchangeable elements of Islam constitute not only beliefs and worship, but also certain social arrangements that he views as in accordance with the eternal principles of individual Islamic virtue.[116] Thus, for Karaman, and for AKP theological discourse more generally, LGBTI+ identities are entirely contrary to Turkish national identity, Islam and human nature itself. The concept of universal human nature is used here to restrict rather than broaden the possible array of theologically acceptable human sexual identities.

As these arguments, and this book, have hopefully demonstrated, modern Turkish theology has reached an extraordinary level of development that has produced an equally extraordinary diversity of viewpoints and theological arguments. Any reader of modern Turkish has access to hundreds of excellent translations and editions of the great theological works of classical Sunnism. In Turkey today there is a wide network of expert academic specialists who have published countless articles and books that both analyse classical Sunni theology and produce new work in constructive and systematic theology. What this means for the future of Islamic theology in Turkey is that its intellectual roots are deep and its academic foundations are secure.

At the same time, this closing chapter demonstrates that the future of Turkish theology remains highly complex and contested. This is due primarily to the capacity of the Turkish state to influence the direction and development of theology in the country. As this book has demonstrated, the intellectual resources of modern Turkish theology are able to support an almost endless array of possible theological projects. Yet because these resources are so closely tied to state control, the exact form that Turkish theology will take in the future will be profoundly impacted by the role the Turkish state chooses to play in Turkish theological academia. The complex relationship between the creativity of Turkish theologians and the imperatives of the Turkish state will, therefore, shape what kinds of theology are possible in the Turkish Republic.

Notes

1. For the history and character of the Diyanet, see Erdem, 'Religious Services in Turkey'; Erşahin, 'Ziya Gökalp's Diyanet Ishları Nazaratı'; Görmez, 'Presidency of Religious Affairs'; Gözaydın, *Diyanet*; and Gözaydın, 'Diyanet and Politics'.
2. Gözaydın, *Diyanet*, 248–9.
3. On the development of this form of secularism in Turkey, see Peker, 'Beyond Positivism', 15–18.

4. Gözaydın, *Diyanet*, 108–9.
5. Schmitt, *The Concept of the Political*, 26.
6. Schmitt, *The Concept of the Political*, 30.
7. Schmitt, *The Concept of the Political*, 43–4.
8. Schmitt, *The Concept of the Political*, 26.
9. Schmitt, *The Concept of the Political*, 27.
10. Schmitt, *The Concept of the Political*, 27.
11. Çağaptay, *Islam, Secularism, and Nationalism in Modern Turkey*, 44.
12. Ciddi, *Kemalism in Turkish Politics*, 6.
13. The most extensive discussion of this concept is Umut Azak's study *Islam and Secularism in Turkey*; see also Soileau, *Humanist Mystics*, 92.
14. Azak, *Islam and Secularism*, 14.
15. Azak, *Islam and Secularism*, 3.
16. Azak, *Islam and Secularism*, 22.
17. Yörükan, *Müslümanlık*, 19.
18. On his notion of national moral progressivism, see 'Ahlakımızın Kökleri I', 7.
19. See Gözaydın, 'Diyanet and Politics'; and Kara, *Cumhuriyet*, 51–118.
20. Yörükan, *Müslümanlık*, 59.
21. Yörükan, *Müslümanlık*, 216.
22. Yörükan, *Müslümanlık*, 219.
23. Hourani, *Arabic Thought in the Liberal Age*, 150.
24. Rida's abhorrence of Sufi ritual is well known and may have played a role in his attraction to Wahhabism. See Hourani, *Arabic Thought in the Liberal Age*, 225.
25. Rahman, *Islam*, 244–5.
26. Şentürk, 'Islamic Reformist Discourses', 236.
27. Ecer, *Büyük Türk Din Alimi Māturīdī*, 156. Ecer's work on this topic seems to have begun in the 1970s.
28. Ecer, *Büyük Türk Din Alimi Māturīdī*, 156.
29. This periodisation is adopted from C. Dorroll, *The Spatial Politics of Turkey's Justice and Development Party*; Kuru, 'Reinterpretation of Secularism in Turkey' and Polat, *Regime Change in Contemporary Turkey*.
30. For summaries of the early rise and founding political ideology of the AKP, see Kuru, 'The Reinterpretation of Secularism in Turkey' and Kuru, 'Shari'a, Islamic Ethics, and Democracy'; Walton, *Muslim Civil Society and the Politics of Religious Freedom in Turkey*, 66–7; and Yavuz, *Secularism and Muslim Democracy in Turkey*, 79–113.
31. Akdoğan, 'Conservative Democratic Political Identity', 61; Dağı, 'The Justice and Development Party', 94; Kuru, 'Shari'a, Islamic Ethics, and Democracy', 165.

32. Yavuz, *Secularism and Muslim Democracy in Turkey*, 113.
33. Kuru, 'Reinterpretation of Secularism in Turkey', 138.
34. Akdoğan, 'Conservative Democratic Political Identity', 54.
35. Yavuz, *Secularism and Muslim Democracy in Turkey*, 82.
36. *AK Parti Kalkınma ve Demokratikleşme Programı*, 7.
37. Dağı, 'The Justice and Development Party', 89; Akdoğan, 'Conservative Democratic Political Identity', 65.
38. Pacaci and Aktay, 'Higher Religious Education', 134.
39. 'Ali Erbaş: Bugün Din Eğitimi Açısından Sıkıntılı Dönemler Geride Kaldı'.
40. According to statistics provided by the Ministry for Higher Education; available at: <https://istatistik.yok.gov.tr> (last accessed 8 October 2020).
41. Maritato, 'To Make Mosques a Place for Women', 39.
42. Maritato, 'To Make Mosques a Place for Women', 39.
43. Maritato, 'Performing Irşad', 436.
44. Maritato, 'To Make Mosques a Place for Women', 45.
45. Shively, 'Religious Bodies and the Secular State', 46–53.
46. Hassan, 'Women Preaching for the Secular State', 457–8; Maritato, 'Performing Irşad', 436–8; Tütüncü, 'The Women Preachers of the Secular State', 595.
47. Hassan, 'Women Preaching for the Secular State', 456.
48. Hassan, 'Women Preaching for the Secular State', 458–60.
49. Maritato, 'Reassessing Women, Religion, and the Secular State', 263–4.
50. Tütüncü, 'The Women Preachers of the Secular State', 599.
51. 'Tüm İllere Bayan Müftü Yardımcıcı'.
52. Kocamaner, 'How New is Erdoğan's "New Turkey"?' 3.
53. Polat, *Regime Change in Contemporary Turkey*, 7.
54. C. Dorroll, 'Hamamönü, Reconfiguring an Ankara Neighborhood', and C. Dorroll, *The Spatial Politics of Turkey's Justice and Development Party*.
55. Polat, *Regime Change in Contemporary Turkey*, 97–103.
56. Polat, *Regime Change in Contemporary Turkey*, 145.
57. Kuru, 'Shari'a, Islamic Ethics, and Democracy', 166; Polat, *Regime Change in Contemporary Turkey*, 162; Walton, *Muslim Civil Society*, 33–4.
58. The coup was organised by a small group of rogue officers in the military who were followers of the secretive religious leader Fethullah Gülen. As M. Hakan Yavuz and Rasım Koç note, the Gülen movement '[comprised] wider circles of peaceful, idealistic followers, as well as an inner circle willing to use violence to attain power' ('The Gülen Movement vs. Erdoğan', 79). The response of the AKP following the coup targeted every member of the Gülen movement, regardless of the fact that the vast majority were innocent of any role in the coup attempt.

The purging of tens of thousands of military and state employees following the coup was 'the most extensive purge in the history of the Turkish Republic' ('The Gülen Movement vs. Erdoğan', 91). For a recent analysis of the threat of jihadist fighters in Turkey, see Yayla, 'Turkish ISIS and AQ Foreign Fighters'.

59. In the summer of 2019, Turkey's ministry of education announced that over 300,000 books had been confiscated across the country and destroyed as part of a larger effort to purge the country of any influences associated with Fethullah Gülen. A 2018 report by the international press freedom organisation PEN concluded that since the 2016 coup attempt '200 media outlets and publishing organisations had been shut down, 80 writers subjected to investigations and prosecutions and 5,822 academics dismissed from 118 public universities' (see Flood, 'Turkish government destroys more than 300,000 books').

60. '2008 Onur Haftası Programı'; Savcı, 'Subjects of Rights and Subjects of Cruelty', 183; Muedini, *LGBTI Rights in Turkey*, 24. The interview cited by Muedini lists 2006 as the date of this panel, but the programme of the original event cited above, along with the other media sources cited below, confirm that it occurred in 2008.

61. 'Kaos GL'den "İslam ve Eşcinsellik"'; 'Kaos GL İslam ve Eşcinselliği Tartıştı: Kim bu İmam Muhsin Hendricks?'; Ergenç, 'Peygamber Eşcinsele Ölüm Cezası Vermedi'.

62. As Fuat Muedini argues, the AKP's reaction to LGBTI+ activism reveals the limits of the party's willingness to conform itself to international human rights standards more generally, revealing a key weakness in the AKP's originally stated commitment to the advancement of individual freedoms for all Turkish citizens (*LGBTI Rights in Turkey* 5, 199). Mehmet Sinan Birdal makes a similar point about the limits of the human rights language used in the AKP platform of 'conservative democracy' (Birdal, 'Queering Conservative Democracy', 119).

63. Muedini, *LGBTI Rights in Turkey*, 110–11.
64. Muedini, *LGBTI Rights in Turkey*, 111–12; Savcı, 'THE LGBTI+ Movement', 125.
65. Muedini, *LGBTI Rights in Turkey*, 111–13.
66. Savcı, 'The LGBTI+ Movement', 128, 130; Muedini, *LGBTI Rights in Turkey*, 116, 133.
67. Muedini, *LGBTI Rights in Turkey*, 20.
68. Polat, *Regime Change in Contemporary Turkey*, 295.
69. Muedini, *LGBTI Rights in Turkey*, 31; Savcı, 'Subjects of Rights and Subjects of Cruelty', 107.

70. Birdal, 'Queering Conservative Democracy', 127; Savcı, 'Subjects of Rights and Subjects of Cruelty', 160, 174–5; Muedini, *LGBTI Rights in Turkey*, 31.
71. Savcı, 'Subjects of Rights and Subjects of Cruelty', 174.
72. Savcı, 'Subjects of Rights and Subjects of Cruelty', 175.
73. Savcı, 'Subjects of Rights and Subjects of Cruelty', 161.
74. Savcı, 'Subjects of Rights and Subjects of Cruelty', 175; Savcı, 'Ethnography and Queer Translation', 77–8.
75. Savcı, 'Ethnography and Queer Translation,', 79; Savcı, 'Subjects of Rights and Subjects of Cruelty', 183; Savcı, 'The LGBTI+ Movement', 129.
76. Muedini, *LGBTI Rights in Turkey*, 218.
77. Kugle, *Living Out Islam*, 22–3.
78. Kugle, *Living Out Islam*, 25–30.
79. Kugle, 'Queer Jihad', 14–15; Osman and Shaikh, 'Islam, Muslims, and Politics of Queerness', 50–5.
80. Kugle, *Living Out Islam*, 25; Kugle, 'Queer Jihad', 15; Osman and Shaikh, 'Islam, Muslims, and Politics of Queerness', 51.
81. 'Qur'an is not against Homosexuality'.
82. Kugle, *Homosexuality in Islam*, 34–5; Kugle, 'Queer Jihad', 14; Osman and Shaikh, 'Islam', 45.
83. Kugle, *Homosexuality in Islam*, 35.
84. Kugle, *Homosexuality in Islam*, 38; Osman and Shaikh, 'Islam, Muslims, and Politics of Queerness', 55.
85. Kugle, *Islam and Homosexuality*, 39–40.
86. Kugle, *Islam and Homosexuality*, 54–5.
87. Habib, 'Queer-Friendly Islamic Hermeneutics', 32–3; see also Habib *Female Homosexuality in the Middle East*, 61–2, 163 n. 31.
88. Ozgur, 'The Ongoing Cause of Hayrettin Karaman', 571.
89. Polat, *Regime Change in Contemporary Turkey*, 154.
90. Karaman, 'Eşcinsellik Problemi'.
91. Karaman, 'Eşcinsellik Problemi'.
92. Karaman, 'Kur'an Eşcinselliği Kınıyor ve Yasaklıyor'.
93. Karaman, 'Kur'an Eşcinselliği Kınıyor ve Yasaklıyor'.
94. Karaman, 'Hadisler de Eşcinselliğe İzin Vermiyor'.
95. Karaman, 'Muhsin Hendrix'in İddiaları'.
96. Karaman, 'Bilim ne Diyor?'.
97. Karaman, 'Eşcinseller vb. ile Aynı Toplulukta Yaşamak'.

98. Karaman, 'Eşcinseller vb. ile Aynı Toplulukta Yaşamak'; Birdal, 'Queering Conservative Democracy', 125–6. Birdal notes that other conservative writers such as Ali Bulaç and Ali Ünal were even more severe in their response at the time, attempting to associate homosexuality with sadomasochism, Nazism, and paedophilia ('Queering Conservative Democracy', 126–7).
99. Kuru, 'Shari'a, Islamic Ethics, and Democracy', 170–1.
100. Polat, *Regime Change in Contemporary Turkey*, 155.
101. Muedini, *LGBTI Rights in Turkey*, 31–4.
102. 'Diyanet İşleri Başkanı Erbaş'tan 'Sapkınlık' Uyarısı'.
103. 'Diyanet İşleri Başkanı Erbaş'tan 'Sapkınlık' Uyarısı'.
104. Yılmaz, '"Strengthening the Family" Policies in Turkey', 375.
105. Yılmaz, '"Strengthening the Family" Policies in Turkey', 381.
106. Yılmaz, '"Strengthening the Family" Policies in Turkey', 379.
107. Kocamaner, 'The Politics of Family Values', 37.
108. Karaman, *İslam'da Kadın ve Aile*, 24.
109. Karaman, *İslam'da Kadın ve Aile*, 28.
110. Karaman, *İslam'da Kadın ve Aile*, 204.
111. Karaman, *İslam'da Kadın ve Aile*, 29.
112. Karaman, *İslam'da Kadın ve Aile*, 37.
113. Karaman, *İslam'da Kadın ve Aile*, 37.
114. Karaman, *İslam'da Kadın ve Aile*, 183.
115. Karaman, *İslam'da Kadın ve Aile*, 191.
116. Karaman, *İslam'da Kadın ve Aile*, 204.

CONCLUSION: WISDOM AND WONDER

'The ways of God are boundless and countless' – İsmail Hakkı İzmirli[1]

The study of modern Turkish theology reveals a number of important insights about the history of modern Turkey in general, as described in detail in the chapters above. As this book has demonstrated, a distinct tradition of Sunni Muslim theology developed in the Republic of Turkey as a consequence of the specific forms of modernisation experienced by Muslims in that country. The process of late Ottoman, and then modern Turkish, modernisation as a series of ever more radical social and political reforms imbued modern Turkish Islamic theology with a fundamental concern for the dynamics of change and permanence. Modern Turkish theology has therefore developed as a way to identify and secure the most fundamental bases of the Muslim faith, so as to preserve these bases and also to reflect on their importance in the ever-changing modern world. Thus, modern Turkish theology constitutes an extended, nuanced and highly variable meditation on what it means to believe in the One God, to believe in *tevhid*, in the context of modernity. The essential truth about the world upon which modern Turkish theology converges is the truth of the existence of the single, omnipotent and infinitely loving and compassionate God – and acknowledgement of this truth necessitates reflection on the consequences that this belief has for human beings living in the modern world.

Like so much of modern Turkish culture, Islamic theology in modern Turkey is rooted in a creative synthesis of classical Islamic traditions and modern cultural and intellectual forms, as demonstrated in Chapter 1. This chapter revealed how the three intellectual streams of Sunni Ottoman systematic theology (*kalām*), late nineteenth- and early twentieth-century Islamic modernism, and late Ottoman and early Republican Turkish sociological theory all came together to lay the groundwork for the development of Islamic theology in the modern Turkish language. Basic arguments, concepts and general theological motifs from all of these sources would emerge time and again as modern Turkish Muslim theologians negotiated the relationship between God and the world, tradition and modernity, the Creator and the created.

The growth of theology in modern Turkey was also enabled by strong institutional contexts for theology that were developed by the Ottomans and then taken over and modified in the Turkish Republic. Theology was an important part of intellectual and educational life in the pre-modern Ottoman *medrese*s, and the highly bureaucratic organisation of these institutions allowed for a specific set of theological texts and traditions to become key components of Ottoman Islamic intellectual culture. Within late nineteenth- and early twentieth-century reformed educational institutions such as the *Darülfünun* and the Ankara University Faculty of Theology, traditional Sunni systematic theology, Islamic theological modernism and sociological theory began to blend together to lay the foundation of a new and distinctive tradition of Islamic theology in the Turkish Republic. Because it emerged from a long process of institutional development that spanned the Ottoman and Republican period, modern Turkish theology has therefore been able to build on classical Sunni theological discourses passed down through the Ottoman period and combine these discourses with specifically modern intellectual influences.

Another key theme in the history of modern Turkey that emerges in the study of modern Turkish theology is the overarching social, political and intellectual importance of nationalism. The nation state of the Republic of Turkey was the final product of decades of reform projects begun in the late Ottoman Empire, and its emergence meant the beginning not only of a new country, but the new language of modern Turkish and a new conception of community among speakers of this language. The Turkish nationalist project created a country whose government was dedicated to the progress of a new nation that could confidently face the modern future. This new nation had to be reconstructed as a distinct cultural, linguistic and historical community by reinterpreting the multi-ethnic, multi-cultural, multi-lingual and multi-religious histories of Turkic-speaking peoples ranging from ancient Central Asia, to Anatolia, to the learned elite of Ottoman Istanbul.

As Chapter 2 demonstrated, this new conception of community enabled the emergence of creative forms of Sunni Muslim theology in the new Turkish Republic. The novel conceptual framework of Turkish nationalism provided key concepts that have come to constitute core features of modern Turkish theological thought, such as notions of progress, national history and the relationship between religion and the secular state. The secularising project of modern Turkish nationalism might, at first glance, seem to be a force that could hinder the development of religious thought. On the contrary, the fact that this project caused Muslim theologians in Turkey to redefine their own history, and thus their own religious tradition, meant that they could develop Sunni theology in ways that were totally impossible before.

The inclusion of Central Asia into the conception of Turkish national history meant that the great Sunni dogmatic theologian al-Maturidi came to be thought of as part of the Turkish heritage. This meant a dramatic revival of Maturidism in modern Turkish theology, a revival that could not have taken place outside of the Turkish nationalist context. In addition, debates over religion and the secular state, conceptions of social progress, and other moral concepts crucial to the nationalist project allowed modern Turkish theologians to reflect on these issues in insightful and interesting ways that could never have developed otherwise. In other words, not only did the concept of the nation state emerge as crucial to the development of modern Turkish theology, it also fostered the growth of some its most important and insightful expressions. In this way, even a concept such as secular nationalism was able, in modern Turkey, to revivify Islamic theological debates on what it means to believe in the One God.

The specific institutional, intellectual and political legacies of the Ottoman Empire and the emergence of Turkish nationalism led, therefore, to new ways of talking about Muslim theology, the core of which is the doctrine of the One God, the doctrine of *tevhid*. This doctrine states the One Omnipotent God created, and continues to sustain, the whole of the cosmos, thus dividing the universe into Creator and created. Chapters 3 and 4 were devoted to exploring ways in which modern Turkish theology analyses this cardinal Islamic theological distinction. Indeed, the central claim of this book is that this distinction is the core concern of Islamic theology in the Turkish Republic, specifically as it relates to what this distinction means for life in the modern world.

As revealed in the third chapter, modern Turkish theologians have met the challenge of modernity by restoring transcendence and sacredness to our conception of the physical world. If the central theme of modern Turkish theology is *tevhid*, the main arguments that modern Turkish theologians make about this doctrine are rooted in the concern to refute materialist and mechanistic visions of the universe. In their arguments about God, the Creator and Sustainer of the universe, Modern Turkish theologians describe the world as inherently sacred because it is a sign of the ultimately transcendent, its Creator. Moreover, human nature itself is sacred because it contains within itself consciousness of its Creator. The created universe and human existence are signs that reveal the existence and attributes of their Creator, the One God who is characterised by endless care and loving compassion. Denying the transcendent significance of the universe and of human nature, as materialism does, means denying not only God's existence, but also denying the loving care of God for all of existence and thus the very meaning of existence itself. This is the foundational argument made in the earliest and most influential works in modern Turkish theology, and the specifics of this argument have been worked out in successive detail over the course of the twentieth and twenty-first centuries.

The fourth chapter focused on the second half of the Creator/created distinction: the ever-changeable world of human experience. Insofar as modern Turkish theology is focused on developing conceptions of *tevhid* within the context of modernity, modern Turkish theologians pay equal attention to conceptions of the changeable world as they do to the unchangeable Creator of the world. This chapter argued that modern Turkish theology discusses the created world as a constantly changing sphere of ethical action within which humans are commanded by God to live out God's eternal will. For this reason, modern Turkish theologians have attempted to define the relationship between the changeable nature of human society and history, and unchangeable theological truth.

The created world is the sphere in which eternal values and truths are actualised by human beings. Modern Turkish theologians, in emphasising the dynamism of historical change via their appropriation of late Ottoman sociology, stress the need for theological reflection on the challenges of living out the commands of God's eternal will in the context of a world whose very nature is ceaseless change and instability. This demand in turns implies the reality of human freedom, meaning here the freedom human beings have to choose to follow God's will or to reject it. This freedom is not only one of the bases of the changeability of the social world, it is also an ethical responsibility given to human beings by God. Thus, Islamic theology in the Turkish Republic becomes a way to use the doctrine of God's Oneness to consider the complexity of the created world, and to meditate on all the ways in which change may or may not be possible in religious practice, such as in the realms of politics and gender relations.

The final chapter of this book considered modern Turkish theology in relation to the Turkish state. While discussions of community in modern Turkey revolve around the concept of the nation, discussions of politics revolve around the concept of the state. The centralised statist supervision of religion by the Turkish state means that the widespread success of any given theological school of thought or particular theological argument is contingent on its acceptance by the Turkish government. This chapter therefore argued that the degree to which the state chooses to assert jurisdiction over theology in Turkey is the most crucial political factor in the future of the development of theology in that county. If the Turkish government chooses to support a given theological school of thought or specific theological argument, that school or argument has the possibility of attaining wide acceptance. If, however, the Turkish government chooses to direct its power towards the suppression of a given school or argument, this makes the widespread acceptance of that argument much more difficult.

This chapter brings our consideration of the relationship between modern Turkish history and modern Turkish theology to the present day. In the same way that theologians associated with previous secular nationalist Turkish governments sought to suppress forms of Islamic theology that they found deviant, such as socially conservative piety, theologians associated with the contemporary conservative nationalist AKP government have sought to suppress forms of Islamic theology that *they* find deviant, most notably LGBT+ affirming Islamic theological arguments. At the same time, the statist control that the AKP has wielded over theology during its tenure in power has also served to radically, and intentionally, increase the participation of women in positions of religious and theological authority. In other words, this chapter shows how in the future, which theological voices are nurtured and which are stifled in contemporary Turkey will have much to do with the prevailing administration's views on what constitutes acceptable forms of Islamic thought. As with its past, the future of modern Turkish theology will continue to be closely connected with the Turkish state.

In all of the ways discussed in these chapters, Islamic theology in the Turkish Republic should be understood as a vital and dynamic part of Turkey's modern history. This tradition of thought is not simply an obscure academic exercise, nor is it divorced from the pressing questions of social and intellectual life in the Turkish Republic. On the contrary, this tradition has been shaped by, and has itself shaped, the historical forces that have driven the development of the Turkish Republic. In searching for the experience of ultimate meaning within the modern flux that produced this nation, modern Turkish theology has since its beginning, and will into the future, track and trace the striving of modern humanity towards communion with changeless Divinity.

* * *

At the same time that it reveals insights about Turkey and the modern world, Islamic theology in the Turkish Republic also reveals something vital and fundamental about Islamic theology as a whole. The extended meditation in modern Turkish theology on the cardinal belief of Islam, the Oneness of God, highlights the basic principle of Islamic theological method in general: Islamic theology is defined by the infinity of God. Somewhat paradoxically, Islamic theology limits itself to the discussion of the limitless: the divine. 'God' as a concept is a kind of aspiration, because the divine by definition remains indefinable, infinite and impossible to delimit. The beginning of theology is open to our mind's understanding, but the end recedes forever into the distance, the mind following its apparent object towards the wordlessness of the divine essence.

As this book has argued, meditation on the theological and social consequences of the belief in the One God (*tevhid*) is the driving question of modern Turkish theology, as this tradition attempted to secure the bases of religion in the changing modern world. This means, as we have seen, that modern Turkish theology features a complex and nuanced, yet rather focused, emphasis on the question of the very concept of God, the very concept of the Infinite. Yet by focusing attention on the fact that the basis of theology is meditation by limited human minds on the Infinite itself, modern Turkish theology invites us to consider a very basic but important question about Islamic theology more broadly: how is it even possible? How can the created talk about the Creator? How can the finite talk about the Infinite? Is the project of Islamic theology logically impossible from the very beginning?

As with so many other topics discussed in this book, İsmail Hakkı İzmirli's *Yeni İlm-i Kelam* provides a possible answer. As discussed, İzmirli's text is notable for its stress on the importance of God's attribute of wisdom (*hikmet*). All of God's acts, such as God's creating and continual sustaining of the cosmos – moment to moment, and from its tiniest to its grandest aspects – are acts that God commits within the divine context of God's attributes. These attributes are of, but not identical to, God's essence. They are the grounding of God's actions because they manifest the perfection of God's essence.[2] How İzmirli talks about these specific attributes, then, tells us a great deal about what İzmirli thinks about God and God's relation to the human being.

It is noteworthy, then, that İzmirli argues that all of God's acts emerge from God's attribute of wisdom. All things in the world, as acts of the One God, evince the supreme order and design of divine wisdom. All of God's acts occur in the context of God's attribute of wisdom because all of God's acts possess an ultimate end, a telos: this is the flourishing (*saadet*) of humanity and the cosmos.[3] At the same time, this telos does not mean that God's acts are based on necessity. On the contrary, though God's actions possess a telos, they are committed by God in total freedom, and there is no inherent need for them to occur in order to fulfil this end. On what basis, then, can we say that God's acts do indeed occur in the Divine Wisdom, and towards fulfilment of the end of human and cosmic flourishing?

The connection between God's actions and God's wisdom is not by necessity – instead, it is by God's goodness and loving concern (*rahmet*).[4] God's actions result in a wisely ordered cosmos not because God *must* order the world this way, but because God *chooses* to do so out of God's love. Because God is inherently wise, and inherently loving, God's actions issue in a cosmos designed to allow human beings and the rest of creation to reach their full potential. This even requires the existence of evil and suffering, because it is only in the context of the possibility of evil and suffering that love, justice and mercy can be experienced by human beings. The ceaseless opposition of hardship and ease, justice and injustice, is necessary if the world is to be a place of free possibility. These oppositions are necessary for humanity to be able to freely recognise God's perfection in its infinite contrast to these oppositions.[5] Moreover, such a world is necessary for human beings to be able to freely strive to reflect God's loving mercy through their own actions towards others; without the possibility of frustration, failure and even despair, moral striving lacks meaning and its own telos of realising the potential of human beings to manifest loving mercy towards one another.[6]

What do İzmirli's thoughts on the Divine Wisdom have to do with Islamic theology as a whole? İzmirli stresses that when human beings contemplate this magnificent order of the cosmos, the product of God's infinite wisdom, they experience one over-riding feeling: wonder.[7] Islamic theology is possible because human beings experience wonder. The experience of wonder is how finite human minds can begin to contemplate the infinite, because wonder is a mental state produced by awareness of the profound disjuncture between the mind and its object. Awareness of our finitude renders possible our contemplation of the Infinite, whose existence and perfection is intimated by our awareness of the wondrous nature of ourselves and the cosmos.

At the same time, and quite paradoxically, wonder is also the feeling that makes us aware of God's closeness to us. This is because, as İzmirli shows above, when we stand in wonder before God's attribute of wisdom, we are also standing in wonder before God's attribute of infinite love and concern.

These divine attributes are the means by which God continuously sustains the cosmos. The wonder that makes theology possible connects us with the signs of an infinitely loving Creator whose actions to create and sustain us constitute the ground not only of our being but also of our transcendent meaning as creation, and our fulfilment as free beings striving to live in accordance with, and as reflections of, God's infinitely loving and wise will.

God is therefore experienced conceptually by the human mind as that within which all contradictions are resolved, all tensions eased, all oppositions reconciled. This is one way to understand what it means to say that God is loving and merciful, *Rahman* and *Rahim*, and the refuge in Whom all human beings find their rest.[8] The tensions that we experience in the world between change and permanence, suffering and ease, justice and injustice, have perhaps been felt with particular acuteness in the tumult of modernity. Modern Turkish theology suggests that these tensions may yet find their resolution in the contemplation and remembrance of the One God, the Creator and Sustainer of all that we experience.

Notes

1. İzmirli, *Yeni İlm-i Kelam*, 2:4 (274).
2. İzmirli, *Yeni İlm-i Kelam*, 2:139 (387).
3. İzmirli, *Yeni İlm-i Kelam*, 2:130 (378–9). See the beginning of Chapter 3 for a fuller discussion of *saadet*.
4. İzmirli, *Yeni İlm-i Kelam*, 2:138 (386).
5. İzmirli, *Yeni İlm-i Kelam*, 2:139–40 (387).
6. İzmirli, *Yeni İlm-i Kelam*, 2:147 (393).
7. İzmirli, *Yeni İlm-i Kelam*, 2:131 (379), 2:152 (397).
8. See for instance Qur'an 13:28, 16:98, and 114.

BIBLIOGRAPHY

'2008 Onur Haftası Programı'. Lambdaistanbul, 12 June 2008. Available at: <http://www.lambdaistanbul.org/s/etkinlik/2008-lgbtt-onur-haftasi-programi> (last accessed 8 October 2020).

Abdel Razek, Ali. *Islam and the Foundations of Political Power*, edited by Abdou Filali-Ansary and translated by Maryam Loutfi. Edinburgh: Edinburgh University Press, 2013.

'Abduh, Muhammad. *The Theology of Unity*. Translated by Ishaq Musa'ad and Kenneth Cragg. Kuala Lumpur: Islamic Book Trust, 2004.

Ahmad, Feroz. *The Making of Modern Turkey*. New York: Routledge, 1993.

Ahmad, Feroz. 'The Political Economy of Kemalism'. In *Ataturk: Founder of a Modern State*, edited by Egun Ozbudun and Ali Kazancigil. London: Archon Press, 1982, pp. 145–63.

Ahmed, Shahab and Nenad Filipovic. 'The Sultan's Syllabus: A Curriculum for the Ottoman Imperial *medrese*s Prescribed in a *fermān* of Qānūnī I Süleyman, dated 973 (1565)'. *Studia Islamica* 98/99 (2004): 183–218.

Ak, Ahmet. *Büyük Alimi Māturīdī ve Māturīdīlik*. Istanbul: Bayrak Matbaası, 2008.

AK Parti Kalkınma ve Demokratıkleşme Programı. February 11, 2002. Available at: <https://acikerisim.tbmm.gov.tr/xmlui/handle/11543/926> (last accessed 8 October 2020).

Akdoğan, Yalçın. 'The Meaning of Conservative Democratic Political Identity'. In *The Emergence of a New Turkey: Islam, Democracy, and the AK Parti*, edited by M. Hakan Yavuz. Salt Lake City, UT: University of Utah Press, 2006, pp. 49–65.

Akpınar, Cemil. 'Davud-i Karsi'. *İslam Ansiklopedisi*. TDV Yayınları, Ankara.

Akseki, Ahmet Hamdi. *İslam Fitri, Tabii ve Umumı Bir Dindir* (1944). In İsmail Kara, *Türkiye'de İslamcılık Düşuncesi 2: Metinler, Kişiler*. Istanbul: Dergah Yayınları, 2014, pp. 845–80.

Aksoy, Hürcan Aslı. 'Invigorating Democracy in Turkey: The Agency of Organized Islamist Women'. *Politics and Gender* 11 (2015): 146–70.

Akşin, Sina. 'The Nature of the Kemalist Revolution'. In *The Turkish Republic at Seventy-Five Years: Progress, Development, Change*. Tallahassee, FL: The Eothen Press, 1999, pp. 14–28.

Aktay, Yasin. 'The Historicist Dispute in Turkish-Islamic Theology'. In *Change and Essence: Dialectial Relations between Change and Continuity in the Turkish Intellectual Tradition*, edited by Sinasi Gunduz and Cafer S. Yaran. Washington, DC: The Council for Research in Values and Philosophy, 2005, pp. 65–86.

Ali, Kecia. *Sexual Ethics and Islam: Feminist Reflections on Qur'an, Hadith, and Jurisprudence*. Revised edition. Oxford: Oneworld, 2016.

'Ali Erbaş: Bugün Din Eğitimi Açısından Sıkıntılı Dönemler Geride Kaldı'. haberler.com. 31 January 2019. Available at: <https://www.haberler.com/ali-erbas-bugun-din-egitimi-acisindan-sikintili-11695687-haberi> (last accessed 8 October 2020).

Alper, Hülya. *İmam Matüridi'de Akıl-Vahıy İlişkisi*. Istanbul: İz Yayıncılık, 2008.

Alper, Hülya. 'Matüridi'nin Akıl ve Vahiy Algısı'. In *Matüridi'nin Düşünce Dünyası*, edited by Şaban Ali Düzgün. Ankara: T. C. Kültür ve Turizm Bakanlığı, 2011, pp. 177–81.

Alper, Ömer Mahir. 'The Conceptions of Islamic Philosophy in Turkey'. In *Change and Essence: Dialectial Relations between Change and Continuity in the Turkish Intellectual Tradition*, edited by Sinasi Gunduz and Cafer S. Yaran. Washington, DC: The Council for Research in Values and Philosophy, 2005, pp. 123–44.

Altıntaş, Ramazan. 'Matüridi Kelam Sisteminde Akıl Nakıl İlişkisi'. *Marife* 5:3 (Winter 2005): 233–46.

Ansari, Zafer Ishaq. 'A Note on Taftazani's Views on taklif, jabr, and qadr: A Note on the Development of Islamic Theological Doctrines'. *Arabica* 16:1 (February 1969): 65–78.

Al-Aqḥisārī, Kāfī Ḥasan Efendi. *Rawḍāt al-Jannāt fī Uṣūl al-I'tiqādāt*. In Edward Badeen (ed.), *Sunnitische Theologie in osmanischer Zeit*, 31–60. Würzburg: Orient-Institut Istanbul, 2008.

Arat, Yeşim. 'Islamıst Women and Feminist Concerns in Contemporary Turkey'. *Frontiers* 37:3 (2016): 125–50.

Atatürk, Mustafa Kemal. 'An Exhortation to Progress'. *The Living Age* 327 (1925): 232–3.
Atay, Hüseyin. *Ben: Akıl ve Kur'an Işığında 1400 Yıllık Süreçte İslam'ın Evreni*. Istanbul: Destek Yayınları, 2019.
Atay, Hüseyin. *Osmanlılarda Yüksek Din Eğitimi*. Istanbul: Dergah Yayınları, 1983.
Aydar, Hidayet. 'Darülfünun'un İlahiyat Fakültesi ve Türk Kültür Hayatına Katkıları'. *İstanbul Üniversitesi İlahiyat Fakültesi Dergisi* 13 (2006): 23–43.
Aydın, Ömer. 'Kelam between Tradition and Change: The Emphasis on Understanding Classical Islamic Theology in Relation to Western Intellectual Effects'. In *Change and Essence: Dialectical Relations between Change and Continuity in the Turkish Intellectual Tradition*, edited by Sinasi Gunduz and Cafer S. Yaran. Washington, DC: The Council for Research in Values and Philosophy, 2005, pp. 103–22.
Aydın, Ömer. *Türk Kelam Bilginleri*. Istanbul: İnsan Yayınları, 2004.
Ayubi, Zahra. *Gendered Morality: Classical Islamic Ethics of the Self, Family, and Society*. New York: Columbia University Press, 2019.
Azak, Umut. *Islam and Secularism in Turkey: Kemalism, Religion, and the Nation State*. London: I. B. Tauris, 2010.
Azak, Umut. 'Secularism in Turkey as a Nationalist Search for Vernacular Islam: The Ban on the Call to Prayer in Arabic (1932–1950)'. *Revue des mondes musulmans et de la Mediterranee* 124 (November 2008): 161–79.
Aydın, Ömer. 'Secularism in Turkey as a Nationalist Search for Vernacular Islam: The Ban on the Call to Prayer in Arabic (1932–1950)'. *Revue des mondes musulmans et de la Mediterranee* 124 (November 2008): 161–79.
Bacik, Gokhan. *Islam and Muslim Resistance to Modernity in Turkey*. Cham, Switzerland: Palgrave Macmillan, 2019.
Bağçeci, Muhiddin. 'Māturīdī'nin Kelam Metodu'. In *Ebu Mansur Semerkandi Māturīdī (862–944) Sempozyumu, Mart 1986*. Kayseri: Ahmet Hulusi Köken, 1990, pp. 23–32.
Baloğlu, Adnan Bülent. 'İzmirli İsmail Hakkı'nın "Yeni İlm-i Kelam"'. In *İzmirli İsmail Hakkı Sempozyumu: 24–25 Kasım 1995*, edited by Mehmet Şeker and Adnan Bülent Baloğlu. Ankara: TDV Yayınları, 1996, pp. 93–107.
Bardakoğlu, Ali. 'Hüsn ve Kubh Konusunda Aklın Rölü ve İmam Māturīdī'. In *Ebu Mansur Semerkandi Māturīdī (862–944) Sempozyumu, Mart 1986*. Kayseri: Ahmet Hulusi Köken, 1990, pp. 33–49.
Bardakoğlu, Ali. 'Teorik Açıdan İslam ve Demokrasi: Yasama'. In *İslam ve Demokrasi*. Ankara: TDV Yayınları, 2005, pp. 361–72.

Bayāḍī Zadeh, Aḥmad ibn Ḥasan. *Ishārāt al-Marām min 'Ibārāt al-Imām*, edited by Aḥmad al-Farīd al-Miziyadī. Beirut: Dār al-Kutub al-'Ilmiyya, 2007.

Bayāḍī Zadeh, Aḥmad ibn Ḥasan. *al-Uṣūl al-Munīfa li-l-Imām Abī Ḥanīfa*. In İlyas Çelebi (ed.), *İmam-ı Azam Ebu Hanife'nin İtikadi Görüşleri*. Istanbul: Marmara Üniversitesi İlahiyat Fakültesi Vakfı Yayınları, 2000, pp. 1–54.

Bein, Amit. *Ottoman Ulema, Turkish Republic: Agents of Change and Guardians of Tradition*. Stanford, CA: Stanford University Press, 2011.

Berger, Lutz. 'Interpretations of Ash'arism and Māturīdism in Mamluk and Ottoman Times'. In *The Oxford Handbook of Islamic Theology*, edited by Sabine Schmidtke. Oxford: Oxford University Press, 2016, pp. 693–706.

Berkes, Niyazi. *The Development of Secularism in Turkey*. New York: Routledge, 1999.

Berkey, Jonathan P. *The Transmission of Knowledge in Medieval Cairo: A Social History of Islamic Education*. Princeton, NJ: Princeton University Press, 1992.

Birdal, Mehmet Sinan. 'Queering Conservative Democracy'. *Turkish Policy Quarterly* 11:4 (Winter 2013): 120–9.

Birinci, Ali and M. Sait Özervarlı. 'İzmirli, İsmail Hakkı'. In *İslam Ansiklopedisi*. Istanbul: TDV Yayınları, 2001, pp. 530–5.

Bozdoğan, Sibel. 'Architecture, Modernism and Nation-Building in Kemalist Turkey'. *New Perspectives on Turkey* 10 (1994): 37–55.

Brodersen, Angelika. 'Divine and Human Acts in Māturīdī *Kalām*'. In *Uluğ bir Çınar İmam Maturidi: Uluslararası Sempozyum Tebliğler Kitabı*, edited by Ahmet Kartal. Istanbul: Doğu Araştırmaları Merkezi 2014, pp. 357–66.

Bruckmayr, Philipp. 'The Spread and Persistence of Māturīdī Kalām and Underlying Dynamics'. *Iran and the Caucasus* 13 (2009): 59–92.

Bulaç, Ali. *Din ve Modernizm*. İstanbul: İz Yayıncılık, 1995.

Bulğen, Mehmet. 'The Criticism of Materialism in Late Ottoman's New Science of Kalām'. *ULUM* 2:1 (July 2019): 133–67.

Ceric, Mustafa. *Roots of Synthetic Theology in Islam: A Study of the Theology of Abū Manṣūr al-Māturīdī*. Kuala Lampur: ISTAC, 1995.

Cetinsaya, Gokhan. 'Rethinking Nationalism and Islam: Some Preliminary Notes on "Turkish Islamic Synthesis" in Modern Turkish Political Thought'. *Muslim World* 89:3–4 (July–October 1999): 350–76.

Ciddi, Sinan. *Kemalism in Turkish Politics: The Republican People's Party, Secularism, and Nationalism*. New York: Routledge, 2009.

Comte, August. *A General View of Positivism*. Translated by J. H. Bridges. London: Routledge, 1908.

Copeaux, Etienne. *Türk Tarih Tezinden Türk-İslam Sentezine*. Translated by Ali Berktay. Istanbul: İletişim Yayınları, 2006.
Correa, Dale. *Testifying Beyond Experience: Theories of Akhbar and the Boundaries of Community in Transoxanian Islamic Thought, 10th–12th Centuries CE*. New York University PhD, 2014.
Çağaptay, Soner. *Islam, Secularism, and Nationalism in Modern Turkey*. New York: Routledge, 2006.
Çelebi, İlyas. *Dini Düşüncede İ'tıdal ve Hoşgörü*. Istanbul: Çamlıca Yayınları, 2009.
Çelebi, İlyas. 'Din ve Mahiyeti'. In Fahrettın Atar et al., *İslam İlmihali*. Istanbul: Marmara Üniversitesi İlahiyat Fakültesi Yayınları, 2012, pp. 9–28.
Çelebi, İlyas. *İmam-ı Azam Ebu Hanife'nin İtikadi Görüşleri*. Istanbul: Marmara Üniversitesi İlahiyat Fakültesi Vakfı Yayınları, 2000.
Çelebi, İlyas. *İslam'ın İnanç Esasları*. Istabnbul: İSAM Yayınları, 2009.
Çelebi, İlyas. 'Modern Dönem Kelam Çalışmalarının Temel Sorunları Üzerine'. In *Modern Dönemde Dini İlimlerin Temel Meseleleri*. Istanbul: İSAM Yayınları, 2007, pp. 73–104.
Çınar, Alev. *Modernity, Islam, and Secularism in Turkey: Bodies, Places, and Time*. Minneapolis, MN: University of Minnesota Press, 2005.
Çorlulu, Kara Halil Pasha. Appendix to *al-Masā'il al-Mukhtalifa bayna al-Ash'ariyya wa al-Māturīdīyya*. Süleymaniye Kütüphanesi İstanbul, Hafid Efendi 150/20.
Daği, Ihsan D. 'The Justice and Development Party: Identity Politics and Human Rights Discourse in the Search for Security and Legitimacy'. In *The Emergence of a New Turkey: Islam, Democracy, and the AK Parti*, edited by M. Hakan Yavuz. Salt Lake City, UT: University of Utah Press, 2006, pp. 88–106.
Daği, Ihsan D. 'Post-Islamism à la Turca'. In Asef Bayat, (ed.), *Post Islamism: The Changing Faces of Political Islam*. Oxford: Oxford University Press, 2013, pp. 71–108.
Daği, Ihsan D. 'Rethinking Human Rights, Democracy, and the West: Post-Islamist Intellectuals in Turkey'. *Critique: Critical Middle Eastern Studies* 13:2 (Summer 2004): 135–51.
Demirci, Osman. 'Osmanlı'da Kelam Eğitimi'. *Türkiye Araştırmaları Literatür Dergisi* 14:28 (2016): 9–39.
Descartes, Rene. *Discourse on Method*. Translated by Donald A. Cress, 3rd edition. Indianapolis, IN: Hackett Publishing Company, 1998.
Dhahani, Alnoor. '*Al-Mawāqif fī 'Ilm al-Kalām* by 'Aḍūd al-Dīn al-Ījī (d. 1355), and its Commentaries'. In *The Oxford Handbook of Islamic Philosophy*, edited by

Khaled El-Rouayheb and Sabine Schmidtke. Oxford: Oxford University Press, 2016, pp. 375–96.

'Diyanet İşleri Başkanı Erbaş'tan 'Sapkınlık' Uyarısı'. *Diyanet Haber.* 2 July 2019. Available at: <https://www.diyanethaber.com.tr/diyanet-haber/diyanet-isleri-baskani-erbastan-sapkinlik-uyarisi-h6308.html> (last accessed 8 October 2020).

Dorroll, Courtney. 'Hamamönü, Reconfiguring an Ankara Neighborhood'. *Journal of Ethnography and Folklore* 1–2 (May 2016): 55–86.

Dorroll, Courtney. *The Spatial Politics of Turkey's Justice and Development Party (AK Party): On Erdoğanian Neo-Ottomanism.* University of Arizona Dissertation, 2015.

Dorroll, Philip. 'Shari'a and the Secular in Modern Turkey'. *Contemporary Islam* 11:2 (July 2017): 123–35.

Dorroll, Philip. 'The Turkish Understanding of Religion: Rethinking Tradition and Modernity in Contemporary Turkish Islamic Thought'. *Journal of the American Academy of Religion* 82:4 (December 2014): 1033–69.

Dorroll, Philip. 'The Universe in Flux: Reconsidering Abū Manṣūr al-Māturīdī's Metaphysics and Epistemology. *Journal of Islamic Studies* 27:2 (2016): 119–35.

Dressler, Markus. 'Rereading Ziya Gökalp: Secularism and Reform of the Islamic State in the Late Young Turk Period'. *International Journal of Middle East Studies* 47 (2015): 511–31.

Duman, Ali. 'Şerafeddin Yaltkaya ve Mu'tezile Husn-Kubh Meselesi Makalesi'. *Dinbilimleri Akademik Araştırma Dergisi* 2 (2002): 53–65.

Dumont, Paul. 'The Origins of Kemalist Ideology'. In *Atatürk and the Modernization of Turkey*, edited by Jacob M. Landau. Boulder, CO: Westview Press, 1983, pp. 25–44.

Durkheim, Emile. *The Elementary Forms of Religious Life.* Translated and abridged by Carol Cosman and Mark S. Cladis. Oxford: Oxford University Press, 2001.

Düzgün, Şaban Ali. 'Matüridi'de Din, Siyaset Kültürü ve Yönetim Erki (Mülk/Devlet)'. In *Matüridi'nin Düşünce Dünyası*, edited by Şaban Ali Düzgün. Ankara: T. C. Kültür ve Turizm Bakanlığı Yayınları, 2011, pp. 349–69.

Ecer, Ahmet Vehbi. *Büyük Türk Din Alimi Māturīdī.* İstanbul: Yesevi Yayıncılık, 2007.

Eichner, Heidrun. 'Handbooks in the Tradition of Later Eastern Ash'arism. In *The Oxford Handbook of Islamic Theology*, edited by Sabine Schmidtke. Oxford: Oxford University Press, 2016, pp. 494–514.

El-Rouayheb, Khaled. 'The Myth of "The Triumph of Fanaticism" in the Seventeenth-Century Ottoman Empire'. *Die Welt des Islams* 48 (2008): 196–221.

El Shamsy, Ahmed. *The Canonization of Islamic Law: A Social and Intellectual History*. Cambridge: Cambridge University Press, 2013.

Erdem, Gazi. 'Religious Services in Turkey: From the Office of Şeyülislām to the Diyanet'. *Muslim World* 98: 2–3 (April 2008): 199–215.

Ergenç, Erdinç. 'Peygamber Eşcinsele Ölüm Cezası Vermedi'. *Sabah*. 1 July 2008. Available at: <http://www.lambdaistanbul.org/s/medya/peygamber-escinsele-olum-cezasi-vermedi> (last accessed 8 October 2020).

Erşahin, Seyfettin. 'The Ottoman Foundation of the Turkish Republic's Diyanet: Ziya Gökalp's Diyanet Ishları Nazaratı'. *Muslim World* 98 (April-July 2008): 182–98.

Flood, Allison. 'Turkish government destroys more than 300,000 books'. *The Guardian*. 6 August 2019. Available at: <https://www.theguardian.com/books/2019/aug/06/turkish-government-destroys-more-than-300000-books?CMP=share_btn_fb> (last accessed 8 October 2020).

Foody, Kathleen. 'Interiorizing Islam: Religious Experience and State Oversight in the Islamic Republic of Iran'. *Journal of the American Academy of Religion* 83:3 (Sept. 2015): 599–623.

Frank, Richard M. 'Elements in the Development of the Teaching of Al-Ashʿarī'. *Le Museon* 104:1–2 (1991): 141–190.

Al-Ghazālī, Abū Ḥāmid Muḥammad. *Moderation in Belief* (*Al-Iqtiṣād fī al-Iʿtiqād*). Translated by Aladdin M. Yaqub. Chicago, IL: The University of Chicago Press, 2013.

Gökalp, Ziya. *The Principles of Turkism*. Translated by Robert Devereux. Leiden: Brill, 1968.

Göle, Nilüfer. *The Forbidden Modern: Civilization and Veiling*. Ann Arbor, MI: University of Michigan Press, 1997.

Görgün, Tahsin. 'Batı Medeniyet İçerisinde İslami İlimler Mümkün müdür? Modern Dönemde Dini İlimlerin Temel Meselelerine Temelli Bir Bakış'. In *Modern Dönemde Dini İlimlerin Temel Meseleleri*. Istanbul: İSAM Yayınları, 2007, 11–30.

Görmez, Mehmet. 'The Status of the Presidency of Religious Affairs in the Turkish Constitution and its Execution'. *Muslim World* 98:2/3 (2008): 242–8.

Gözaydın, İstar B. 'Diyanet and Politics'. *The Muslim World* 98 (April/July 2008): 216–27.

Gözaydın, İstar B. *Diyanet: Türkiye Cumhuriyeti'nde Dinin Tanzımı*. Istanbul: İletişim Yayınları, 2009.

Griffith, Sydney. *The Church in the Shadow of the Mosque: Christians and Muslims in the World of Islam*. Princeton, NJ: Princeton University Press, 2008.

Guida, Michelangelo. 'The New Islamists' Understanding of Democracy in Turkey'. *Turkish Studies* 11:3 (September 2010): 347–70.

Guida, Michelangelo. 'Nurettin Topçu and Necip Fazıl Kısakürek: Stories of "Conversion" and Activism in Republican Turkey'. *Journal for Islamic Studies* 34 (January 2014): 98–117.

Güler, İlhami. *Sabit Din, Dinamik Şeriat*. Ankara: Ankara Okulu, 2015.

Al-Gümülcinevī, Muḥammad ibn Aḥmad. *Risāla fī Baḥth al-Irādāt al-Juz'iyya*. Süleymaniye Kütüphanesi, Istanbul. Esad Effendi 01180.

Habib, Samar. *Female Homosexuality in the Middle East: Histories and Representations*. New York: Routledge, 2007.

Habib, Samar. 'Queer-Friendly Islamic Hermeneutics'. ISIM Review 21 (Spring 2008): 32–3.

Haidar, Yahya Raad. *The Debates between Ash'arism and Māturīdism in Ottoman Religious Scholarship: A Historical and Bibliographical Study*. Australian National University PhD, 2016.

Haj, Samira. *Reconfiguring Islamic Tradition: Reform, Rationality, and Modernity*. Stanford, CA: Stanford University Press, 2009.

Hale, William. *The Political and Economic Development of Modern Turkey*. Kent: Croom Helm, 1981.

Abū Ḥanīfa, al-Nu'mān ibn Thābit. *Kitāb al-'Ālim wa al-Muta'allim*. Edited by Muḥammad Zāhid al-Kawtharī. Cairo: Al-Maktaba al-Azharīyya li al-Turāth, 2001.

Hanioğlu, M. Şükrü. 'The Historical Roots of Kemalism'. In *Democracy, Islam, and Secularism in Turkey*, edited by Ahmet T. Kuru and Alfred Stepan. New York: Columbia University Press, 2012, pp. 32–60.

Hashemi, Nader. *Islam, Secularism, and Liberal Democracy: Toward a Democratic Theory for Muslim Societies*. Oxford: Oxford University Press, 2009.

Hassan, Mona. 'Women Preaching for the Secular State: Official Female Preachers (Bayan Vaizler) in Contemporary Turkey'. *International Journal of Middle Eastern Studies* 43:3 (August 2011): 452–73.

Heneghan, Tom. 'Turkey Presents Prophet's Sayings for the 21st Century'. *Reuters UK*. 22 May 2013. Available at: <https://www.reuters.com/article/us-turkey-islam-hadiths/turkey-presents-prophets-sayings-for-the-21st-century-idUSBRE94L0OJ20130522> (last accessed 8 October 2020).

Heper, Metin. 'Islam and Democracy in Turkey: Toward a Reconciliation?' *Middle East Journal* 5 (1997): 32–45.

Hidayatullah, Aysha A. *Feminist Edges of the Qur'an*. Oxford: Oxford University Press, 2014.

Hizmetli, Sabri. 'İzmirli İsmail Hakkı'nın İlmi Şahsiyeti'. In *İzmirli İsmail Hakkı Sempozyumu: 24–25 Kasım 1995*, edited by Mehmet Şeker and Adnan Bülent Baloğlu. Ankara: TDV Yayınları, 1996, pp. 3–25.

Holmes Katz, Marion. *Prayer in Islamic Thought and Practice*. Cambridge: Cambridge University Press, 2013.

Hourani, Albert. *Arabic Thought in the Liberal Age: 1798–1939*. Cambridge: Cambridge University Press, 1983.

Ibn Abī 'Udhba, Ḥasan. *Rawḍat al-Bahīyya fīmā bayna al-Ashāʿira wa al-Māturīdiyya*, edited by 'Alī Farīd Daḥrūj. Beirut: Dār Sabīl al-Rishād, 1996. Also edited by Edward Badeen in *Sunnitische Theologie in osmanischer Zeit*. Würzburg: Orient-Institut Istanbul, 2008, pp. 133–209.

Ibn Rushd. *Al-Kashf 'an Manāhij al-Adilla fī 'Aqā'id al-Milla*. Edited by Muḥammad 'Ābid al-Jābrī. Beirut: Markaz Markaz Dirāsāt al-Waḥda al-'Arabīyya, 1998.

Al-Ijī, 'Aḍūd al-Dīn. *Al-Mawāqif fī 'Ilm al-Kalām*. Beirut: 'Ālam al-Kutub. N.D.

Imber, Colin. 'How Islamic was Ottoman Law?' In *İSAM Papers: Ottoman Thought, Ethics, Law, Philosophy-Kalam*, edited by Seyfi Kenan. Istanbul: İSAM Yayınları, 2013, pp. 77–90.

Inalcik, Halil. *The Ottoman Empire: The Classical Age, 1300–1600*. London: Phoenix, 2002.

Iqbal, Muhammad. *The Reconstruction of Religious Thought in Islam*, edited by M. Saeed Sheikh. Lahore: Iqbal Academy Pakistan and Institute of Islamic Culture, 1989.

Isbirī, Qāḍi Zadeh. *Mumayyizat Madhhab al-Māturīdiyya 'an al-Madhāhib al-Gharīyya*. In Edward Badeen (ed.), *Sunnitische Theologie in osmanischer Zeit*. Würzburg: Orient-Institut Istanbul, 2008, 61–80.

İhsanoğlu, Ekmeleddin. 'The Emergence of the Ottoman Medrese Tradition'. *Archivum Ottomanicum* 25 (2008): 283–338.

İhsanoğlu, Ekmeleddin. 'Institutionalisation of Science in the *Medrese*s of Pre-Ottoman and Ottoman Turkey'. In *Turkish Studies in the History of Philosophy and Science*, edited by Gürol Irzık and Güven Güzeldere. Dordrecht: Springer, 2005, pp. 265–83.

İmece, Mustafa Selim. *Atatürk'ün Şapka Devriminde Kastamonu ve İnebolu Seyahatları, 1925*. Ankara: Türk Tarih Kurumu Basımevi, 1959.

İnan, Arı. *Gazi Mustafa Kemal Atatürk'ün 1923 Eskişehir-İzmit Konuşmaları*. Ankara: Türk Tarih Kurumu Yayınları, 1996.

İzmirli, İsmail Hakkı. 'İcma, Kıyas ve İstihsanın Esasları', edited by Ali Duman. *Hikmet Yurdu* 1:1 (January 2008): 149–60.

İzmirli, İsmail Hakkı. 'Sosyal Bir Fıkıh Usulüne İhtiyaç Var mı?', edited by Ali Duman. *Hikmet Yurdu* 2:3 (January–June 2009): 399–412.

İzmirli, İsmail Hakkı. *Yeni İlm-i Kelam*. I–II. Istanbul, 1923–4.

İzmirli, İsmail Hakkı. *Yeni İlm-i Kelam*, edited by Sabri Hizmetli. Ankara: Ankara Okulu Yayınları, 2013.

Al-Jawharī, Abū al-ʿAbbās Aḥmad ibn Ḥasan. *Risāla Tataʿallaqa bayna Kalām al-Māturīdī wa al-Ashʿarī*. Istanbul: Topkapı Sarayı Müzesi, 2004.

Jelen, Brigitte. 'Educated, Independent, and Covered: The Professional Aspirations and Experiences of University-educated Hijabi in Contemporary Turkey'. *Women's Studies International Forum* 34 (2011): 308–19.

Al-Jurjānī, al-Sayyid al-Sharīf. *Sharḥ al-Mawāqif*. Istanbul: 1894.

Kafadar, Cemal. *Between Two Worlds: The Construction of the Ottoman State*. Berkeley, CA: University of California Press, 1995.

Kamali, Mohammad Hashim. '*Maqāṣid al-Sharīʿah*: The Objectives of Islamic Law'. *Islamic Studies* 38:2 (1999): 193–208.

Kamali, Mohammad Hashim. *Shariʿah Law: An Introduction*. Oxford: Oneworld, 2008.

Kamali, Mohammad Hashim. *Shariah Law: Questions and Answers*. London: Oneworld, 2017.

'Kaos GL'den 'İslam ve Eşcinsellik''. Kaos GL. 13 November 2008. Available at: <http://www.lambdaistanbul.org/s/medya/peygamber-escinsele-olum-cezasi-vermedi> (last accessed 8 October 2020).

'Kaos GL İslam ve Eşcinselliği Tartıştı: Kim bu İmam Muhsin Hendricks?' odatv.com. 14 November 2008. Available at: <https://odatv.com/kaos-gl-islam-ve-escinselligi-tartisti-1411081200.html> (last accessed 8 October 2020).

Kara, İsmail. *Cumhuriyet Turkiye'sinde Bir Mesele Olarak Islam*. İstanbul: Dergah Yayınları, 2008.

Kara, İsmail. 'Turban and Fez: Ulema as Opposition'. In *Late Ottoman Society: The Intellectual Legacy*, edited by Elisabeth Özdalga. New York: Routledge, 2011, pp. 163–202.

Karal, Enver Ziya. 'The Principles of Kemalism'. In *Ataturk: Founder of a Modern State*, edited by Egun Ozbudun and Ali Kazancigil. London: Archon Press, 1982, pp. 11–36.

Karaman, Hayreddin. 'Bilim ne Diyor?' *Yeni Şafak*. 24 May 2009. Available at: <https://www.yenisafak.com/yazarlar/hayrettinkaraman/bilim-ne-diyor-16921> (last accessed 8 October 2020).

Karaman, Hayreddin. 'Eşcinsellik Problemi'. *Yeni Şafak*. 21 May 2009. Available at: <https://www.yenisafak.com/yazarlar/hayrettinkaraman/ecinsellik-problemi-16864> (last accessed 8 October 2020).

Karaman, Hayreddin. 'Eşcinseller vb. ile Aynı Toplulukta Yaşamak'. *Yeni Şafak*. 31 May 2009. Available at: <https://www.yenisafak.com/yazarlar/hayrettinkaraman/ecinseller-vb-ile-ayni-toplulukta-yaamak-17042> (last accessed 8 October 2020).

Karaman, Hayreddin. 'Hadisler de Eşcinselliğe İzin Vermiyor'. *Yeni Şafak*. 29 May 2009. Available at: <https://www.yenisafak.com/yazarlar/hayrettinkaraman/hadisler-de-ecinsellige-izin-vermiyor-16994> (last accessed 8 October 2020).

Karaman, Hayreddin. *İslam'da Kadın ve Aile*. Istanbul: Ensar Neşriyat, 2011.

Karaman, Hayreddin. 'Kur'an Eşcinselliği Kınıyor ve Yasaklıyor'. *Yeni Şafak*. 29 May 2009. Available at: <https://www.yenisafak.com/yazarlar/hayrettinkaraman/kuran-ecinselligi-kiniyor-ve-yasakliyor-16978> (last accessed 8 October 2020).

Karaman, Hayreddin. 'Laikliğin Kur'an'la savunulması'. *Yeni Şafak*. 22 October 2004.

Karaman, Hayreddin. 'Muhsin Hendrix'in İddiaları'. *Yeni Şafak*. 22 May 2009. Available at: <https://www.yenisafak.com/yazarlar/hayrettinkaraman/muhsin-hendrixin-iddialari-16881> (last accessed 8 October 2020).

Karasipahi, Sena. *Muslims in Modern Turkey: Kemalism, Modernism, and the Revolt of the Islamic Intellectuals*. London: I. B. Tauris, 2009.

Karaveli, Halil M. 'An Unfulfilled Promise of Enlightenment: Kemalism and its Liberal Critics'. *Turkish Studies* 11:1 (March 2010): 85–102.

Karpat, Kemal. *The Politicization of Islam: Reconstructing Identity, State, Faith and Community in the Late Ottoman State*. Oxford: Oxford University Press, 2002.

Al-Karsī, Dāvūd. *Rısāla fī Bayān Mas'alat al-Ikhtiyārāt al-Juz'iyya wa al-Idrākāt al-Qalbiyya*, Süleymaniye Kütüphanesi, Istanbul. Serez 1422.

Kasaba, Reşat. 'Kemalist Certainties and Modern Ambiguities'. In *Rethinking Modernity and National Identity in Turkey*, edited by Sibel Bozdoğan and Reşat Kasaba. Seattle, WA: University of Washington Press, 1997, pp. 15–36.

Kazım, Musa. 'Hürriyet–Müsavat'. *Sırat-ı Müstakim* 1,2,3 (1908–1909). In İsmail Kara, *Türkiye'de İslamcılık Düşuncesi 1: Metinler, Kişiler*. Istanbul: Dergah Yayınları, 2014. pp. 109–16.

Kazım, Musa. 'İslam ve Terakki'. *İslam Mecmuası* 27 March 1904. In İsmail Kara, *Türkiye'de İslamcılık Düşuncesi 1: Metinler, Kişiler*. Istanbul: Dergah Yayınları, 2014, pp. 123–8.

Kazım, Musa. 'Medeniyet-Din İlişkisi'. *Terüman-ı Hakikat* 23 July (1898). In İsmail Kara, *Türkiye'de İslamcılık Düşuncesi 1: Metinler, Kişiler*. Istanbul: Dergah Yayınları, 2014. pp. 117–22.

Kılavuz, Ahmet Saim. 'Hayreddin Karaman'. In *Çağdaş İslam Düşünürleri*, edited by Cağfer Karadaş. İstanbul: Ensar Neşriyat, 2007, pp. 301–46.

Al-Kırşehrī, Muḥammad ibn Velī ibn Resūl. *Sharḥ al-Khilāfiyyāt bayna al-Ashʿarī wa al-Māturīdī*. Süleymaniye Kütüphanesi, Istanbul. Şehit Ali Paşa 1650.

Kısakürek, Necip Fazıl. *İman ve İslam Atlası*. Istanbul: Büyük Doğu Yayınları, 2011.

Kocamaner, Hikmet. 'How New is Erdoğan's "New Turkey"?' *Middle East Brief* 91 (April 2015): 1–9.

Kocamaner, Hikmet. 'The Politics of Family Values in Erdoğan's New Turkey'. *Middle East Report* 288 (Fall 2018): 36–9.

Kocar, Musa. 'Mâtürîdî'de Akılcılık ve Uygulama Alanları'. *Süleyman Demirel Üniversitesi İlahiyat Fakültesi Dergisi* 17:2 (2006): 27–54.

Korteweg, Anna C. and Gökçe Yurdakul. *The Headscarf Debates: Conflicts of National Belonging*. Stanford, CA: Stanford University Press, 2014.

Koştaş, Münir. 'Ankara Üniversitesi İlahiyat Fakültesi'. *Ankara Üniversitesi İlahiyat Fakültesi Dergisi* 31:1 (1990): 1–27.

Koyuncu, Nuran. 'İslami Yönetimde Demokrasi var mıdır?' *Türk-İslam Medeniyeti Akademik Araştırmalar Dergisi* 4 (2007): 245–56.

Köprülü, Fuad. *Early Mystics in Turkish Literature*. Translated by Gary Leiser and Robert Dankoff. New York: Routledge, 2006.

Körner, Felix. *Revisionist Koran Hermeneutics in Contemporary Turkish University Theology: Rethinking Islam*. Würzburg: Ergon Verlag, 2005.

Köse, Saffet. *Çağdaş İhtiyaçlar ve İslam Hukuku*. Istanbul: Rağbet Yayınları, 2004.

Köse, Saffet. *İslam Hukukuna Giriş*. Istanbul: Hikmetevi Yayınları, 2013.

Köse, Saffet. 'Kuran Hükümlerini Doğru Anlamak'. *Ribat Dergisi* 394 (October 2015): 58–61

Köylü, Mustafa. 'Religious Education in Modern Turkey'. In *Change and Essence: Dialectical Relations between Change and Continuity in the Turkish Intellectual Tradition*, edited by Sinasi Gunduz and Cafer S. Yaran. Washington, DC: The Council for Research in Values and Philosophy, 2005, pp. 45–64.

Kugle, Scott Siraj al-Haqq. *Homosexuality in Islam: Critical Reflections on Gay, Lesbian, and Transgender Muslims*. Oxford: Oneworld, 2010.

Kugle, Scott Siraj al-Haqq. *Living Out Islam: Voices of Gay, Lesbian, and Transgender Muslims*. New York: NYU Press, 2014.

Kugle, Scott Siraj al-Haqq. 'Queer Jihad: A View from South Africa'. *ISIM Review* 16 (Autumn 2005): 14–15.

Kurt, Umit. 'The Doctrine of "Turkish-Islamic Synthesis" as Official Ideology of the September 12 [Regime] and the "Intellectuals' Hearth"- Aydınlar Ocağı as the Ideological Apparatus of the State'. *European Journal of Economic and Political Studies* 3:2 (2010): 111–25.

Kuru, Ahmet T. 'The Reinterpretation of Secularism in Turkey: The Case of the Justice and Development Party'. In *The Emergence of a New Turkey: Islam, Democracy, and the AK Parti*, edited by M. Hakan Yavuz. Salt Lake City, UT: University of Utah Press, 2006, pp. 136–59.

Kuru, Ahmet T. 'Shari'a, Islamic Ethics, and Democracy: the Crisis of the 'Turkish Model'.' In *Shari'a Law and Modern Muslim Ethics*, edited by Robert W. Hefner. Bloomington, IN: Indiana University Press, 2016, pp. 158–76.

Kutlu, Sönmez. 'Bilinmeyen Yönleriyle Türk Din Bilgini: İmam Māturīdī'. *Dini Araştırmalar* 5:15 (2003): 5–28.

Kutlu, Sönmez. 'İmam Matüridi'ye Göre Diyanet Siyaset Ayrımı ve Cağdaş Tartışmalarla Mukayesi'. *Islamiyat* 8:2 (2005): 55–69.

Kutlu, Sönmez. 'Matüridi Akılcılığı ve Bunun Günümüz Sorunları Çözmeye Katkısı'. In *Büyük Türk Bilgini İmam Matüridi ve Matüridilik Milletlerarası Tartışmalı İlmi Toplantı, 22–24 Mayıs 2009, İstanbul*. İstanbul: Marmara Üniversitesi İlahiyat Fakültesi Yayınları, 2012, pp. 549–75.

Kutlu, Sönmez. 'Matüridi Akılcılığı ve Günümüz Sorunlarını Çözmeye Katkısı'. *Mezhep Araştırmaları* 2:1 (Spring 2009): 7–41.

Leaman Oliver and Sajjad Rizvi. 'The Developed *Kalām* Tradition'. In *The Cambridge Companion to Classical Islamic Theology*, edited by Tim Winter. Cambridge: Cambridge University Press, 2008, pp. 77–98.

Madelung, Wilferd. 'The Spread of Māturīdism and the Turks'. *Actos do IV Congresso de Estudos Arabes e Islamicos, Coimbra-Lisboa*, 1968 (1971): 109–68.

Makdisi, George. 'Muslim Institutions of Learning in Eleventh Century Baghdad'. *Bulletin of the School of Oriental and African Studies* 24:1 (February 1961): 1–56.

Makdisi, George. *The Rise of Colleges: Institutions of Learning in Islam and the West*. Edinburgh: Edinburgh University Press, 1981.

Manastırlı, İsmail Hakkı. *Telhis'ül Kelam fi Berahini Akaid'il İslam*, edited by Arif Kübraoğlu. Istanbul: Fatih Gençlik Vakfı Matbaası.

Mardin, Şerif. *The Genesis of Young Ottoman Thought: A Study in the Modernization of Turkish Political Ideas*. Syracuse, NY: Syracuse University Press, 2000.

Mardin, Şerif. 'The Nakşibendi Order in Turkish History'. In *Islam in Modern Turkey: Religion, Politics, and Literature in a Secular State*, edited by Richard Tapper. London: I. B. Tauris, 1994, pp. 121–42.

Mardin, Şerif. *Religion and Social Change in Modern Turkey : The Case of Bediüzzaman Said Nursi*. Albany, NY: State University of New York Press, 1989.

Maritato, Chiara. 'Performing Irşad: Female Preacher's (Vaizeler's) Religious Assistance within the Framework of the Turkish State'. *Turkish Studies* 16:3 (2015): 433–47.

Maritato, Chiara. 'Reassessing Women, Religion, and the Secular State in the Light of the Professionalization of Female Preachers (Vaizeler) in Istanbul'. *Religion, State, and Society* 44:3 (2016): 258–75.

Maritato, Chiara. '"To Make Mosques a Place for Women": Female Religious Engagement within the Turkish Presidency of Religious Affairs'. In *Contemporary Turkey at a Glance II: Turkey Transformed? Power, History, Culture*, edited by Meltem Ersoy and Esra Ozyurek. Wiesbaden: Springer VS, 2017, pp. 39–52.

Mattson, Ingrid. 'How to Read the Quran'. In *The Study Quran*, edited by Seyyed Hossein Nasr, Caner K. Dagli, Maria Massi Dakake, Joseph E. B. Lumbard and Mohammed Rustom. New York: HarperOne, 2015, pp. 1587–1606.

Al-Māturīdī, Abū Manṣūr. *Kitāb al-Tawḥīd*. Edited by Bekir Topaloğlu and Muhammad Aruçı. Istanbul: Irshad Kitap Dağıtım Yayınları, 2007.

Al-Māturīdī, Abū Manṣūr. *Kitabü't-tevhid Tercümesi*. Translated by Bekir Topaloğlu. Ankara: İSAM, 2002

McCarthy, Richard J. *The Theology of Ash'ari*. Beirut: Imprimerie Catholique, 1953.

Meeker, Michael E. 'The New Muslim Intellectuals in the Republic of Turkey'. In *Islam in Modern Turkey: Religion, Politics, and Literature in a Secular State*, edited by Richard Tapper. London: I. B. Tauris, 1994, pp. 189–219.

Memiş, Murat. 'Yusuf Zıya Yörükan ve Kelam'. In Yusuf Ziya Yörükan, *İslam Akaid Sisteminde Gelişmeler: İmam-ı Azam Ebu Hanife ve İmam Ebu Mansur-ı Māturīdī*, edited by Turhan Yörükan. Istanbul: Ötüken Neşriyat, 2006, pp. 17–30.

Mestcizāde, 'Abdullāh ibn Osmān ibn Mūsā. *al-Masālik fī Bayān al-Madhāhib li al-Ḥumamā' wa al-Mutakallimūn wa al-Ash'ariyya wa al-Māturīdiyya*. Süleymaniye Kütüphanesi, Istanbul. Hekimoğlu Ali Paşa 402.

Miller, Ruth A. 'The Turkish Republic'. In *The Oxford Handbook of Islamic Law*, edited by Anver M. Emon and Rumee Ahmed. Oxford: Oxford University Press, 2018, pp. 653–71.

Mir-Hosseini, Ziba. 'Muslim Legal Tradition and the Challenge of Gender Equality'. In *Men in Charge? Rethinking Authority in Muslim Legal Tradition*, edited by Ziba Mir-Hosseini, Mulki al-Sharmani and Jana Rumminger. Oxford: Oneworld, 2015, pp. 13–43.

Muedini, Fuat. *LGBTI Rights in Turkey: Sexuality and the State in the Middle East.* Cambridge: Cambridge University Press, 2018.

Müftüler-Baç, Meltem. *Turkey's Relationship with a Changing Europe.* Manchester: Manchester University Press, 1997.

Al-Nawaʿī, Yaḥyā Efendi ibn ʿAlī. *Risāla fī al-Farq bayna Madhhab al-Ashāʿira wa al-Māturīdiyya.* In Edward Badeen (ed.), *Sunnitische Theologie in osmanischer Zeit.* Würzburg: Orient-Institut Istanbul, 2008, pp. 25–30.

Nguyen, Martin. *Modern Muslim Theology: Engaging God and the World with Faith and Imagination.* Lanham, MD: Rowman and Littlefield, 2019.

Nursi, Said. *Sözler.* Istanbul: Sözler Yayınevi, 2002.

Nursi, Said. *The Words.* Translated by Huseyin Akarsu. Somerset, NJ: The Light, 2005.

Ocak, Ahmet Yaşar. 'Cumhuriyet Dönemi Türkiyesi'nde Devlet ve İslam'. In *Türkler, Türkiye ve İslam: Yaklaşım, Yöntem, ve Yorum Denemeleri.* Istanbul: İletişim Yayınarlı, 2009, pp. 113–28.

Ocak, Ahmet Yaşar. 'Değişen Dünyada İslam'ın Batı'ya Dönük Yüzü: Günümüz Türkiye Müslümanlığına Genel Bir Bakış'. In *Türkler, Türkiye ve İslam: Yaklaşım, Yöntem, ve Yorum Denemeleri.* Istanbul: İletişim Yayınarlı, 2009, pp. 129–40.

Ocak, Ahmet Yaşar. 'Günümüz Türkiye'sinde İslami Düşüncenin Bir Tahlil Denemesi ve Tarihi Perspektifi'. In *Türkler, Türkiye ve İslam: Yaklaşım, Yöntem, ve Yorum Denemeleri.* Istanbul: İletişim Yayınarlı, 2009, 97–112

Ocak, Ahmet Yaşar. 'Islam in the Ottoman Empire: A Sociological Framework for a New Interpretation'. *International Journal of Turkish Studies* 9:1–2 (2003): 183–197.

Osman, Mujahid and Sa'diyya Shaikh. 'Islam, Muslims, and Politics of Queerness in Cape Town'. *Journal of Gender and Religion in Africa* 23:2 (December 2017): 43–67.

Ozbudun, Ergun. 'The Nature of the Kemalist Political Regime'. In *Ataturk: Founder of a Modern State*, edited by Egun Ozbudun and Ali Kazancigil. London: Archon Press, 1982, pp. 79–192.

Ozgur, Iren. 'Social and Political Reform through Religious Education in Turkey: The Ongoing Cause of Hayrettin Karaman'. *Middle Eastern Studies* 47:4 (July 2011): 569–85.

Öçal, Şamil. 'Osmanlı Kelamcıları Eş'ari miydi?: Muhammed Akkirmani'nin İnsan Hürriyeti Anlayışı'. *Dini Araştırmalar* 2/5 (1999): 225–54.

Öğük, Emine. *Kelam Geleneğinde Temel Kaynaklardan İstifade Yöntemleri: Matüridi Örneği*. Istanbul: Rağbet Yayınları, 2015.

Özcan, Hanifi. *Māturīdī'de Dini Çoğulculuk*. Istanbul: Marmara Üniversitesi İlahiyat Fakültesi Vakfı Yayınları, 1999.

Özcan, Hanifi. 'Modern Çağda Dinin Birey ve Toplum için Anlamı', *Akademik Araştırmalar Dergisi* 32 (2007): 134–41.

Özcan, Hanifi. 'Türk Din Anlayışı: Matüridilik'. In *İmam Māturīdī ve Māturīdīlik: Tarihi Arka Planı, Hayatı, Eserleri, Fikirleri ve Māturīdīlik Mezhebi*, edited by Sönmez Kutlu. Ankara: Kitabiyat, 2003, pp. 305–10.

Özcan, Hanifi. 'Türk Düşünce Hayatında Matüridilik'. *Türkiye Günlüğü* 101 (2010): 141–51.

Özdinç, Rıdvan. *Akıl, İrade ve Hürriyet: Son Dönem Osmanlı Dini Düşüncesinde İrade Meselesi*. Istanbul: Dergah Yayınları, 2013.

Özervarlı, M. Sait. 'Alternative Approaches to Modernization in the Late Ottoman Period: İzmirli İsmail Hakkı's Religious Though against Materialist Scientism'. *International Journal of Middle East Studies* 39:1 (February 2007): 77–102.

Özervarlı, M. Sait. 'Attempts to Revitalize Kalām in the Late 19th and Early 20th Centuries'. *Muslim World* 89:1 (January 1999): 90–105.

Özervarlı, M. Sait. 'İzmirli İsmail Hakkı'nın Kelam Problemleriyle İlgili Görüşleri'. In *İzmirli İsmail Hakkı Sempozyumu: 24–25 Kasım 1995*, edited by Mehmet Şeker and Adnan Bülent Baloğlu. Ankara: TDV Yayınları, 1996, pp. 109–25.

Özervarlı, M. Sait. *Kelamda Yenilik Arayışları 19. Yüzyıl Sonu 20. Yüzyıl Başı*. Istanbul: İSAM, 2008.

Özervarlı, M. Sait. 'Theology in the Ottoman Lands'. In *The Oxford Handbook of Islamic Theology*, edited by Sabine Schmidtke. Oxford: Oxford University Press, 2016, pp. 567–86.

Özervarlı, M. Sait. 'Transferring Traditional Islamic Disciplines into Modern Social Sciences in Late Ottoman Thought: The Attempts of Ziya Gökalp and Mehmed Serafeddin'. *Muslim World* 97 (April 2007): 317–30.

Öztürkmen, Arzu. 'The Role of the People's Houses in the Making of National Culture in Turkey'. *New Perspectives on Turkey* 11 (1994): 159–81.

Pacaci, Mehmet and Yasin Aktay. '75 Years of Higher Religious Education in Modern Turkey'. In *The Blackwell Companion to Contemporary Islamic Thought*, edited by Ibrahim M. Abu-Rabi'. Oxford: Wiley-Blackwell, 2006, pp. 122–44.

Peker, Efe. 'Beyond Positivism: Building Turkish *Laiklik* in the Transition from the Empire to the Republic (1908–1938)', *Social Science History* 44:2 (2020): 1–27.

Polat, Necati. *Regime Change in Contemporary Turkey: Politics, Rights, Mimesis*. Edinburgh: Edinburgh University Press, 2016.

Quataert, Donald. *The Ottoman Empire: 1700–1922*. Cambridge: Cambridge University Press, 2005.

'Qur'an is not against Homosexuality'. Kaos GL. 7 January 2013. Available at: <https://kaosgl.org/en/single-news/quotquran-is-not-against-homosexuality-quot> (last accessed 8 October 2020).

Al-Qurashī, 'Abd al-Qādir ibn Abī al-Wafā'. *al-Jawāhir al-muḍiyya fī ṭabaqāt al-Ḥanafiyya*, edited by 'Abd al-Fattāḥ Muhammad al-Ḥilū. Cairo: Dar Iḥyā' Kutub al-'Arabiyya, 1980–1982.

Rahman, Fazlur. *Islam*. Chicago, IL: University of Chicago Press, 1979.

Rahman, Fazlur. *Islam and Modernity: Transformation of an Intellectual Tradition*. Chicago, IL: University of Chicago Press, 1982.

Raudvere, Catharina. *The Book and the Roses: Sufi Women, Visibility, and Zikir in Contemporary Istanbul*. London: I. B. Tauris, 2003.

Reed, Howard. 'Revival of Islam in Secular Turkey'. *Middle East Journal* 8:3 (1954): 267–82.

Repp, Richard. *The Müfti of Istanbul: A Study in the Development of the Ottoman Learned Hierarchy*. Oxford: Ithaca Press, 1986.

Repp, Richard. 'Some Observations on the Development of the Ottoman Learned Hierarchy'. In *Scholars, Saints, and Sufis: Muslim Religious Institutions since 1500*, edited Nikki R. Keddie. Berkeley, CA: University of California Press, 1972, pp. 17–32.

Rudolph, Ulrich. 'Das Entstehen der Māturīdīya'. *Zeitschrift der Deutschen Morgenländischen Gesellschaft* (1997): 394–404.

Rudolph, Ulrich. 'Ḥanafī Theological Tradition and Māturīdism'. In *The Oxford Handbook of Islamic Theology*, edited by Sabine Schmidtke. Oxford: Oxford University Press, 2016, pp. 280–96.

Rudolph, Ulrich. 'Al-Māturīdī's Concept of God's Wisdom'. In *Büyük Türk Bilgini İmam Matüridi ve Matüridilik: Milletlerarası Tartışmalı İlmi Toplantı, 22–24 Mayıs 2009, İstanbul*. Marmara Üniversitesi İlahiyat Fakültesi Vakfı Yayınları, 2012, pp. 45–53.

Rudolph, Ulrich. *Al-Māturīdī and the Development of Sunnī Theology in Samarqand*. Translated by Rodrigo Adem. Leiden: Brill, 2015.

Safi, Omid. *The Politics of Knowledge in Premodern Islam: Negotiating Ideology and Religious Inquiry*. Chapel Hill, NC: The University of North Carolina Press, 2006.

Ṣaḥīḥ Muslim: Being Traditions of the Sayings and Doings of the Prophet Muhammad. Translated by Abdul Hameed Siddiqui. Lahore: Sh. Muhammad Ashraf, 1973.

Sariyannis, Marinos. 'Ruler and State, State and Society in Ottoman Political Thought'. *Turkish Historical Review* 4 (2013): 83–117.

Savcı, Evren. 'Ethnography and Queer Translation'. In *Queering Translation, Translating the Queer: Theory, Practice, Activism*, edited by Brian James Baer and Klaus Kaindl. New York: Routledge, 2018, pp. 72–83.

Savcı, Evren. 'THE LGBTI+ Movement'. In *Authoritarianism and Resistance in Turkey: Conversations on Democratic and Social Challenges*, edited by Esra Özyürek, Gaye Özpınar and Emrah Altındış. Cham: Springer, 2019, pp. 125–32.

Savcı, Evren. 'Subjects of Rights and Subjects of Cruelty: The Production of an Islamic Backlash against Homosexuality in Turkey'. *Political Power and Social Theory* 30: 159–86.

Sayeed, Asma. *Women and the Transmission of Knowledge in Islam*. Cambridge: Cambridge University Press, 2013.

Schacht, Joseph. 'An Early Murji'ite Treatise: The *Kitāb al-ʿĀlim wa al-Mutaʿallim*'. *Oriens* 17 (1964): 96–117.

Schimdtke, Sabine. 'Early Ašʿarite Theology: Abū Bakr al-Bāqillānī (d. 403/1013) and his 'Hidāyat al-mustaršidīn'. *Bulletin d'études orientales* 60 (2011): 39–71.

Schimdtke, Sabine. 'Introduction'. In *The Oxford Handbook of Islamic Theology*, edited by Sabine Schmidtke. Oxford: Oxford University Press, 2016, pp. 1–26.

Schmitt, Carl. *The Concept of the Political*. Translated by George Schwab. Chicago, IL: The University of Chicago Press, 1996.

Siddiqui, Sohaira. *Law and Politics Under the ʿAbbasids: An Intellectual Portrait of al-Juwayni*. Cambridge: Cambridge University Press, 2019.

Spellberg, Denise. *Politics, Gender, and the Islamic Past: The Legacy of ʿA'isha bint Abi Bakr*. New York: Columbia University Press, 1994.

Şentürk, Recep. 'Intellectual Dependency: Late Ottoman Intellectuals between Fiqh and Social Science'. *Die Welt des Islams*, New Series 47:3/4 (2007): 283–318.

Şentürk, Recep. 'Islamic Reformist Discourses and Intellectuals in Turkey: Permanent Religion with Dynamic Law'. In *Reformist Voices of Islam: Mediating Islam and Modernity*, edited by Shireen T. Hunter. Armonk, NY: M. E. Sharpe, 2009, pp. 227–46.

Shefer-Mossensohn, Miri. *Ottoman Medicine: Healing and Medical Institutions, 1500–1700*. Albany, NY: SUNY Press, 2010.

Shively, Kim. 'Religious Bodies and the Secular State: The Merve Kavakci Affair'. *Journal of Middle Eastern Women's Studies* 1:3 (Fall 2005): 46–72.

Silverstein, Brian. *Islam and Modernity in Turkey*. New York: Palgrave Macmillan, 2010.
Sinanoğlu, Mustafa. 'Türkiye'de Son Dönem Kelam Çalışmaları: Gelenek ve Modernite Arasında Bir Arayış'. In *Modern Dönemde Dini İlimlerin Temel Meseleleri*, Istanbul: İSAM Yayınları, 2007, pp. 115–40.
Soileau, Mark. *Humanist Mystics: Nationalism and the Commemoration of Saints in Turkey*. Salt Lake City, UT: The University of Utah Press, 2018.
Somer, Murat. 'Democratization, Clashing Narratives, and "Twin Tolerations": Between Islamic Conservative and Pro-Secular Actors'. In *Nationalisms and Politics in Turkey: Political Islam, Kemalism, and the Kurdish Issue*, edited by Marlies Casier and Joost Jongerden. London: Routledge, 2010, pp. 28–47.
Soroush, Abdolkarim. 'The Changeable and the Unchangeable'. In *New Directions in Islamic Thought: Exploring Reform and Muslim Tradition*, edited by Kari Vogt, Lena Larson and Christian Moe. London: I. B. Tauris, 2008, pp. 9–15.
Stokes, Martin. *The Arabesk Debate: Music and Musicians in Modern Turkey*. Oxford: Oxford University Press, 1993.
The Study Quran. Edited by Seyyed Hossein Nasr, Caner K. Dagli, Maria Massi Dakake, Joseph E. B. Lumbard and Mohammed Rustom. New York: HarperOne, 2015.
Subaşı, Necdet. 'İlahiyat(çı)lar Üzerine'. In *Öteki Türkiye'de Din ve Modernleşme*. Ankara: Vadi Yayınları, 2002. Also available at: <www.necdetsubasi.com/index/php/makale/67-ilahiyatcilar-uzerine> (last accessed 8 October 2020).
Al-Subkī, Tāj al-Dīn. *Nūnīyya al-Subkī*. In Edward Badeen (ed.), *Sunnitische Theologie in osmanischer Zeit*. Würzburg: Oriental-Institut Istanbul, 2008, pp. 2–18.
Suluoğlu, Muhammet Hanefi. 'İlahiyat Fakültelerindeki Güzel Gelişmeler'. *E-İlahiyat Dergisi* 1 (2011): 14.
Tanner Lamptey, Jerusha. 'Boko Haram: Not My Shariah'. *Time* magazine. 8 May 2014.
Al-Ṭahṭāwī, see Rifāʿa Rāfiʿ. *An Imam in Paris: Account of a Stay in France by an Egyptian Cleric (1826–1831)*. Translated by Daniel L. Newman. London: Saqi, 2004.
Tajali, Mona. 'Islamic Women's Groups and the Quest for Political Representation in Turkey and Iran'. *The Middle East Journal* 69:4 (Autumn 2015): 563–81.
Taşköprülzade, Aḥmad ibn Muṣṭafā. *al-Shaqāʾiq al-Nuʿmāniyya fī ʿUlamāʾ al-Dawla al-ʿUthmāniyya*. Beirut: Dār al-Kitāb al-ʿArabī, 1975.
Taylor, Charles. *A Secular Age*. Cambridge, MA: Harvard University Press, 2007.

Thiele, Jan. 'Between Cordoba and Nīsābūr: The Emergence and Consolidation of Ashʿarism'. In *The Oxford Handbook of Islamic Theology*, edited by Sabine Schmidtke. Oxford: Oxford University Press, 2016, pp. 225–41.

Topaloğlu, Bekir. *Allah İnancı*. Istanbul: İSAM Yayınları, 2006.

Topaloğlu, Bekir. *İslam Kelamcıları ve Fılozoflarına göre Allah'ın Varlığı (İsbat-ı Vacib)*. Ankara: Diyanet İşleri Başkanlığı Yayınları, 1983.

Topaloğlu, Bekir. *Kelam İlmine Giriş*. Ankara: Damla Yayınevi, 2014.

Topaloğlu, Bekir and İlyas Çelebi. *Kelam Terimleri Sözlüğü*. Istanbul: İSAM Yayınları, 2009.

Toprak, Binnaz. 'Islam and Democracy in Turkey', *Turkish Studies* 6:2 (June 2005): 167–86.

Toprak, Binnaz. 'Islamist Intellectuals of the 1980s in Turkey'. *Current Turkish Thought* 62 (1987): 1–19.

Toprak, Zafer. 'The Family, Feminism, and the State during the Young Turk Period, 1908–1918'. In *Première Rencontre Internationale sur l'Empire Ottoman et la Turquie Moderne, Institut National de Langues et Civilizations Orientales, Maison des Sciences de l'Homme. Varia Turcica, XIII*. Istanbul & Paris: Edition Isis (1991).

Treiger, Alexander. 'Origins of *Kalām*'. In *The Oxford Handbook of Islamic Theology*, edited by Sabine Schmidtke. Oxford: Oxford University Press, 2016, pp. 27–43.

Tuğal, Cihan. 'Islam and the Retrenchment of Turkish Conservatism'. In *Post Islamism: The Changing Faces of Political Islam*, edited by Asef Bayat. Oxford: Oxford University Press, 2013, pp. 109–33.

Tuksal, Hidyet Şefkatli. 'Kadın Gözüyle Hz. Peygamber'. In *İslam'da Kadın ve Toplum*. Ankara: Türkiye Diyanet Vakfı, 2008, pp. 70–6.

Tuksal, Hidyet Şefkatli. *Kadın Karşıtı Söylemin İslam Geleğendeki İzdüşümleri*. Ankara: OTTO Yayınları, 2014.

Tuksal, Hidyet Şefkatli. 'Misogynistic Reports in the Hadith Literature'. In *Muslima Theology: The Voices of Muslim Women Theologians*, edited by Ednan Aslan, Marcia Hermansen and Elif Medeni. New York: Peter Lang, 2013, pp. 133–54.

Turner, Colin and Hasan Horkuc. *Said Nursi*. London: I. B. Tauris, 2009.

'Tüm İllere Bayan Müftü Yardımcıcı'. dinibulten.com. Available at: <http://www.dinibulten.com/diyanet/tum-illere-bayan-muftu-yardimcisi/7725> (last accessed 11 March 2018).

Tütüncü, Fatma. 'The Women Preachers of the Secular State: The Politics of Preaching at the Intersection of Gender, Ethnicity, and Sovereignty in Turkey'. *Middle Eastern Studies* 46:1 (July 2010): 595–614.

Uludağ, Süleyman. 'Teorik Açıdan İslam ve Demokrasi: Yargı'. In *İslam ve Demokrasi*. Ankara: TDV Yayınları, 2005, pp. 397–410.

Van Ess, Josef. *Theology and Society in the Second and Third Centuries of the Hijra: A History of Religious Thought in Early Islam*, Vol. I. Translated by John O'Kane. Leiden: Brill, 2017.

wadud, amina. *Qur'an and Woman: Rereading the Sacred Text from a Woman's Perspective*. Oxford: Oxford University Press, 1999.

Walton, Jeremy F. *Muslim Civil Society and the Politics of Religious Freedom in Turkey*. Oxford: Oxford University Press, 2017.

Watt, W. Montgomery. *The Formative Period of Islamic Thought*. Oxford: Oneworld, 1998.

Weiss, Bernard. 'Interpretation in Islamic Law: The Theory of *Ijtihād*'. *The American Journal of Comparative Law* 26:2 (Spring 1978): 199–212.

Weiss, Jenny. 'State Feminism, Modernization, and the Turkish Republican Woman'. *NWSA Journal* 15:3 (Fall 2003): 145–59.

Wilkinson, Taraneh R. *Dialectical Encounters: Contemporary Turkish Muslim Thought in Dialogue*. Edinburgh: Edinburgh University Press, 2019.

Wilson, Brett. *Translating the Qur'an in an Age of Nationalism: Print Culture and Modern Islam in Turkey* Oxford: Oxford University Press, 2014.

Wood, Simon A. *Christian Criticisms, Islamic Proofs: Rashīd Riḍā's Defense of Islam*. Oxford: Oxford Oneworld, 2008.

Yafeh, Hava-Lazarus, Mark R. Cohen, Sasson Somekh and Sidney H. Griffith (eds). *The Majlis: Interreligious Encounters in Medieval Islam*. Wiesbaden: Harrasowitz Verlag, 1999.

Yaltkaya, M. Şerefettin. *Dini Makalelerim*. Ankara: T. C. Diyanet İşleri Reisliği, 1944.

Yaltkaya, M. Şerefettin. 'Türk Kelamcıları'. *Darülfünun İlahiyat Fakültesi Mecmuası* 23 (1932): 1–19.

Yaman, Hikmet. 'Small Theological Differences, Profound Philosophical Implications: Notes on Some of the Chief Differences between the Ash'arīs and Māturīdīs'. *Ankara Üniversitesi İlahiyat Fakültesi Dergisi* 51:1 (2010): 177–94.

Yavuz, M. Hakan. *Secularism and Muslim Democracy in Turkey*. Cambridge: Cambridge University Press, 2009.

Yavuz, M. Hakan and John L. Esposito (eds). *Turkish Islam and the Secular State: The Gülen Movement*. Syracuse, NY: Syracuse University Press, 2003.

Yavuz, M. Hakan and Rasım Koç. 'The Gülen Movement vs. Erdoğan: The Failed Coup'. In *Turkey's July 15th Coup: What Happened and Why*, edited by M.

Hakan Yavuz and Bayram Balcı. Salt Lake City, UT: The University of Utah Press, 2018, pp. 78–97.

Yayla, Ahmet S. 'Turkish ISIS and AQ Foreign Fighters: Reconciling the Number and Perception of the Terrorism Threat'. *Studies in Conflict and Terrorism* (2019). Available at: <doi: 10.1080/1057610X.2019.1628613> (last accessed 8 October 2020).

Yazır, Elmalılı Muhammed Hamdi. 'Müslümanlık Mani-i Terakki Değil, Zamin-i Terakkidir, *Sebilürreşad* 21, July–August 1923. In İsmail Kara, *Türkiye'de İslamcılık Düşuncesi 1: Metinler, Kişiler*. Istanbul: Dergah Yayınları, 2014, 484–501.

Yildiz, Ahmet. 'Transformation of Turkish-Islamic Thought since the 1950s'. In *The Blackwell Companion to Contemporary Islamic Thought*, edited by Ibrahim Abu Rabi'. London: Wiley-Blackwell, 2006, pp. 39–54.

Yıldırım, Arif. 'Ebu Mansur Matüridi'nin Din-Devlet İlişkisine Bakışı ve Bazı Değerlendirmeler'. *EKEV Akademi Dergisi* 10:27 (Spring 2006): 147–68.

Yılmaz, '"Strengthening the Family" Policies in Turkey: Managing the Social Question and Armoring Conservative-Neoliberal Populism'. *Turkish Studies* 16:3 (2015): 371–90.

Yörükan, Turhan. 'Açıklama ve Teşekkür'. In Yusuf Ziya Yörükan, *İslam Akaid Sisteminde Gelişmeler: İmam-ı Azam Ebu Hanife ve İmam Ebu Mansur-ı Māturīdī*, edited by Turhan Yörükan. Istanbul: Ötüken Neşriyat, 2006, pp. 9–16.

Yörükan, Yusuf Ziya. 'Ahlakımızın Kökleri I'. *Kutlu Bilgi* 1 (1944): 5–9.

Yörükan, Yusuf Ziya. 'Ahlakımızın Kökleri II'. *Kutlu Bilgi* 2 (1944): 37–40.

Yörükan, Yusuf Ziya. 'Dincilik Düşman Bir Fikir midir?' *İslam-Türk Mecmuası* 2:76 (1947): 4–6.

Yörükan, Yusuf Ziya. 'Dini İnkilap ve İslahat Hakkında'. *İslam-Türk Mecmuası* 2:73 (1947): 9–10.

Yörükan, Yusuf Ziya. 'Diyanet Nedir?' *Kutlu Bilgi* 7 (1945): 193–97.

Yörükan, Yusuf Ziya. Editor and translator. *Islam Akaidine dair Eski Metinler. I. Ebu Mansur-i Māturīdī'nin Iki Eseri: Tevhid kitabi ve Akaid risalesi*. Istanbul, 1953.

Yörükan, Yusuf Ziya. 'İlim ve Din'. *Kutlu Bilgi* 5 (1944): 129–32.

Yörükan, Yusuf Ziya. 'İslam İlm-i Hali'. *Ankara Üniversitesi İlahiyat Fakültesi Dergisi* 1 (1952): 5–20.

Yörükan, Yusuf Ziya. 'İslam Nedir? I'. *Kutlu Bilgi* 8 (1945): 225–9.

Yörükan, Yusuf Ziya. 'İslam Nedir? II'. *Kutlu Bilgi* 9 (1945): 257–61.

Yörükan, Yusuf Ziya. *Müslümanlık* Ankara: Doğuş Matbaacılık, 1993.

Yurdagür, Metin. *Ünlü Türk Kelamcıları: Maveraünnehir'den Osmanlı Coğrafyasına*. Istanbul: Marmara Üniversitesi İlahiyat Fakültesi Vakfı Yayınları, 2017.

Zilfi, Madeline C. *The Politics of Piety: The Ottoman Ulema in the Post-Classical Age (1600–1800)*. Minneapolis, MN: Bibliotheca Islamica, 1988.

Zorlu, Tuncay. 'The Medical *Medrese* of Süleymaniye'. In *International Congress on Learning and Education in the Ottoman World, Istanbul April 12–15, 1999*, pp. 63–87.

Zurcher, Erich. *Turkey: A Modern History*. London: I. B. Tauris, 2004.

INDEX

'Abduh, Muhammad, 30, 172–3
Abu Hanifa, 63, 65, 131
activism, Islamic, 75–6; *see also* Karaman, Hayreddin
AKP (Justice and Development Party)
    authoritarianism of, 76, 77, 174, 179, 180–1, 190
    conservative social vision, 77, 179–81
    definition of secularism, 175
    discourse on the LGBTI+ community, 182–3, 190–2
    early years, 174–9, 184
    gender equality under, 174, 176–8
    human rights discourses, 176, 182
    ideological programme, 174–6
    later years, 174, 179–81
    parallels with Kemalist statism, 180
    policy of women in the Diyanet, 177–8
    rise of, 75, 76, 173–5
    statist supervision of religion, 165, 178–9
    support for academic theology, 173–4, 176, 178
    theology of the family, 192, 195
Akseki, Ahmet Hamdi, 58–9
al-Fitra foundation, 186
Alper, Hülya
    the nature of reason, 96–7
    reason and human morality, 99–100
    role of revelation, 98, 99, 100
    theology of, 14, 89
    transcendent significance (*saadet*), 93

Ankara University, Faculty of Theology, 43–4, 71, 202; see also *Darülfünun*
al-Aqhisari, Kafi Hasan Efendi, 64–5
Aruçi, Muhammad, 67
al-Ash'ari, Hasan, 4–5
Ash'ari school
    al-Taftazani and, 24
    in the *medrese* system, 21, 24, 64
    Molla Fenari, 21
    in Ottoman Sunni theology, 41
    synthesis of the Ash'ari and Maturidi schools, 24–5, 64
    theological methods, 4–5
Atatürk, Mustafa Kemal, 28, 57, 129, 169; *see also* Kemalism
Atay, Hüseyin, 125–7
authoritarianism
    of the AKP, 76, 77, 174, 179, 180–1, 190
    conservative religious authoritarianism, 76, 127
    liberal theological critiques of, 77–82
    nationalist secularism of the early Turkish Republic, 79, 80, 81
Aydın, Ömer, 66–7
Ayubi, Zahra, 92
Azak, Umut, 170

Bacık, Gökhan, 75
Bardakoğlu, Ali, 145
Bulaç, Ali, 75–6

Çelebi, İlyas, 135, 137

Darülfünun
   faculties of theology, 38–9, 43, 44
   foundation of, 37–8, 202
   report on religious reform, 60–2
   see also Ankara University

democracy
   critiques of state intervention into religious affairs, 78, 80
   Islamic activism's challenge to, 75–6
   Islam's compatibility with, 143–6

Democrat Party, 71

Descartes, René, 115

devotional associations (*cemaat*s), 74–5

Diyanet (*Diyanet İşleri Başkanlığı*)
   under the AKP, 177
   female religious leadership, 178
   formation of, 28, 165, 167
   gender equality policies, 177–8
   secular Kemalist policies, 170

Dorroll, Courtney, 179, 180

Durkheim, Emile, 34, 35, 40, 61

Düzgün, Şaban Ali, 146

Ecer, Ahmet Vehbi, 173

education, Islamic, 72–3; *see also* faculties of theology (*ilahiyat fakülteleri*); *medrese* system

Erbakan, Necmettin, 74, 75, 76

Erbaş, Ali, 176, 191–2

Erdoğan, Recep Tayyip, 77, 175, 179, 190, 192

ethics
   adalet (justice) concept, 55–6
   ethical action of human life, 124, 125–6
   human rights discourses, 55, 56
   Islamic ethical values, 59
   liberty, 56–7
   moral judgements, 133
   moral threat of dissident religions, 166
   reason and human morality, 93–4, 99–100

faculties of theology (*ilahiyat fakülteleri*)
   AKP support for, 176
   Ankara University, 43–4, 71, 202
   conservative politics in, 76–7
   female students, 176–7
   numbers of, 44
   state relations with, 43, 45
   under the Turkish nationalist regime, 37, 42–3

gender
   changeable/unchangeable distinction in Islam and, 30, 146–7, 154–5
   Diyanet's gender equality policies, 177–8
   gender equality in Ottoman theology, 57
   gender equality in Turkism, 33
   misogynistic discourse in the hadith, 147, 148, 149–54
   the patriarchal social system, 147–8, 149
   Quranic message of human equality, 147, 148–9
   in Said Nursi's theology, 72
   theology of the family, 192, 194–5
   see also women

Gezi Park protests, 77, 180, 183

al-Ghazali, Abu Hamid, 94

God
   argument from design, 96, 109–11
   attribute of loving mercy, 93, 186–7
   changeable/unchangeable distinction in Islam and, 123
   Creator/created distinction, 96, 99, 123–4, 193
   freedom to know God's will, 125–7
   God's existence and inner knowledge of the self, 112–16
   knowledge of through intellectual freedom, 127
   loving care and concern (*inayet*), 87, 88, 97–8, 109–10, 112, 116
   wisdom (*hikmet*), 97, 109, 110–11, 116, 207–9
   see also Oneness of God doctrine (*tevhid*)

Gökalp, Ziya (Mehmed Ziya)
   culture/civilisation distinction, 34–5
   on national identity, 34
   separation of state from religion, 35–6
   social *fiqh* theory, 35, 41
   sociological interpretation of religion, 33–6, 40, 61, 138
   support for Maturidism, 65
   Turkish as the language of worship, 62
   as a Young Turk, 33

Görgün, Tahsin, 7

Gozaydın, İştar, 165–6

Gülen, Fethullah, 181

Güler, İlhami, 135–6, 138–9

hadith
  A'isha's authority as a transmitter and interpreter of Prophetic tradition, 152–4
  misogynistic discourse in, 149–54
Hanifa, Abu, 63
Hendrix, Muhsin
  Hayreddin Karaman's rebuttal of, 188–90
  Kaos GL interview, 181–2, 184
  life of, 185–6
  theological hermeneutics, 184, 186–8, 191, 193
  use of the story of Lot, 182, 184, 185, 187–8
  see also LGBTI+ affirming theology; LGBTI+ community
human freedom
  dynamism of humanity in the world, 125
  ethical consequences of, 125–6
  freedom of human reason, 126–7
  humanist theological rationalism, 125–9
  in Hüseyin Atay's theology, 125–7, 129
  intellectual freedom and knowledge of God, 127–8
  Quranic message of human equality, 147, 148–9
  revelation as affirmation of, 128–9
  traditional theological discourses of, 129–30
  see also liberty
human rights discourses
  in early AKP programmes, 176, 182
  Islamic duty for the advancement of, 59, 137–8
  in Ottoman theology, 55, 56, 167
  as Western imperialist concepts, 77
  see also liberty
humanist theological rationalism, 125–9
humanity
  absolute truth/human life relationship, 134–9
  dynamism of human action, 124, 127–8, 137–8, 142–3
  friend-enemy distinction, 168
  gift of reason, 93
  human nature in Karaman's theology, 193–4
  inborn nature of the human individual, 186, 193
  moral capacity of, 93–4, 99–100
  necessity of God's revelation, 98–9
  realms of human life, 144–5
  transcendent significance (*saadet*), 92–4
  the world and humanity as signs of the sacred, 88, 116, 204

Ibn Rushd, 109
al-Iji, 'Adud al-Din, 5, 23–4, 26, 102, 104, 113–14
ikhtilāf treatises, 24–5
ilahiyat, term, 3, 6
institutions
  development of modern Turkish theology and, 9, 17, 37, 42–3, 202
  of the Ottoman Empire, 18
  state supervision of religious institutions, 29, 45, 166
  see also faculties of theology (*ilahiyat fakülteleri*)
Islamic modernism
  changeable/unchangeable distinction, 29–30, 31
  critiques of Sufism, 172–3
  in modern Turkish theology, 17, 31, 42
  Ottoman Islamic modernism, 31–2
  overview of, 29
  rationalism in, 30–1
  renewal (*yenilenme*) of Islamic thought, 31, 39–40
Islamic theology
  arabo-centrism in, 9
  definition, 2–3
  in the Turkish Republic, 1–2
  see also modern Turkish theology
İzmirli, İsmail Hakkı
  absolute truth/human life relationship, 134
  argument from design, 109–10, 111
  Darülfünun report on religious reform, 60
  the existence of the One God, 108–9
  forms of religious judgements, 132–4, 136
  God's attribute of wisdom, 207–9
  God's existence and inner knowledge of the self, 112, 114–15
  immutable beliefs and practices of Islam, 60, 167
  on literalistic Quranic interpretation, 104
  renewal of Islamic theology, 39–40
  social progress and theology, 55, 56
  on theological knowledge, 94–5, 115
  theological texts, 39, 55, 60, 89, 207
  theology of, 41, 70, 71, 72, 75, 89, 108
  transcendent significance (*saadet*), 92–3
  value of empirical sciences, 91–2

al-Jurjani, Al-Sayyid al-Sharif, 5–6, 23–4, 26, 95, 102, 113–14
Justice and Development Party (AKP) *see* AKP (Justice and Development Party)
justice concept (*adalet*), 55–6

kalām theology
  definitions of, 5–6, 63
  inner knowledge of the self, 113–14
  in the *medrese* system, 22–6
  in modern Turkish theology, 3, 5–7, 17, 114, 202
  Oneness of God doctrine (*tevhid*), 5, 6
  schools of, 4
  term, 3–4
Kaos GL, 181–2, 183, 186, 188
Karaman, Hayreddin
  academic career, 188
  alignment with AKP social conservatism, 77, 188, 190
  rebuttals of Muhsin Hendrix's theological argument, 188–9
  rejection of Islamic secularist state, 76–7
  theology of, 192–4
  theology of the family, 192, 194–5
Katip Çelebi, 23
Kazım, Musa, 54, 56–7
Kemal, Namık, 32
Kemalism
  AKP parallels with Kemalist statism, 180
  control over religious affairs, 167
  irtica (reactionism) discourses, 170, 171, 173
  Menemen Incident, 170–1
  secular Kemalism (*laiklik*), 165, 169–70, 175
  suppression of conservative religious thought, 165, 170–4
Kısakürek, Necip Fazıl, 73–4, 75
Köse, Saffet, 136, 139–42, 144–5
Körner, Felix, 8–9
Kotku, Mehmet Zahid, 74–5
Kutlu, Sönmez, 78–80, 127–8

language, modern Turkish
  alphabet, 29
  ilahiyat term, 3
  Islamic thought in, 1–2
  kalām term, 3

  as the language of worship, 62
  modern Turkish theology and, 37
  translations of the Qur'an, 69
  Turkish identity and, 169
law/jurisprudence
  imperial laws on the *medreses*, 23
  office of the *Şeyhülislam*, 21
  social *fiqh* theory, 35
  see also Shari'ah
LGBTI+ affirming theology
  coverage in the Turkish media, 181–2, 188
  Hayreddin Karaman's rebuttal of, 188–90
  Hendrix's theological hermeneutics, 184, 186–8, 191, 193
  politicisation of theology and, 182
  reluctance to utilise, 185
  story of the Prophet Lot, 182, 184, 187–8
LGBTI+ community
  AKP political discourse on, 182–3, 190–2
  coverage in the Turkish media, 181–2, 188
  history of, 183–4
  Istanbul Pride celebrations, 183, 185
  in relation to theology of the family, 194–5
  relations with pious Muslim groups, 184–5
  as a threat to Turkish identity, 179, 189–90, 195
liberty
  freedom of religion alongside secular national politics, 78
  as Islamic ethical value, 59
  in Ottoman theology, 56–7
  as a Western concept, 77
  see also human freedom

materialism
  empirical science and, 91
  modern/contemporary Turkish theological critiques of, 88, 90–4
  in relation to natural law, 111
Mattson, Ingrid, 3
al-Maturidi, Abu Mansur
  in Ahmet Vehbi Ecer's thought, 173
  in contemporary Turkish theology, 67–8
  definition of *kalām*, 5, 63
  God's determination of events, 129–30
  within modern Turkish nationalism, 63–4, 65–7, 68–9, 203
  on *nazar*, 102

Oneness of God doctrine (*tevhid*), 79, 203–4
religion/*Shari'ah* distinction, 131–2
role of human reason, 99
theology of, 4–5, 63
Turkish ethnicity of, 63, 64, 66, 203
Maturidi school
   human free will (*ikhtiyār*), 65
   Oneness of God doctrine (*tevhid*), 79, 203–4
   in Ottoman Sunni theology, 41, 64–5
   Sunni concept of the secular, 79
   synthesis of the Ash'ari and Maturidi schools, 24–5, 64
   theological methods, 4–5
medrese system
   abolition of, 29
   dominance of the Ash'ari school, 21, 24, 64
   establishment of, 19, 20
   Mulla Hafız's career, 26–7, 65
   within state religious orthodoxy, 20, 21
   Sunni Islamic theology in, 18, 19–20, 21, 22–6, 202
   Tanzimet period, 37
Menemen Incident, 170–1
Mir-Hosseini, Ziba, 30
modern Turkish theology
   as authentically Islamic theology, 8
   changeable/unchangeable distinction, 29, 31, 62, 87–8, 123–4, 130–1, 143, 167, 204–5
   critique of materialism, 90–4
   in dialogue with modernity and social change, 7–8, 36–7, 58–9
   distinction between the 'divine' and 'human' elements of religion, 61–2
   dynamism of human action, 124, 127–8, 137–8, 142–3
   early Republican sociological theory, 17, 33–7, 42, 60–1, 62, 124, 135, 202, 205
   foundational systematic works, 88, 89
   institutional locus of, 9, 17, 37, 42–3, 202
   Islamic modernism and, 17, 31, 42
   Islam's compatibility with representative democracy, 143–6
   kalām theology in, 3, 5–7, 17, 114, 202
   limits of social progress, 59–62
   links with Ottoman Islamic tradition, 3, 5–7, 9, 25–6, 31, 42, 202
   links with pre-modern Sunni theology, 25
   in modern Turkish, 1–2
   nationalist political context, 9
   Oneness of God doctrine (*tevhid*), 1, 2, 6, 17, 31, 59, 60, 108–9, 206–7
   religious belief/practice distinction, 59–60, 62, 131–43, 167
   re-sacralisation of modern ways of knowing, 91–2, 94
   scholarship on, 7–10
   secularism and the development of, 53, 57–8, 69
   statist supervision of religion, 164–5, 195
   transcendent significance (*saadet*) and, 92–4, 203
   Turkish nationalism and, 53–4, 57–8, 63, 70, 202–3
   the world and humanity as signs of the sacred, 88, 116, 204
Molla Fenari, 21
Mulla Hafız, 26–7, 65

national identity
   culture/civilisation distinction, 34–5
   LGBTI+ community as a threat to, 179, 189–90, 195
   Turkishness concept, 34
   in Ziya Gökalp's thought, 34
nationalism, Turkish
   adoption of al-Maturidi by, 63–4, 65–7, 68–9, 203
   conservative theological critiques of, 69–77, 81
   ethnocentrism in, 71–2
   liberal theological critiques of, 77–82
   limits of social progress, 57–62
   in Necip Kısakürek's thought, 73–4, 75
   reinterpretations of Sufism, 68–9
   in relation to modern Turkish theology, 53–4, 57–8, 63, 70, 202–3
   in Said Nursi's theology, 71–3
   social progress and, 54–7
   Turkish-Islamic synthesis, 76, 203
Nursi, Said, 71–3, 75

Ocak, Ahmet Yaşar, 20, 21
Öğük, Emine
   on human freedom, 129
   the law of Islam, 95
   on literalistic Quranic interpretation, 104, 107
   theological hermeneutics, 106
   on theological method (*nazar*), 101–4
   theology of, 89
Oneness of God doctrine (*tevhid*)
   as an absolute truth, 87, 88, 100–1, 108
   argument from design, 109–11
   changeable/unchangeable distinction in Islam and, 29, 31, 62, 87–8, 123–4, 130–1, 143, 167, 204–5
   God's existence and inner knowledge of the self, 112–16
   inborn nature of the human individual, 186
   within Islamic theology, 1, 2
   within *kalām* theology, 5, 6
   as the main message of the Qur'an, 106
   in Maturidi theology, 79, 203–4
   in modern Turkish theology, 1, 2, 6, 17, 31, 59, 60, 108–9, 206–7
   in Necip Kısakürek's thought, 74
   positivistic discourses and, 171
   theological knowledge and, 95
   transcendent significance (*saadet*) and, 88, 90, 93–4, 204
Ottoman Empire
   centralised religious authority of, 20–2
   kanun and *Shari'ah* distinction, 22
   Maturidi theology in, 41, 64–5
   Ottoman Islamic modernism, 31–2
   reforms of late Ottoman era, 33
   renewal (*yenilenme*) of Islamic thought, 31, 39–40
   social progress and theology, 54–7, 58
   state/religion distinction, 21–2
   Sunni theology, 18–19, 22–5, 41, 54, 64, 69–70
   transition to nation state, 27–8
Özcan, Hanifi, 128, 129, 138, 142
Özdinç, Rıdvan, 55, 56, 66

Polat, Necati, 180
politics
   defined, 168
   politics and culture as secondary to statism, 166
   politicisation of theology, 164, 171
   threat of the Other, 168–9

Qur'an
   Abraham's theological reasoning, 96, 109
   argument from design, 96
   contextual framework of, 106
   Creator/created distinction, 96
   ethical consequences of human freedom, 125–6
   inborn nature of the human individual, 186, 193
   literalistic interpretations of, 104, 106–7
   message of human equality, 147, 148–9
   role of revelation, 99, 101, 105–6, 128–9
   story of the Prophet Lot, 182, 184, 185, 187–8
   theological hermeneutics, 106
   translations into Turkish, 69
   the world and humanity as signs of the sacred, 116
   see also hadith

Rahman, Fazlur, 173
reason (*akıl*)
   and absolute truth, 100–1
   contrasted with uncritical imitation (*taklit*), 103–4
   faculty of reason, 93
   human morality and, 99–100, 126–7
   nature and function of within theology, 96–7, 115
   relationship with divine revelation (*vahiy*), 94–6, 97–101, 105, 126, 146
   in theological method (*nazar*), 101–5, 106–7
revelation (*vahiy*)
   as affirmation of human freedom, 128–9
   human reason/divine revelation relationship, 94–6, 97–101, 105, 126, 146
   misogynistic discourse in the hadith as contrary to, 147, 148
   revelation and Prophetic tradition, 101, 105–7
   role of revelation, 98–9, 100–1, 105–6, 128–9
Rida, Rashid, 172–3
Rumi, Jalal al-Din, 68

Savcı, Evren, 184–5
Schmidtke, Sabine, 2–3
Schmitt, Carl, 168
sciences
  within Islamic curricula, 71
  in modern systematic theology, 91–2
  natural laws, 111
  in relation to materialism and the transcendental, 91
  stance of devotional associations on, 75
secularism
  under the AKP, 175
  conservative theological critiques of, 69–77
  critique of secular nationalism, 89
  and the development of modern Turkish theology, 53, 57–8, 69
  of the early Turkish Republic, 29, 32, 35, 79, 80, 81
  laicism (*laiklik*), 29, 42, 45, 166, 170, 175
  liberal theological critiques of, 77–81
  as mutually compatible with religion, 78, 80–1
  nationalist secularism of the early Turkish Republic, 79, 80, 81, 89
  religion/secular state relationship, 35–6, 53
  secular Kemalism (*laiklik*), 165, 169–70, 175
  within Sunni theology, 53–4, 78–9, 81
  of Turkish nationalism, 53, 57–8, 69
  Western conceptions of religion in, 139
Shari'ah
  dynamic structure of (*ictihat*), 139–41, 142
  in faculties of theology, 38, 43, 44
  formalist rulings, 141–2
  in İlhami Güler's thought, 138–9
  kanun/Shari'ah distinction, 22
  in Necip Kısakürek's thought, 74
  practical elements of, 56
  reinterpretation and renewal of rulings, 32, 58
  religious belief/practice distinction, 131–43, 167, 172
  rituals of worship, 134
  rules of worldly interactions, 134
  Shari'ah judgements, 133–4
  term, 46
  textual literalism, 142
social progress
  adalet (justice) concept, 55–6
  under Atatürk, 56–7

Darülfünun report on religious reform, 60–2
in late Ottoman theology, 54–7, 58
liberty and equality, 56–7
as an modern Turkish Islamic value, 57–9
religious rulings on human interactions, 137
theological limits of, 59–62
Turkish nationalism and, 54–7
sociology
  early Republican sociological theory, 17, 33–7
  in Hidayet Tuksal's thought, 147–8, 150
  in Mehmed Yaltkaya's thought, 40–1
  in modern Turkish theology, 36–7, 42–3, 45, 60–1, 62, 124, 135, 202, 205
  in Yusuf Yörükan's thought, 40–1
  in Ziya Gökalp's thought, 33–6, 40, 61, 138
Soileau, Mark, 68
Soroush, Abdolkarim, 29
statism (*devletçilik*)
  AKP parallels with Kemalist statism, 180
  defence of the state, 169
  laicism (*laiklik*), 29, 42, 45, 166, 170, 175
  politics and culture as secondary to, 166
  as repressive, 179
  tradition of statist supervision of religion, 164–5, 167–8, 169, 178–9, 205
al-Subki, Taj al-Din, 25
Sufism
  contemporary scholarship on, 68
  devotional associations and, 74–5
  early Islamic educational institutions, 19, 20
  Islamic modernists' critiques of, 172–3
  in Necip Kısakürek's thought, 73
  outlawed Sufi shrines and lodges, 28
Sunni theological orthodoxy, 4
Sunni theology
  concept of the secular, 78–9, 81
  ikhtilāf treatises, 24–5
  institutionalisation in, 25
  'late' tradition of, 24
  links with modern Turkish theology, 25
  medieval theological education, 19–20
  during the Ottoman era, 18–19, 20–5, 41, 54, 64, 69–70
  pan-Sunni Islamists, 71–2, 74
  religion/*Shari'ah* distinction in medieval theology, 131–2

Sunni theology (*Cont.*)
　synthesis of the Ash'ari and Maturidi schools, 24–5, 64
　see also Ash'ari school; *kalām* theology; Maturidi school

al-Taftazani, Sa'd al-Din, 23–4
theological knowledge
　as dogmatic, 108
　forms of, 94
　as holistic, 107–8
　human reason/divine revelation relationship, 94–6, 97–101, 105, 126, 146
　intellectual freedom and knowledge of God, 127–8
　in İzmirli's thought, 94–5, 115
　the law of Islam, 95
　the nature and function of reason, 96–101, 115
　revelation and Prophetic tradition, 101, 105–7
　role of revelation, 98–9, 100–1
　state power over religious discourse, 166
　theological hermeneutics, 106
　theological method (*nazar*), 101–5, 106–7
　theological truth, 133, 135, 136
　uncritical imitation (*taklit*), 103–4
Topaloğlu, Bekir
　argument from design, 109–10
　critique of secular nationalism, 89
　inner knowledge of the self, 112–13, 114
　relationship with divine revelation (*vahiy*), 95–6
　theological texts, 67, 89
　theology of, 89
truth
　absolute truth/human life relationship, 134–9
　immutable theological truths, 133, 135, 136
　Oneness of God doctrine (*tevhid*) as an absolute truth, 87, 88, 100–1, 108
　theological truth, 144

Tuksal, Hidayet Şefkatli, 147–55
Turkish Republic
　early social reforms, 28–9
　first multi-party elections, 70–1
　statist approach to religion, 164–5, 195
　Turkism, 32–3
Turkish-Islamic synthesis ideology, 76

Wilkinson, Taraneh R., 8–10
women
　equality of, early Turkish republic, 28
　female preachers, 178
　female students in faculties of theology, 176–7
　LGBTI+ identities and women's groups, 185
　Muslim women's advocacy groups, 184–5
　participation and influence in religious life, 177
　wearing of headscarves, 162, 170, 175, 177, 184
　see also gender

Yaltkaya, Mehmed Şerefettin
　al-Maturidi as Turkish, 66
　at the Diyanet, 41
　inner perception of God, 113
　list of 'Turkish' theologians, 66–7
　sociological framework of, 40–1
　theology of, 39, 40, 69
Yazır, Elmalılı Muhammed Hamdi, 54–5, 56
Yıldırım, Arif, 80–1
Yörükan, Yusuf Ziya
　academic career, 41–2
　Darülfünun report on religious reform, 60
　Islamic modernism/ Turkish laicism, 42
　positivistic discourses of, 171–3
　theology of, 39
Young Turk Revolution, 33, 36
Yurdagür, Metin, 67

EU representative:
Easy Access System Europe
Mustamäe tee 50, 10621 Tallinn, Estonia
Gpsr.requests@easproject.com

www.ingramcontent.com/pod-product-compliance
Lightning Source LLC
Chambersburg PA
CBHW070344240426
43671CB00013BA/2400